PRIORITY MAIL

The Investigation and Trial of a Mail Bomber Obsessed with Destroying Our Justice System

MARK WINNE

A LISA DREW BOOK

SCRIBNER

New York • London • Toronto • Sydney • Tokyo • Singapore

SCRIBNER
Rockefeller Center
1230 Avenue of the Americas
New York, NY 10020

Designed by Jennifer Dossin

Manufactured in the United States of America

1 3 5 7 9 10 8 6 4 2

Library of Congress Cataloging-in-Publication Data
Winne, Mark.
Priority mail: the investigation and trial of a mail bomber obsessed with
destroying our justice system/Mark Winne.
p.   cm.
"A Lisa Drew Book."
Includes index.
1. Moody, Walter Leroy—Trials, litigation, etc. 2. Trials (Assassination)—
Minnesota—St. Paul. 3. Trials (Murder)—Minnesota—St. Paul. 4. Bombings—
Georgia. 5. Bombings—South Carolina. 6. Bombings—Florida. I. Title.
KF224.M58W56   1995
364.1'523'09776581—dc20   94-40279
CIP

ISBN 0-02-630240-3

Contents

Contents

Author's Note

The American system of jurisprudence, along with the people who comprise it, has become a target, the stage for violent soliloquies screamed by shrill people who seem to believe they have been treated unfairly, who would risk everything to gain nothing beyond the expurgation of some inner rage. Of all such attacks in recent years on courthouses, law offices and even personal residences, perhaps none has been more darkly ambitious and expertly executed than those that became known as the Southeastern mail bombings. What follows is the story of those bombs and related crimes and the struggle to bring the bomber to justice.

This story is a composite of accounts drawn from thousands of pages of documents, including voluminous court records; from interviews with investigators, lawyers, witnesses, victims, survivors and others; from countless tapes, and from my firsthand observations as a television reporter covering the mail-bomb case for its duration. Exact quotes, when used, come from documents, tapes, observation or the recollections of participants in the conversations. For the sake of a readable, compelling narrative, no further attribution is used, except in cases of particular controversy, litigious concern or other extraordinary circumstances.

And we know that all things work together
for good to them that love God, to them that
are called according to His purpose.
　　　　　　　　—Romans 8:28

Prologue

Birmingham's fringes crawl up the north slope of Red Mountain, but down the other side affluence and influence cascade into Mountain Brook, a shady suburb ranking first in Alabama in per capita income, property tax for schools and probably debutantes, German luxury cars and huge homes on lush lawns. In one big, white-columned, brick colonial house on a hill, Helen Vance had lived twenty-seven years with her husband Bob, who for the last eleven years had been a U.S. Circuit Court of Appeals judge. No matter the neighborhood, it would be a mistake to pigeonhole Helen Vance as some supercilious matron of the post–Junior League variety. From a distance she could look the part, but the dignity, the correctness of her carriage, is tempered by the dark effervescence in her eyes, the heartiness of her handsome face, and a winking wisdom born in part of years spent around politics—*Alabama* politics, the George Wallace way, made all the more interesting when Bob Vance occasionally stood in George Wallace's way.

On Saturday afternoon, December 16, 1989, Helen Vance was wrapping Christmas presents when the mailman brought two packages to the big house on Shook Hill Road. One package, from in-laws, contained more Christmas gifts. The sender of the second parcel may have hurried to get it in the Christmas mail, but it wasn't packed with presents. The return address suggested it was from another judge on the Eleventh Circuit bench, Lewis "Pete" Morgan of Georgia. But the return address was a lie.

Close to two o'clock in the afternoon, Helen Vance heard her husband come in the back door into the kitchen. She headed downstairs, picking up the mail in the front hall as she came off the steps. She sat down four feet across from where he stood at the kitchen table. The package ostensibly from Judge Morgan was on top, so he opened it first.

Bob Vance wasn't a country-club man. Shoal Creek, which because of the racial furor surrounding the 1990 P.G.A. Championship would forever alter the nation's notions of the exclusivity of country clubs,[*] was not far south of Mountain Brook, but a mere upstart in social standing compared to Birmingham Country Club and The Mountain Brook Club. Bob Vance might have gotten into either of those two had he desired, but exclusivity was consistent neither with his politics nor the personal code he chose to project. He'd dabbled in dog shows, but the big house was as much a hobby as anything was, and whether he was cutting the grass or, as on this day, running, as Helen called them, "regular Saturday errands," he was apt to be in those belted poplin coveralls you can buy from Sears for work around the house. And lately, though far short of a full-blown avocation, horses held some casual interest for Bob Vance, particularly with the recent opening of Birmingham's new track. Judge Pete Morgan raised horses.

"I guess Pete's sending me more horse magazines," he said. Maybe a year before, Pete Morgan had given him others.

From the package, Bob ripped off the plain brown wrapping paper with the neatly typed red-and-white label and stamps depicting an American flag flying over Yosemite Park. He lifted the cardboard lid. Inside the box that motion brought together two carefully cut slivers of aluminum pie plate, completing an electrical circuit powered by a pair of flashlight batteries. The current coursed into a detonator rigged from a ballpoint pen barrel loaded with high explosive. The makeshift detonator was jammed through a hole in one of the end caps screwed on a five-and-a-half-inch steel pipe.

---

[*]Shortly before the tournament, Shoal Creek founder Hall Thompson reportedly told the *Birmingham Post-Herald*, "We have the right to associate with whomever we choose. . . . I think we've said that we don't discriminate in every other area except blacks." Huge controversy erupted, then eased when the club accepted its first black member.

The inside of the pipe was packed with smokeless powder, and on the outside, rubber bands held eighty finishing nails in place.

A furious fireball flashed. The pipe burst into pieces, becoming jagged, whirring, tearing propellers ripping up the middle of Judge Vance's body. Fragments of the end caps became missiles hurtling in opposite directions. The nails added to the fusillade of deadly shrapnel. Judge Robert Vance was tossed into a corner, crumpled, bloody and still.

Helen Vance looked up from the floor and saw the ceiling light was out. She thought momentarily a lightbulb had blown, but quickly she knew it was more.

The Vances read English mysteries at night and had once discussed how characters in those books seemed to scream so often. Helen had never in her memory screamed. But now, still supine, she tried, and she did, not knowing whether anything was coming out. She waited for Bob to come see about her, wondering why he didn't.

She looked around and began to realize a bomb had exploded. For a time she heard nothing from Bob. Then he made noises she thought sounded as if someone's breath had been knocked out after a belt to the stomach. That was the last sound she heard him make.

There was no dial tone when Helen picked up the phone, or maybe there was; her hearing was for the moment numbed by the blast. Just as the template of logic cannot be laid neatly over the mind of a murderer, often there is no explaining the immediate priorities of the victim of crime. Helen Vance was compelled to get a towel from her bedroom. She put it over Bob's belly, or where his belly had been.

The Vance home lot was four acres, and the houses on Shook Hill Road spaced far apart, so when Helen went for help, she drove the family van. At the end of the driveway she turned left because she was afraid to turn right, toward Highway 280, a main thoroughfare where she imagined someone might be waiting, someone who, seeing her alive, would try again to kill her.

There was nobody at the first house she tried, and as she drove into the driveway across the street, she was hitting the horn. Margaret Ashby came out, recognized Helen and started to invite her in. The neighbor's words caught in her throat when she caught sight of the blood. Sanguineous slits were scattered over Helen's face, arms and legs, but she hadn't thought herself seriously hurt—maybe because she hadn't thought of herself much at all in the past few minutes. Only much later, at the hospital, would worsening shoulder pain prompt a cautionary X ray. That is how doctors discovered the explosion had rocketed a nail into her chest, a nail that then sliced through a lung, lacerated her liver and wedged near her back.

"Would you call the police?" Helen asked the neighbor woman. "A bomb has gone off."

Helen returned home in the van. When Margaret Ashby's husband, Charles, pulled up soon after, Helen was still sitting in the van. She stayed in the van even as police and paramedics arrived. She already knew what they would soon know for themselves. Bob Vance was dead.

An ambulance took Helen down Highway 280 to St. Vincent's Hospital, where she would recuperate for two weeks. Both of her sons—Bob junior, who'd followed his father into the law, and Charles, in doctoral studies at Duke—had rushed to her side. Deputy marshals watched the door. The waiting room teemed. When FBI agents came to question her, she was in pain, tubes running into her abdomen, which was cut nearly its full length and perpendicularly across. But their presence was fine with Helen. She wanted to catch whoever killed Bob.

Helen knew of no threats, not recently. Certainly there'd been times over the years when menacing phone calls, anonymous and annoying, came often. Bob Vance became chairman of the Alabama Democratic Party in 1966 because he and other young progressives wanted to stop the Wallace crowd from turning it into the Wallace party, divorced from the national body. Two years later, he presided over the seating of Alabama's first black delegates at the Chicago convention. But Helen knew Bob believed he most effectively induced change working behind the scenes, a coalition builder, a pragmatist preferring to get things done by not asking people to do what they absolutely could not do. And as she searched her psyche for why this had happened, she simply could not think of anyone who hated Bob Vance enough to kill him, not with a package bomb that could've killed anybody else in his family who might open it. This had to be part of something bigger, she intuited almost from the start. Somebody, she decided, had to be after the court.

She was not alone in considering the possibility.

The telex-style message was marked December 17, thirty-one minutes after midnight, and addressed to all U.S. marshals from

Marshals Service headquarters in Arlington, Virginia. It related Vance's death and updated Mrs. Vance's condition:

> *U.S. Marshals are advised to notify all circuit judges, district judges, magistrates, bankruptcy judges, as well as other members of the judicial family, to report any packages received via the U.S. Postal Service, the United Parcel Service or hand delivery. Any packages received should be reported to the U.S. Marshal immediately.*
>
> *The FBI is currently investigating this incident and we will keep each district advised of further developments.*

1

The Atlanta Bomb

With an easy blush and an unruly smirk, Brian Hoback was boyish but balding, brown eyes at once bright and dark, luminous and bituminous. Square-jawed and square-living, modest and polite, almost self-effacing, he seemed well suited to the role of rising young manager for a Memphis manufacturer, the part he played until, after five years of trying, he took a $14,000-a-year pay cut to become a federal agent with the Bureau of Alcohol, Tobacco and Firearms. Hoback loved the new job. But in two years with ATF in the Atlanta office, he had been principal investigator in just two explosives cases, one of those a measly Molotov-cocktail case federal prosecutors declined to handle. So when he learned about the Vance bombing from a TV news report, he thought little about it, other than how awful it was and how busy the ATF agents in Birmingham would be. It did not occur to him he might get involved in the case, or that it would forever change the way he looked at his job and the way he looked at himself.

Elsewhere in Georgia, news of the Vance bombing meant more to a couple of other ATF agents. Assigned to Savannah, Frank Lee had been handling big cases since 1971, when he worked an explosion that killed close to two dozen people at a plant near the Georgia coast. Now he was on ATF's National Response Team, a cadre of veteran arson and explosives investigators, and as soon as he'd heard about the Vance bombing, he packed a bag, expecting to be scrambled. Sunday morning he'd worn his beeper to church, then to the golf course when his wife urged him to quit fidgeting and get out of the house.

In Macon, the network news had confirmed for ATF Agent Joe Gordon the rumor he'd learned from a buddy with the Marshals Service, that a judge had been killed in Alabama. Gordon was pissed off, stunned in a deeply personal way at the audacity of it, harboring, already, a visceral animus toward attackers of public servants, an enmity bathed in his own blood. He'd been a Georgia state patrolman out of the Atlanta post when he'd boarded a Metropolitan Atlanta Rapid Transit Authority bus looking for a fugitive who'd wrecked a stolen car at the end of a chase. The felon fired the first shot point-blank and knocked Gordon back with a gory wound under the belt, but the next five rounds belonged to the wounded trooper. Gordon left in an ambulance. The gunman, a coked-up prison escapee and career criminal whose pockets were stuffed with stolen jewelry, left his life spilled down the aisle of the MARTA bus.

By Monday in Macon, Joe Gordon was looking for a way to insinuate himself into the bomb case. In Savannah, Frank Lee was still waiting for a call from Birmingham. In Atlanta, Hoback was assigned to fill in for a vacationing agent in what he considered a frustrating, pencil-pushing job at district headquarters, where he had to wear one of the three suits he owned and scan other investigators' case reports for typos and bad grammar. But the drudgery barely lasted until nine A.M. Rich Rawlins, the assistant special agent-in-charge, told him the Birmingham office had called. The Vance package bomb had been mailed from Newnan, about a fifty-minute ride down Interstate 85 from downtown Atlanta. Rawlins wanted Hoback to get up a list of federal firearms licensees for the Newnan area to send back to Birmingham. The young agent decided to include the rest of Georgia, and when he called Ruth Poole, the administrator who handled such information for ATF in Atlanta, she offered to run a list of Alabama licensees too. Hoback marveled at his involvement, however small, in such a big case as the Vance murder.

Barely a block and a half from Hoback's office was the Eleventh Circuit Court of Appeals—where Judge Vance sat on the bench—in a converted post office, one big gray stone box the size of a city block, less sidewalks. Inside, through a boxy X-ray machine, one

package after another moved on a conveyor belt while Steven Grant
stood before the viewing screen. With close-cropped hair, a muscular
build, smooth, dark skin, aviator glasses and posture as if he had a
yardstick for a spine, Grant looked like what he was: an ex–military
policeman, ten years in the Marines, and a court security officer for
the Eleventh Circuit Court of Appeals. At first, each time Grant was
ready to inspect the bluish, monochromatic image of another parcel, he pushed a button to move the conveyor belt. But by the time
he'd worked his way to the second ragged canvas bin of mail, his finger had tired. He switched to using a floor pad he activated with
foot pressure.

All this was a precaution, and a final one at that. Mail passing
Steve Grant's inspection went to the court clerk's office, to be
opened as usual, by one of four or five people clustered around a
table. Just then, nobody, save the killer and conspirators, could have
known why Judge Vance had been targeted. No one else knew
whether other bombs had been mailed—until Steve Grant found
the answer with the tenth or eleventh package from that second bin,
a package wrapped in brown paper, with a neatly typed red-and-
white label and American-flag-over-Yosemite stamps.

Grant saw on his screen the opaque silhouette of a seven-inch
pipe, with wires leading to a pair of flashlight batteries. He'd studied
explosives in the Marines and again at the Federal Law Enforcement Training Center down on the Georgia coast. The configuration
was so classic it could be a training aid.

Grant showed what he saw to the deputy marshal on the phone
behind him—who agreed it was a bomb—and then told his supervisor. Grant and the others went from room to room evacuating the
building.

———

At the ATF office, Rawlins told Hoback there was a bomb at the
Eleventh Circuit. *A serial bomber*, Hoback said to himself. Rawlins,
who looked and spoke amazingly like Dan Dierdorf, the ex–NFL
lineman of *Monday Night Football* and diet-commercial fame, told
Hoback ATF agents were already on the scene and Hoback was
needed at the FBI office to help at the command center. The young
agent was crestfallen; the biggest bomb case he'd probably ever be
close to was unfolding a block and a half away and he was headed in
the opposite direction, probably to play gofer for the FBI.

———

Within minutes, a small crowd of lawmen clustered at Grant's post, not all of them versed in the operation of the X-ray machine in which the package bomb reposed. Only later would it register that somebody had unwittingly tripped the "reverse" switch on the machine—only later, when a bomb dog stepped on that floor pad Grant had been using. Everyone stood near one end of the machine, but the suddenly rolling conveyor belt moved the package steadily, inexorably toward the other end. The box holding a bomb longer, thicker and deadlier even than the one that had killed Judge Vance teetered on the edge. Then it dropped.

Pete McFarlane was at a pawnshop just south of downtown when he got a message to call in and in turn got word about the package at the Eleventh Circuit. He hustled into his tan, government-issue Chevy Blazer, hit the lights and siren and chose surface streets over the interstate as the most direct route. Straight off, of course, the Vance bomb came to mind. For a change, this one he was rolling on *had* to be real. He grabbed the mike and radioed a request that the Atlanta Police bomb squad meet him. When he finally got inside the old courthouse, McFarlane made a quick observation. People were there who didn't need to be, and he started clearing them out.

McFarlane was a twenty-year veteran FBI agent and a bomb technician. Quantico doesn't pop every agent out of the same mold. If some match the cinematic, bureaucratic, stiff and stuffy stereotype, others are less starchy, more streetwise, savvy, almost lusty about the job. Some like their crime and their attire strictly white-collar. Some crave to wear a rope wrapped about the crotch of the dark blue fatigues of the SWAT team and to practice rappelling off skyscrapers and maybe affirm that amid all that coiled nylon rope are big balls of brass, the kind needed to kick in doors when the unknown awaits on the other side. And then in any outfit there are those who defy grouping, and Pete McFarlane was one of the FBI's.

With his silver-brown, droopy mustache, wire-rim glasses, dress-Stewart plaid, button-down shirt and sweater with elbow patches, he looked professorial, except that when he bent over the package resting facedown on the floor at the base of the X-ray machine, the sweater rode up his back to reveal a gun shoved in his baggy blue jeans.

A deputy marshal briefed him about how the device wound up on the deck. McFarlane was amused and amazed it didn't detonate.

Somebody found another parcel that, though much heavier, looked enough like the bomb package that the finder wanted to run it through the X-ray machine too. McFarlane gave him the go-ahead, glanced at the benign image the second box made on the screen— this one contained only lawbooks—then, hearing voices from the clerk's office, started that way to urge whoever was there to get out. But the man who'd checked the second package had his problems with the conveyor belt too. Again, it was in reverse. McFarlane was barely a few feet away when out of the corner of his eye he saw the box of books, maybe fifteen pounds of books, falling off the conveyor belt, plummeting toward the bomb package on the floor. He froze. He felt as if his heart were sucked into his gullet, and he sucked a big breath as if it were his last.

After a hard thud, a quiet moment, then flooding relief and nervous laughter, the other man's visage wore the realization of major screwup.

"We gave it the lawbook test," McFarlane cracked with reassuring humor. Then he continued on toward the clerk's office.

One man McFarlane didn't clear out of the building, Atlanta Police bomb-tech Bill Briley, had a similarly affable, implacable demeanor. There aren't many jumpy, impatient bomb techs, not, at least, who reach McFarlane's or Briley's age. Briley wore what looked like hip waders, but a flycaster could drown in britches like these, lined with Kevlar, the material in bulletproof vests. He had a matching jacket reinforced with ceramic plate and a helmet shaped like Darth Vader's. McFarlane wore a vest of similar construction. For all the gear, McFarlane knew a detonation would probably kill them.

———

Another ATF agent dispatched to the FBI command center was senior to Hoback and Hoback was jealous, assuming the senior man would be assigned as ATF's case agent on the Eleventh Circuit bomb. Hoback's main role was to figure out what else ATF could do to help, a backup agent on a backup mission. Then he heard an FBI supervisor say, "Let's get it the hell out of there and take it apart." Hoback called Rawlins, filled him in, then sought and got permission to go to the Atlanta Police Academy on the edge of town where, if things went well, the mail bomb would be, in the parlance of bomb technicians, "rendered safe."

———

Now all the bomb techs McFarlane and Briley had to do was get the deadly device out of what, at this time of day, was possibly the most populous square mile in the South. Using a shoebox-sized, portable X-ray machine Briley had brought, the pair of them scrutinized the mail bomb from other angles besides the one Steve Grant's machine captured. Briley slowly lifted it into a fiberglass bucket, wide as a trash barrel but shorter, with nylon netting inside. They swathed the package in a blue ballistic blanket constructed similarly to their bomb suits. One on each side, they hefted the big bucket as two people might tote a heavy footlocker, or as two pallbearers on opposite sides of a casket.

A wet and windy chill whipped down Forsyth Street, and at either end the block was lined with federal agents, police, reporters, photographers and court workers. Both bomb techs bristled to see how close the crowd was allowed. McFarlane and Briley, bomb bucket between them, walked across the street toward a trailer hitched to a white police van. The entire trailer bed was taken up by a big red tube standing on end, roughly five thousand pounds of double-layered steel insulated with sand, so that if a bomb placed inside it went off, the blast would be directed skyward. They climbed on the trailer and gingerly laid the fiberglass bucket in the tube. Moments later, a siren yelped, and Briley at the wheel, the van towing the trailer headed out, leading a procession including a police car, McFarlane's Blazer and a Ford Bronco carrying a television news crew.

Bill Briley knew what exploding metal could do to human flesh, having carried reminders since 1965 when a hand grenade left him decorated with scars on his left leg and arm, a misshapen finger and a Purple Heart. The teenager from Atlanta learned how to blow things up in Vietnam; only years later did his hometown police department send him off to learn how to stop things from blowing up. Now he thought the same awful things he thought around other bombs. He thought about what it would be like in the vacuum-vortex of the explosion, whether he'd get flat-out killed or die squirming or live maimed. He thought about it blowing his hands off and thought about guys he'd seen in Vietnam without arms. He worried about his hearing, about his sight. And he thought about whether, when he toted the box, the pipe within would be parallel to his hips or perpendicular, since in the latter case he knew he might take an end cap like a point-blank cannon shot right in the belly.

The bomb range, entered through a high, sliding chain-link gate, was a sort of chasm, the towering, massive dirt banks of the city landfill forming the rear wall. Toward that ran the vestige of an old road, asphalt bleached to a pearly gray and substantially encroached upon by dense brush, tawny and frail for the winter. And here, technically, the bomb techs had a choice.

Often, the safest, surest way to render safe an improvised bomb is simply to blow it up. Take it out in a field, countercharge it, clear out and watch the show. And watch the body of evidence eviscerated. There was no doubt; there would be no countercharge here. A judge was dead, a court under attack. This bomb would be dismantled piece by piece, preserving precious evidence. And that meant risk.

The risk in what Briley and McFarlane did soon after their arrival at the bomb range lay partly in the jostling the bomb might have sustained in the crosstown journey. That the package had made it through the U.S. mail was mitigation; nonetheless, neither man knew what parts might have rearranged themselves in the trailer trip, what pieces of metal might have come together to—with another jiggle—complete the electrical circuit and ignite the power of the powder-packed pipe.

Both bomb techs climbed on the trailer, bent awkwardly and picked up the edges of the ballistic blanket, cradling the package. They placed blanket and package on the ground, and a police captain whose cheek seemed permanently formed around a hank of tobacco directed two SWAT officers to place the bomb bucket on its side several paces away. Then Briley had the package again, this time by himself, holding it out in front of him the way a man in a new suit might carry a leaky bag of kitchen garbage. His elbows were bent almost at right angles, his stride level, no amble, ramble, or bounce, as if you might be able to balance a glass on his head. Or a bomb between his palms.

He placed it inside the bomb bucket, which was fortified with at least one sandbag and the ballistic blanket on top. A remotely controlled tool was readied to begin dismantling the package bomb piece by piece. The range, meanwhile, was a burgeoning bustle of badges—Atlanta Police, agents from the FBI, ATF, the Postal Inspectors. Among them, Hoback deemed it proper procedure to hang back, and the number who ventured forth for close-up looks at the package surprised him. A line of tripods trained TV cameras from just outside the gate. Too close, thought Hoback. But then again, the young agent reminded himself, this is big stuff, bigger than I've ever been involved with. These other guys must know what they're doing.

"Fire in the hole!" yelled J. W. Powell, another Atlanta Police bomb tech of Briley's vintage, hustled up from a nearby academy room where he'd been teaching a firearms class.

"Fire in the hole!" meant get ready for a blast, in this case as the render-safe device functioned. The lawmen took cover. But the blast was a bust. The tool was misaligned and managed only to knock a hole clean through the package, apparently failing to neutralize a single component of the bomb assembly. And that was a problem. For much of the day, the sheaf of X rays Briley and McFarlane had made tremendously enhanced the odds of survival, providing at least a partial diagram of the package. But now, as the bomb techs approached the bomb package to realign the render-safe tool, they moved toward it not knowing what the impact of the first, futile attempt might have wrought in the bomb configuration. The shifting of something as flimsy as a small piece of cardboard might have caused the detonation system to kick in.

It didn't, not this pass. The second time, the de-arming tool did its job, knocking out the two flashlight batteries the bomber had obviously intended to power the detonator. This made the package safer, but not safe. Terrorist bombers had been known to hide a secondary power source inside the pipe itself, where the X rays can't penetrate. The next step was McFarlane's call, and he took two things into account. First, the pipe itself would be difficult to attack with the box and the wrapping still around it. Second, while the paper and cardboard could be torn away remotely, evidence might be destroyed in the process. Again the bomb techs had to balance protecting themselves and protecting the evidence.

McFarlane and Powell knelt on the asphalt on opposite sides of the parcel, both wearing rubber gloves. Using his fingertips, McFarlane took delicate hold of a piece of the wrapping paper and held it back so he could look inside with his flashlight. He carefully opened the back of the box. Then he stuck his hand in and took hold of the pipe bomb. It didn't blow, but it didn't budge.

"Hold the box," said Powell to McFarlane. The policeman peered into it. Over and over, it had been hammered into him: remove remotely, use a rope to gut a bomb from a position of safety. But he told himself a *monkey* can pull a rope. He'd never tell that to a class of police recruits, knew it was anathema to the close-knit bomb-tech community. Nonetheless, possessing supreme confidence in his mechanical ability, his instincts, he would probably have stuck his hand into this box even if the wrapping wasn't important.

Powell reached in, feeling his way, searching for booby traps the X rays might have missed, ready to withdraw if he felt anything that shouldn't be there. Don't force anything, he reminded himself. He pulled out a piece of the homemade ignition system, which looked to Powell like a sliver of disposable pie pan.

"Pie pan!" blurted one of the feds on hand.

"Yeah, like a pie comes in," retorted the middle-aged cop. "I realize that y'all think it comes sliced on a saucer."

Powell fished back inside the box. The pipe was fastened to the box with heavy-gauge aluminum wire, which he twisted free of the cold steel. Then he slowly pulled the bomb out.

The pipe, naked and exposed for the first time, struck McFarlane as much bigger than the X rays suggested. Two more observations: he'd never seen a pipe bomb like it, and this guy meant to kill somebody. The pipe itself was ordinary, galvanized steel, at seven inches long and two inches in diameter, larger than the bomb that had rent Judge Vance and his kitchen two days before. Nails, juicing the capability to tear flesh and inflict pain, were affixed to the pipe with rubber bands. What stood out were the ends of the bomb. A pipe bomber interested only in terrorism, in being noticed or sending a warning, might simply enclose the powder in the pipe by screwing commercially available caps on each end. Instead, this bomb had square metal plates welded on each end of the pipe. Then the bombmaker inserted a long threaded rod through holes drilled in each end plate. The rod, three-eighths of an inch thick, ran the length of the pipe and was bolted snug at each end. The effect, as a bomber who knew chemistry and physics might figure, was to bolster the bomb at what otherwise would be its two weakest points. This would delay by milliseconds the bursting of the pipe after detonation, causing a greater buildup of explosive force within and a more powerful, perilous blast.

Bolting the bomb like this was more dangerous not only for whoever might have felt its force in the Eleventh Circuit clerk's office, but for the bomber also. Combined with a stray grain or two of powder in the wrong place, the friction of a mere turn of the threaded rod or the slight tightening of a nut could vent the same viciousness on the bomber as he intended for someone else. He'd gone to enormous trouble—and risk—simply, it seemed, to make a more efficient machine of destruction.

Hoback had made a point in his short career to latch onto the canny veterans in bomb investigations, to partner up, tag along and soak up expertise. Such was his personal mission this day, his mentor of the moment Bob Holland, a crusty ATF veteran, an architect of the Bureau's National Response Teams and a former director of the International Association of Bomb Technicians and Investigators.

When Holland said he too had never seen a bomb like this before, Hoback heard him.

"What do you mean?"

The older agent pointed out the square end plates and the threaded rod, and Hoback was awed and cowed—awed that somebody with a quarter century of experience was seeing something for the first time, and cowed that when he himself had first looked upon the bomb, he noticed nothing unusual. Hoback felt inadequate.

But what is to the rest of us merely a morbid mosaic of cardboard, steel and wire can become, canted from the angle of a bomb tech, a sort of hologram, from which emerges shimmering hints of the bombmaker's mind-set. Terry Byer was an explosives expert at his first day of work since transferring to the ATF lab in Atlanta, and he wound up joining the crowd of cops on the range. The pipe bomb impressed him, one of the best he'd seen. The metal-plates-and-bolt feature reminded him of military ordnance that used the same principle to boost kill power. The builder is a methodical thinker, Byer told himself, and smart, very smart.

Two wires dangling from a tiny hole drilled in one of the end caps meant a firing device was still inside the pipe. McFarlane still didn't know how dangerous was the heavy object in his hands, but he trimmed the wires and shunted them together to prevent static electricity or other stray current from touching off the bomb. The nails were removed by hand.

The feeling was that the tool used to get this far wouldn't do the next job: taking apart—without blowing apart—the pipe bomb itself. And a more powerful and suitable disarming device was within reach. Bob Holland had only to reach into his trunk, which might seem odd to those who know that the ATF forbids agents from disarming bombs. Investigate them, yes; render them safe, no. Leave that to local bomb techs or Army explosive-ordnance disposal teams, or, in dire emergencies, to ATF lab guys like Byer. But Holland had transgressed that rule before, and now, barely two weeks from retirement, he wasn't worried about the regulations. He wanted in on this one and volunteered not only his machine but himself.

"We're not supposed to be doing this, are we?" asked Hoback.

"Nope," Holland replied.

Powell carried the pipe farther down the range and placed it on sandbags against the dirt slope, a better backdrop for the violent rendering of the pipe this stage of the operation would entail—or for an explosion. Holland's device was aligned, a long wire affixed so it could be activated remotely from cover. He'd come this far, rules or no . . . Bob Holland pulled the trigger.

From the pipe, orange flame geysered several feet into the sky.

It's ready to go off! Hoback thought.

Aw shit, Holland said to himself.

For just that instant, Holland waited for either a thunderous boom or a whooshing sound like an acetylene torch makes. He got the whoosh, and he knew that meant the tool had worked, had hammered back the corner of an end cap. Unfortunately, the render-safe device also ignited the smokeless powder within the bomb, but bomb techs on the range knew the whooshing sound meant the vacuum in the pipe was broken, the compression necessary for the explosion neutered. So the powder simply burned. The seconds it sizzled said there was a lot of it.

McFarlane went up to a pipe still warm and smoking. Inside he could see residue from the powder, flecked with crimson. Hercules Red Dot brand. Also still in the metal tube, and still intact, the detonator, jammed with a high explosive far more unstable than the powder had been.

"Here, hold this," McFarlane said as he handed the pipe to his boss, Bill Hinshaw, special agent-in-charge of the FBI in Georgia. McFarlane untied the wires he'd earlier shunted together, then, using a pair of hemostats—a surgical tool that looks like scissors and works like tweezers—he grabbed hold of the detonator and pulled it out. So meticulously crafted that some surmised at first it may have been commercially produced, the detonator was actually homemade from the barrel of a ballpoint pen, an efficient but time-consuming device far in excess—like the threaded-rod construction—of what was needed had the bomber been merely cavalier about whether he killed or maimed. The pen-barrel rig would make for fierce, white-hot detonation. The higher the temperature, the more forceful the reaction inside the pipe, the more violent the explosion.

———

Bill Hinshaw was an ex–Army officer and college football player with a crooked smile, square shoulders and a reputation as a square shooter, even in quarters where the FBI wasn't always greeted fondly.

Hours before the eduction of the pipe at the police bomb range, even before he knew there was a bomb at the Eleventh Circuit courthouse, Hinshaw's first full week as the new special agent-in-charge—"SAC" in fed jargon—of the FBI's Atlanta field office had begun with word the package that killed the judge in Alabama wore a postmark from Hinshaw's jurisdiction, from Newnan, Georgia. Hinshaw had his folks setting up a small command post in the small town and planned to show up in person and show the flag to the troops. As he walked out of his office for the trip, his secretary, Mary Jane Caudill, stopped him.

"You'll want to take this call," she said. "It's the director."

And that's how Hinshaw found out about the Eleventh Circuit bomb. FBI director William Sessions told Hinshaw he'd been informed about it by Gerald Tjoflat, chief judge in the Eleventh Circuit.

"I knew you'd want to know about it right away," Sessions told Hinshaw, "so I decided to just call you directly."

The Atlanta SAC promised to get details. He hung up and looked at Mary Jane.

"We got a bomb in the Eleventh Circuit. Where the hell is the Eleventh Circuit?"

He stuck his head in on one of his assistants.

"Get off the phone," Hinshaw urged.

"I'm talking about the bombing," the subordinate replied, apparently meaning the Vance bombing.

"We got a bomb here in Atlanta. I need you to get off the phone."

The assistant was on the phone to somebody big in headquarters, somebody who, upon hearing there was a bomb in Atlanta, wanted details. The Washington official, Hinshaw suspected, wanted to score points as the one to inform the director of this major development. But Hinshaw told his man not only did the director already know, but the director had been the one who called *him*. He insisted

again his man get off the phone, knowing his handling of the Washington guy was bad political form. It was the beginning of a sometimes contentious, adversarial relationship between Hinshaw and
headquarters concerning the bomb case.

In the commotion around the Atlanta FBI office, Gary Robinette
wasn't sure anybody was listening to him. So he took a pair of bolt
cutters to the chain of command and went to Hinshaw himself. The
return address spurred him, when he heard a downtown lawyer's
name had been used on the Eleventh Circuit package. The lawyer,
of course, had nothing to do with the bomb, other than the bomber
may have randomly grabbed his name from the phone book. Such
had been the case with another package, one Robinette had been
investigating, containing not a bomb in the classic sense but a tear-
gas grenade rigged to trip when the package lid lifted. The case
had gone to Robinette because he worked civil rights violations,
and the tear gas had been mailed to the Southeastern regional office of the National Association for the Advancement of Colored
People—the NAACP—in downtown Atlanta. It arrived on August
21, 1989, about four months before the mail bombs to Vance and
the courthouse.

The thing was clean—no fingerprints, no DNA, no obvious suspects. The age of the tear-gas canister made it virtually untraceable.
But the sender's fastidiousness fascinated the veteran agent. The
box looked at first to be die-cut for some special purpose, with a
creased, corrugated attachment to the lid housing the trip wire, and
precisely matching partitions cradling the canister in place. Even
box-manufacturing insiders at first thought a professional box man
had made it. But finally microscopic scrutiny with a commercial box
expert dispelled that notion. The cuts were fine but not exactly sym-
metrical, the work careful, artful, but not professional.

Robinette related this to Hinshaw and pulled evidence photos for
the SAC to see. Hinshaw left for the bomb range. On his way, he got
a call relaying concerns from a headquarters official about how the
bomb should be handled.

"Tell him," Hinshaw replied, "there is only one SAC who is a
qualified bomb technician and that SAC is on the way to the range
and will be personally responsible."

Hinshaw was not only a bomb tech, but author of the FBI's only
manual on bomb investigations. Page 11:

Idiosyncrasies found in the construction of one particular device may surface in another case. While this is not positive proof that the same person is involved, it is a source for a viable investigative lead.

On the range, Hinshaw looked upon a work of extraordinary craftsmanship. The metal pipe and other components had been firmly and meticulously affixed to the inside of the container, with attention not only to function but symmetry, and the entire assembly had been bathed in black paint, probably to drown any fingerprints.

Hinshaw glanced up. "NAACP bomb?"

A postal lab guy who'd examined the tear-gas package seemed to buy it. The Atlanta Police bomb techs, Briley and Powell, had been at the NAACP that day in August, had discussed months ago whether the tear gas might be a trial balloon to test the civil rights groups' defenses, and on the range with the pipe bomb both saw similarities in the packaging. Hoback, too, had been at the NAACP, but hadn't laid eyes on the tear-gas package itself.

Murlene Murray thought her eyesight was gone and her face on fire. A secretary at the NAACP for close to thirty years, she and regional director Earl Shinhoster had opened the box. There were sparks, two pops, and white and yellow smoke plumed. Shinhoster jumped back, tripping over a table and breaking a lamp. He yelled to Ms. Murray to get out, and they knocked on doors to warn other tenants. Out of the office building, which housed a number of doctors' offices, came old people, children and others, crying, coughing or falling down.

ATF Agent Ed Hemsath got a call from Atlanta Fire about what officials feared might be an undetonated explosive device. He fetched Hoback from his cubbyhole of an office. Hemsath had been the young investigator's training officer until a few months before and continued to coach what he considered the best trainee he had ever tutored, earnest and tenacious, the way he liked to think of himself at that stage. And he saw his reflection in another way; each man could nearly see his reflection in the other's gleaming pate, not lost on other agents when the pair partnered up.

"If we put our heads together," Hemsath would say, "Hoback and I make an ass out of ourselves."

They took Hemsath's brown Oldsmobile, under lights and siren, and were the first feds on the scene. There was no need for Hoback to head inside since he had little experience with bombs, and the building still belched smoke. Hemsath stuffed his tall, muscular body into a firefighter's overclothes, slung a borrowed air tank on his back and waded into the murk. After he looked at the package in the NAACP office, he and APD bomb tech Powell, who wore a gas mask, prowled the premises in search of other suspicious packages.

When Hemsath finally emerged and peeled off the fire gear, Hoback noticed his partner's light gray suit was now black with sweat. The older man huddled with agents from the FBI and postal inspectors and decided the package, since it was not really a bomb, didn't come under ATF's jurisdiction.

A man who seemed affiliated with the NAACP approached Hemsath and asked him what could be done to stop such things in the future. Hemsath told him everything should be suspect.

———

Now, as Hinshaw headed back to his office from the bomb range, he dispatched an alert to the regional NAACP office about the similarities between the August tear-gas package and this latest bomb from the courthouse. But he was still in the car, just minutes later, when he heard a radio news broadcast. The story was out of Savannah, on the coast four hours east of Atlanta. Another bomb. This one went off.

2

The Savannah Bomb

Late on the afternoon of December 18, Abercorn Street in downtown Savannah was dripping with Spanish moss and cold rain. The north side of the 1300 block consisted of a pink row of offices side by side, town-house style. One of them belonged to Robbie Robinson, a lawyer. Two doors down were the offices of Emerson Brown, doctor of optometry.

Dr. Brown was on the phone near five P.M. when he heard not exactly a crash, not a thud, but something loud. Not an accident on the corner . . . maybe more like a gas explosion. Carol Cutter, his receptionist, told him the windows had blown out of Robbie Robinson's office. Dr. Brown told the party on the phone he had to leave and he ran out the door.

Smashed glass from Robinson's second-story windows littered the ten paces of sidewalk to the lawyer's front door. Smoke drifted through the jagged openings left overhead. Dr. Brown opened the heavy salmon-colored front door to the whining buzz of a smoke alarm.

He saw Joyce Tolbert, Robinson's secretary. She hadn't been upstairs to Robinson's private office since the loud explosion shook the building. She'd started up, but then turned around and called the 911 emergency number. Then she called her mother. Then she called her minister.

Dr. Brown hurried up the steps and turned sharply to the left at the top of the staircase. He knew Robinson, of course, though not so well that he'd call him a friend, but an acquaintance. Robinson was a city alderman, known in the community but, in Dr. Brown's mind, low-key and hardly controversial in spite of some mildly publicized legal work for the NAACP on a school desegregation case. Both men were NAACP members, but in different chapters.

When Dr. Brown turned the corner, he saw Robinson kneeling where his chair would normally be, close to what was left of his large, cherry-colored wooden desk. The desk was almost blown in two splintered, blood-drenched pieces, with a big semicircle of desktop, about where a blotter would go, obliterated. Nails were embedded at wild angles in the pale blue walls, which were spattered too with what looked at a distance like small wisps of blown fiberglass insulation. It was actually Robinson's flesh, bone and hair. A chaotic pile of books, manila folders, legal papers, office supplies, glass shards and other debris covered the floor. A hole the size of a child's fist pierced a wall across the room from the desk, and through that hole could be discerned another in another wall, and in turn a chunk of metal lodged in a third wall about forty-five feet away from Robinson.

Robinson said nothing. Dr. Brown couldn't tell if he was conscious. Blood poured from tiny cuts about Robinson's face. The optometrist moved behind the lawyer, squatted and slid his left hand under Robinson's left armpit to keep him from pitching forward into the rubble. Robinson's left hand was mangled and attached to the arm by only a shred of skin. The right arm was gone from near the elbow, and as Dr. Brown held Robinson, he looked down to see the right side of Robinson's chest ripped apart. A gory hole gaped from his thigh, possibly where a palm-sized hunk of steel had bored through before it ricocheted off a windowsill and sliced through the wall of a metal file cabinet. Robinson's shoes were off, not as a lawyer would slip them off as he settled into his desk chair to look at the mail, but as if he'd literally been blown out of them.

Dr. Brown, an Army reservist, was trained in triage, in treating battlefield wounded. *Stop the bleeding*, he thought reflexively. But Robinson bled in too many places for Brown even to try. He just kept holding him. *Hold on* . . . Brown spoke softly to encourage the ravaged man, but Robinson said nothing in reply. Dr. Brown could feel the fading pulse in the armpit. It seemed like minutes passed, leg-cramping, desperate minutes, the two men locked in their pose, one just holding on to the other, one just holding on to the last, dimming strands of life. Finally, the doctor looked up to see emergency workers in the doorway—frozen there, it seemed to Dr. Brown. He heard them ask something about whether it was safe to come in. Dr. Brown was, for a moment, irritated at their hesitation. But they did come in, took charge of Robbie Robinson, and helped Dr. Brown to stand up.

———

Steffanie Baker's new boss was giving her a lift to her car at the end of the workday when they heard the alarm over the radio. The dispatcher sent out the call as a structure fire. But soon the battalion chief's voice crackled over the air.

"Call the investigators over here. We've had an explosion."

Steffanie Baker had become one of those investigators barely a month and a half before. The chief fire investigator, Louis McLendon, was sitting next to her, at the wheel, and they were only about two blocks away from Robinson's office. As they got out of the car, a siren sound said an ambulance was close and getting closer. A firefighter came to the door of the law office. "It's upstairs," he said.

"In the front room, Mac," said the battalion chief at the top of the stairs. McLendon headed toward Robinson and Baker started to follow, but the battalion chief grabbed her by the shoulders.

"Shug," he said, "you don't need to go in there. The man's been blown apart."

Steffanie Baker pushed him back against a wall. She pushed not hard enough to hurt him, but enough to get past him—and enough that she would worry later whether she would face disciplinary charges. She focused immediately on Robinson's right side, which faced toward the door through which she entered. *Where's his arm?* she thought. She scanned the room and spotted it, virtually intact, next to the trash can. The ambulance crew was right behind her, and one of them grabbed a sheet from his jump kit and helped Baker swaddle the limb.

Christopher Scalisi, a lanky paramedic with seventeen hundred hours of training and seven years on the job, couldn't take a radial pulse on a man with virtually no wrist left. Now Robinson was no longer still, no longer silent. As the paramedics began to treat him, he became restless, intermittently wailing or moaning in high-pitched tones. They tried to bandage him but the tape wouldn't stick to his bloody skin. He struggled as the emergency crew moved him to the long board used to immobilize a patient's spine. A restraint fastened over his brow, a cervical collar around his neck and straps across what remained of his large frame, he thrashed violently now, infused, perhaps by adrenaline or the semiconscious, agonized will to live, with awesome strength.

Securing Robinson sufficiently to move him took close to five minutes. He fought, screaming as Scalisi and partner Dana Bauers carried him down the stairs. What was left of his arms left on the wall a dripping crimson streak the length of the staircase, as broad and defined as if painted with a brush. To Scalisi, some of the experienced firemen witnessing the scene looked to be in shock, unable to bring themselves close enough to Robinson's screaming, bloody paroxysms to help.

Dr. Brown was downstairs with Joyce Tolbert when the paramedics brought her boss down from his office. Dr. Brown told her not to look, but she looked anyway and saw the remains of Robinson's right arm continually catch in the spindly banister supports as they descended.

Robinson screamed and struggled after he was in the ambulance. Scalisi was driving but could hear the screaming behind him. At the hospital, emergency-room workers gathered to help. Robinson was still fighting when Scalisi left the room, still screaming, still trying, Scalisi thought, to free himself.

———

A sack of stocking stuffers in hand, Frank Lee was walking through the Wal-Mart parking lot when his pager went off. Checking the display and seeing it was his office calling, Lee headed not for a phone but for his car, from which he could call in on the radio. Lee was the senior agent in the ATF Savannah office, maybe the senior federal agent of *any* kind in Savannah. When he switched on the ignition in his gold Mercury, a young ATF colleague was already shouting for him on the air. Calming when Lee finally answered, the agent on the radio told him about the explosion at Robinson's office.

Frank Lee signed on young in 1966, when the ranks of ATF's predecessor, the Alcohol and Tobacco Tax Division, swelled for Operation Dry-Up, a Sherman-like march on the thousands of stills cooking moonshine in Georgia. Lee was an ex-schoolteacher lured by the chance to kick in doors, drive fast cars and run bootleggers through the swamps, but when escalating sugar prices and the increased availability of legal or "red" liquor began drying up the illegal "white" liquor industry in the South, ATF shifted focus to arson, explosives and guns. Lee early on made the conversion to the painstakingly methodical arson-explosives speciality.

The veteran agent knew Robinson and where his office was. Only a week or so before they'd been in court together. Lee had helped DEA on a drug case, and Robinson represented one of a half dozen or so defendants. Lee was six foot one, thickset but not fat, thick hair and mustache a sandy red to meld into a face burnished by fishing and golfing in the coastal sun and wind. He didn't exude flexibility, but had a rocklike bearing, with chiseled chin and flinty eyes. He heard the fading siren from an ambulance as he badged his way through police roadblocks to park across the street from the law office. Walking over through the cold rain, he went in to find a number of city officials, among others, on the first floor. He also saw Everette Ragan, a lieutenant with the Savannah Police, and fire department investigator Louis McLendon, two men with whom he'd worked for years and knew well. Ragan told him a bomb had gone off upstairs and Lee would supervise the crime-scene work.

"You're in charge and anything you want from us, we'll give you," Ragan said.

Lee asked for and got a big police officer at the front door. Ragan personally handled his request to get as many of the political types out as he could. For all Lee knew at that point, there could've been a zillion tiny pieces of evidence waiting to be crunched by an untrained if well-intentioned foot. There might also yet be explosive material that hadn't detonated, which weighed on Lee as he and Steffanie Baker went upstairs, where the bomb had blown.

The windows were broken. In an office lit by a single dangling bulb, fine grains of smokeless powder hung thick in the chill. They returned to the first floor.

"Nobody goes upstairs," Lee told a police supervisor. "We're not in any rush. The scene is not going anywhere."

Postal Inspectors, FBI and ATF agents, Savannah Police, and fire department investigators assembled in Robinson's law library for the parceling out of the work. Lee and Baker would use thumbtacks and string and grid the whole office, then others would work in shifts, grid by grid, picking up every piece of potential evidence down to stuff that could only be vacuumed up. After each grid was vacuumed, the vacuum bag and filter would be marked, saved and replaced for the next grid. Somebody had been sent to find some big, empty fertilizer bags to store large items of debris. A Savannah cop got the job of photographing every car within three blocks, and a still camera was set up on the first floor to shoot bomb remnants. The Savannah PD public relations officer was assigned to videotape the entire scene.

A good man was needed for one of the grittiest, grisliest jobs of all.

Frank Bennett knew something about pipes. But at seventeen, he had left home in Knoxville, Tennessee, headed for Washington, D.C., never seriously considering following his dad into the plumbing business. Instead he took a job in the FBI mailroom, the first of a succession of clerical jobs he held at the Bureau while going to college full-time. He graduated magna cum laude and hired on almost immediately as a special agent. Close to two decades later, he was at home near five-thirty P.M. when the office called and dispatched him to the site of a bombing at a local attorney's office. He'd barely steered out of his neighborhood in his gold Dodge government car when a supervisor came on the air and told Bennett he needed to swing by the office first to gather boxes, labels and bags—the stuff of crime-scene investigation—before going to Abercorn Street. Minutes later, another change: head for the hospital.

When Frank Lee had asked for somebody to take custody of the pieces of the bomb, now pieces of evidence, as they were one by one removed from Robinson in the operating room, he was insistent the investigator must not leave Robinson for a moment.

"I don't give a shit if he has to piss in a sink."

To Lee, the FBI made a good choice in the experienced Bennett, who parked near the emergency entrance at Memorial Medical Center, then learned Robinson was already on his way into surgery. A Savannah officer approached Bennett in the emergency room about Robinson's clothing and towels used to cover the wounded man in the ambulance, all of which might contain bomb residue. The FBI agent hastily scribbled the cop's name off his ID plate, then peremptorily told him to stay with the stuff and they'd hook up later. For now, Bennett knew where he had to be and knew he had to move quickly.

His request to be in the operating room was not roundly welcomed. The doctors could retrieve the evidence for him, it was explained, and simply hand it over after surgery without worrying about a stranger in the OR. The trim, slim agent with neat red hair and glasses made known in careful, measured tones he *must* be in there, and he sensed the opposition was not to him, but rather to anything extrinsic to the medical mission. The lines were clear in his mind. The doctors and nurses were there to save Robinson. Bennett's job was to save evidence, and he could do nothing for the agonized lawyer but help catch his assailant. The agent remained quietly, stubbornly insistent and was finally shown to a room to wash his hands and throw on blue scrubs over his street clothes. He grabbed a steno pad and a pen.

About six-fifty P.M., roughly five minutes after arriving at the hospital, Bennett stood in the operating room, perhaps a yard from Robinson's feet. A nurse pushed toward him a tray draped with a white cloth and standing about waist high, on rollers. Stay behind it, she told him, and try to stay out of the way.

At the FBI office in downtown Atlanta, Gary Robinette heard that the packaging from the Eleventh Circuit bomb had been brought in from the range. As soon as he saw it, he knew the same typewriter addressed its mailing label as typed the label on the NAACP tear-gas package in August. He knew, now, the tear-gas bomb had been a trial run. And that goofy letter suddenly made sense.

Copies had been sent to television outlets in Philadelphia, Pennsylvania; St. Paul, Minnesota; Milwaukee, Wisconsin; Cleveland, Ohio; Baltimore, Maryland; Raleigh, North Carolina; Columbia, South Carolina; Montgomery, Alabama; Little Rock, Arkansas; Jackson, Mississippi; and Atlanta. He'd checked it only because it was postmarked on August 21, the same day the tear gas went off at the NAACP. But the neat typing in the malicious missive and the neat typing on the tear-gas package label did not match, and there had been no apparent nexus between the NAACP and the subject matter of the letter. There was a nexus now. The letter was about the Eleventh Circuit Court of Appeals and was entitled *DECLARATION OF WAR*.

> THE UNITED STATES COURT OF APPEALS FOR
> THE ELEVENTH CIRCUIT DOES DELIBERATELY AND
> WRONGFULLY REFUSE TO FULFILL ITS OBLIGATION
> TO PROTECT THE INNOCENT.

THE COURT'S FAILURE TO RENDER IMPARTIAL
AND EQUITABLE JUDGMENTS IS DUE TO RANK BIAS
AND THE MISTAKEN BELIEF ITS VICTIMS CAN NOT
EFFECTIVELY RETALIATE.

THEREFORE, CITIZENS OF DENSELY POPULATED
CITIES SHALL BE SUBJECTED TO HIGH
CONCENTRATION LEVELS OF CARBONYL CHLORIDE
AND CYANODIMETHYLAMINOETHOXYPHOSPINE
OXIDE. THE ATTACKS SHALL CONTINUE UNTIL
WIDESPREAD TERROR FORCES THE COURT TO
ADDOPT [sic] THE IMPARTIAL AND EQUITABLE
TREATMENT OF ALL AS ITS HIGHEST PRIORITY.

THE MEDIA IN TARGET CITIES HAVE BEEN
NOTIFIED OF THE TERRORIST ATTACKS AND THAT
THEY CAN OBTAIN GAS SAMPLE DATA BY
CONTACTING THE COURT.

SUBSEQUENT TO EACH ATTACK, THE MEDIA
SHALL BE REMINDED THE COURT'S CALLOUS
DISREGARD FOR JUSTICE MADE THE ATTACK
NECESSARY.

Also in from the range were Bill Hinshaw and a trio of Washington-based crime-lab experts who had rushed over from Alabama, where they'd been working on the Vance case. About as unofficious as an FBI SAC can get, and a perpetual motion machine besides, Hinshaw was in character when he volunteered to drive the lab guys to Hartsfield International Airport for their flight back to Birmingham.

The ride was dominated, naturally, by talk of what had just happened in Savannah, and on the interstate, just north of the airport, Hinshaw decided that's where they should go. Now. The crime scene in Birmingham was already old. It would wait.

"Hey, you're the boss," somebody replied.

Hinshaw knew Savannah, having been the FBI's number two there in the early eighties, and he knew there was a Delta flight to the old coastal city about now. He parked and popped the trunk in search of gear. In a kit bag he kept blue fatigues, clean underwear and a pair of boots, the kind of stuff for a manhunt in the woods, not for an out-of-town trip as point man on the Bureau's biggest case.

On the plane, they spoke in subdued tones once learning the cocked ear in the aisle ahead belonged to a Cable News Network reporter. The agent who picked them up at the airport was well known to Hinshaw from his time in Savannah, as was Frank Lee, who thought the Savannah FBI, when Hinshaw was there, had been the most creative, innovative group he'd ever seen.

Lee's methodical crime-scene investigation was still in the early stages when Hinshaw arrived, lab people in tow.

Someone had made a startling discovery, fishing from a trash can brown wrapping paper replete with a neat red-and-white address label and stamps. Apparently, Robinson had walked over to the trash can and deposited the paper, complete and intact, before returning to his desk to open the box. Hinshaw immediately recognized it as almost identical to the wrapping he had seen on the Atlanta Police bomb range only hours before.

This time, the return addressee wasn't a lawyer but the Reverend John E. Jackson, from Warner Robins, just south of Macon. Hinshaw picked up a phone and told the Atlanta command post to roll people out of Macon to find out about this reverend, believing instantly he had nothing to do with the bombing, but hoping to glean insight into what the minister's selection might tell them about the bomber.

Few organizations can match the FBI's ability to delegate and mobilize. At about ten-twenty P.M., two agents out of Macon were talking to Rev. John E. Jackson, who told them he never goes by John, that those who know him know his first name as "Emory." Jackson was a white, retired, seventy-three-year-old evangelist who no longer led a congregation but would preach at revivals around the Southeast when asked. Not surprisingly, he said he hadn't sent any mail to Savannah in quite some time. He was not a member—nor had he ever been a member—of the Klan, any other white-supremacist group or, for that matter, the NAACP. He hadn't received any threats or hate mail. And, he told the agents, he hadn't been involved in any litigation.

Repeatedly, the old preacher lamented the destruction folks brought upon themselves with drugs and weapons. But as to why somebody was destroying other people with these particular weapons, his interview yielded little.

––––––––

Paula Denitto considered herself slightly jaded after five years as a resident and a year of practice on her own. But this was a combination of all the worst. The chief resident on call had called her because this case was too much to handle alone and Dr. Denitto was on deck in the trauma-surgeon rotation. Now Robbie Robinson was before her and the team of doctors and nurses, so much of his arms gone, the right side of his chest like hamburger. Before she'd even seen him, the IV fluids, oxygen, and sedation were begun. A laryngoscope went in his mouth to push the tongue out of the way, so a tube could be snaked down his trachea. A needle and catheter were inserted below Robinson's belly button to check for blood in the abdomen, which would indicate internal injuries. Not surprisingly, there was blood.

Denitto and a resident did the exploratory laparotomy. A scalpel made an incision down the lawyer's abdomen. Denitto, diminutive and dark-haired, stuck her hands inside, groping, looking. The diaphragm was ruptured. Superficial cracks were discovered in the liver, which was then packed in pads to be left inside when the abdomen was closed. Later they could go back to take them out. The idea now was to keep him alive.

The chest didn't have to be opened surgically. The explosion had done that. A chest tube was in place to drain blood. While Paula Denitto was doing her work, an orthopedist and another resident were completing the amputation the bomb had begun, of the left hand.

The closest Frank Bennett had ever been to the inside of an operating room was for the births of his three children, the last two twins delivered by C-section. Happy as he was at the delivery, he had cringed at the setting of scalpel to flesh. And nothing he'd seen had prepared him for what Robinson looked like now. Even the doctors, it seemed to Bennett, were amazed at the damage, amazed Robinson still lived. But awed as he was at the gore, at the spectacle of a man's life on the line, Bennett was fixed on his job, on the evidence.

Dr. Denitto removed much of it. A second doctor typically gave it a quick look and his opinion of whether it was cardboard, metal, or a wood fragment. The items went in small cups, which were placed on the tray in front of Bennett. Skin tissue from Robinson's chest that might show gunpowder traces. Cardboard from inside the chest. Black, powdery residue off his left heel. Scrapings from his right thigh. Later, Bennett would search for dry ice in which to pack the severed hands. Eventually a Savannah Police officer got an ice-company owner to open his business so there would be enough.

Even to the layman Bennett, Robinson's vital signs seemed to worsen for about an hour. His blood pressure became immeasurable. His carotid pulse undetectable. For fifteen or twenty minutes, the medical team tried chest compressions, drugs to increase the heart rate, electric shocks.

The floor of the OR was a red puddle. Bennett, his shoe coverings saturated, made his way to a phone in the corner and called his office near eight twenty-five P.M. Robbie Robinson, he told his boss, was dead.

By three A.M., Frank Lee had bags of debris, lawbooks perforated by nails and steel, flesh-flecked manila file folders, steel end plates, the batteries used to power the bomb, the stainless-steel nuts, the wrapping and more. He knew the placement of the bomb when it exploded. He had a mental image of the package and of the aluminum wire used as a harness for the pipe. But the threaded rod he'd found sitting on what was left of the desk bothered him. He'd never seen a bomb with a threaded rod through it and couldn't understand how the bomber loaded the powder inside with end plates welded to the pipe. He was confident smokeless powder had been the main filler, but figured a more powerful explosive must have been used in a detonator to create the kind of force evidenced here, shredding steel pipe.

Lee had somebody call the Federal Law Enforcement Training Center, just down the Georgia coast in Brunswick, to borrow sifting screens, which he put to use the morning after the bombing. After the large, obvious bomb remnants were picked up from a given grid, the grid was vacuumed, always with a fresh filter in the vacuum cleaner. The yield from each grid was bagged and marked. Then each bag was emptied atop stacked screens of a progressively finer gauge to separate the contents for closer examination. Remnants of the soldering turned up this way, as did small pieces of the detonator.

By the next morning, reporters and photographers descended on Savannah, along with Lee's boss, Tom Stokes, ATF's agent-in-charge from Atlanta. Stokes flanked Hinshaw—who had gone to the mall for a new shirt and tie and borrowed an iron to revive his suit—at a news conference in a wood-paneled meeting room at Savannah Police headquarters. The FBI man warned the public what to look out for:

"We believe the three packages were essentially the same type of package and device. That's based on our investigation. And the package, based on what we recovered in Atlanta, measured twelve inches long, nine inches wide and was four and a half inches thick. It was wrapped in brown paper. It has a red, parcel-post mailing label in the upper left-hand corner. It bears stamps, rather than a metered postage stamp. And it also has string that is tied around it to form a cross."

He revealed to the public at least two of the packages had been mailed in Georgia. But there was little he could reveal, at a news conference or anywhere else, about the bomber's motive, a void underscored when Savannah Mayor John Rousakis went on camera.

"He was never high profile nor extremist or radical in any way on any issue," the mayor told a reporter of Robinson. "He was just involved and interested. A good man. Had no reason why he should have been connected, either drug-wise or through his efforts a year ago when he represented the NAACP in a desegregation case.

"Which," Rousakis added, "he lost."

But the most telling video that day came because of a plan hatched by Hinshaw and Stokes, incubated partly by sympathy for cold, wet news crews so far frozen out of the crime scene and partly by the SACs' sense nothing they could say would adequately depict the bloody horror of Robinson's office. And it was a crime about which the public needed to know and be outraged. So plastic drop cloths and strict guidelines were laid down, Frank Lee was won over to the idea, and in the afternoon news cameras came in to convey the carnage blown, spattered and smeared across every dimension of Robbie Robinson's office.

———

In Atlanta and Birmingham, the multiagency task force to investigate the bombings was already taking shape. The FBI and ATF joined postal inspectors, the Georgia Bureau of Investigation (GBI), the Marshals Service and others.

Brian Hoback called his old training officer, Ed Hemsath, who a month and a half earlier had transferred to Internal Affairs, at a regional office across town.

"I think they're gonna assign this to me," Hoback said almost plaintively. "It's a big case. I don't think I have enough experience for this."

Hemsath ran down the roster of cases they'd worked together.

"It's just another investigation," the older agent reassured. This case just had more leads to follow, and more press. Hemsath related the story of a bomb-murder case about which he'd felt the same way when he was a green, twenty-four-year-old investigator. But it had worked out.

And, Hemsath said, "I consider you a better investigator than I was."

Hemsath told him to call anytime he needed help and assured him he'd do fine on his own. The veteran agent's stint in Internal Affairs so far had lacked the action he craved, and after Hemsath hung up he envied Hoback's chance to work the bomb case, but not the bureaucratic headaches he knew would go with it.

As predicted, in the 1970s-style, smoked-glass office tower housing ATF and an alphabet soup of other governmental agencies, Rich Rawlins, the assistant special agent-in-charge, told Hoback the Eleventh Circuit bomb case was his.

"You sure about that?" Hoback replied.

3

A Revenuer Remembers

Georgia moonshiners made their white liquor in myriad styles of stills, but almost always the mash box required lots of water, sugar, grain (wheat bran was popular) and time, lots of time for the mash to work, to start heaving, bubbling, foaming, churning, until it looked like some weird, breathing, living thing. Then the sweetly pungent, sawdust-colored mess was slopped into the cooker and heated until the vapor rose and slunk like a ghostly snake into the tubes that led to the condenser, often an old engine radiator sitting in a streambed. The coolness of the branch water condensed the steam into liquor. The problem for the boys from the Treasury Department's Alcohol and Tobacco Tax Division was, even in the scorching Georgia summer, the mash could take days to ferment, so a moonshiner might visit the stillsite only once or twice a week. That meant agents could be on a stakeout for days, burrowed in the brush, sustained by Vienna sausages, crackers and whatever diversion they could manufacture; legendary still-stakeout artist Frank Frazier passed time composing songs for accompaniment by his ukulele. But near the end of the whiskey wars, other investigative methods emerged.

In 1964, Lloyd Erwin, a lanky youngster from Young Harris, deep in the north-Georgia mountains, went to work as a chemist at the Treasury Department's Atlanta lab, and a big part of the job was proving the link between a moonshiner and his still even if nobody spotted him there. That might have meant sneaking into a stillsite to spread fluorescent grease, so that later, if the bootlegger balked in questioning, agents could shine a black light on him to see if he glowed. Or Erwin might've matched the red clay caulked into the seams of a stillworker's brogans with the soil from the pine thicket where investigators had discovered jugs of finished product. He learned about the marks tools made on metal, so, for instance, he could prove a suspect's wire cutters matched the cuttings on the wire holding parts of a still together, and he became proficient in analyzing liquor and the volatile fuels sometimes used to fire the cookers. These technical skills stood him in good stead when the laws changed governing what Erwin, Frank Lee and their buddies did for a living. By December 19, 1989, Lloyd Erwin had been analyzing bombs and incendiary devices for close to two decades.

Jimmy Carter Boulevard is a clogged artery in the heart of southern Gwinnett County, a major landing strip for the white flight just north of Atlanta. Ryan's Steakhouse is just down Jimmy Carter from Interstate 85 and has a partition to turn one end of the restaurant into a meeting room suitable for Kiwanians, Rotarians or, on this day, the Metro Bomb Meeting. The name is unofficial; an attendance record is kept, but nobody ever decided what to formally call the dozen or more local, state and federal bomb experts who get together for lunch about once a month. After eating, their discussions are about the latest wrinkles in local bombs, who's building what where and how to beat them. In police parlance it is "sharing intelligence."

The notices for the December 19, 1989, meeting had gone out in the mail perhaps a week and a half in advance, before any of the invitees could know something else would soon be in the mail to make the meeting extraordinarily timely. The day before the meeting and just a few miles away, the Eleventh Circuit bomb was disarmed; only a few hours' drive away, the Robinson bomb wasn't. Suddenly the main item on the menu was the mail-bomb case.

ATF veteran Bob Holland, who pulled the trigger to render safe the Eleventh Circuit bomb, had a flattop haircut, jowls like a bulldog, and a growl to match. And as he told the lunch crowd about events the day before at the police range, Lloyd Erwin digested, along with his soup and salad, what his old friend from the moonshine days had to say. Holland talked about how the bomb was defeated and about its unusual configuration, with square end plates and a boltlike threaded rod running its length. When Holland

passed around pictures, Erwin, still slender if now grizzled, asked
for one. As the meeting broke up, he got Holland off to the side,
along with the ATF ASAC Rich Rawlins.

"I know a person that has made a bomb of this style," Lloyd told
them. "I don't know where he's at, but I know he's gotta be out of
prison because it's been such a long time ago.

"His name is Roy Moody. It happened in Macon. Sometime in
1972."

Erwin had done the lab work in the case, in which a young wife
was injured when she opened a package bomb she found in her
home. It was addressed, but not mailed, to a car dealer whose company had repossessed her husband's car when it was almost paid off.
The husband was Roy Moody. The case agent was Chester Bryant,
well known in ATF since he had gone on to become the Bureau's
comptroller.

Erwin grabbed an announcement for Holland's upcoming retirement party at the Decatur Elks Lodge, flipped it over and sketched,
from memory, an amazingly accurate diagram of the '72 bomb.
"Flashlight bulb igniter," he wrote, drawing an arrow to the appropriate place in his sketch. "Metal plates." Another arrow. He remembered the thickness of the metal plate and the material used to
construct it, the size and material of the pipe, the smokeless powder,
the bolt size. Though the '72 bomb used four rods instead of one,
Erwin said he'd never seen another one that had both the end plates
and the long bolts in it—until now. And as senior chemist at the ATF
lab in Atlanta, he'd known about every bomb that came through
there, more than three thousand of them.

Rawlins was rapt. He took the sketch and beside it wrote in black
ballpoint:

> *Chet Bryant case.*
> *Moody*
> *had square pieces of metal*
> *on ends of a cylinder*

Erwin took Jimmy Carter Boulevard past nearly every conceivable brand of fast-food franchise and gas station, across the over-
pass, then turned left and cruised down the on-ramp to I-85
southbound, toward the lab. Moody had to have something to do
with those bombs, Erwin decided. Or maybe it was somebody with
whom he did prison time; somehow, Roy Moody was connected. It

was his design. Nobody else, in Erwin's recollection, had ever used it, and his recollection included enough explosive devices to wage a small war.

Once back at the lab, Erwin's mission was to dig out the 1972 case number to pass back to the field agents. That number was the key to tracking down potentially crucial information about the old case. He checked storage cabinets and storage boxes. He hunted for the old logbook. But he couldn't find the number. He couldn't even find the logbook. Then a supervisor told him about a "management decision" that was news to Lloyd. Case files older than ten years had been trashed, tossed to make room. Erwin picked up the phone and called Chester Bryant.

Chet Bryant started out as a whiskey chaser too, barely believing he could get money for something so fun, though other agents maybe figured the same about his old job—selling bras for Playtex. Seven years after starting, he was ATF's Agent of the Year in Georgia. It was the year he nailed Roy Moody, but the newspaper write-up barely alluded to the case. "Bryant, and the eleven agents under him, were responsible for the seizure of 42 illicit distilleries last year with a mash capacity of 45,120 gallons," it said. "They seized 2,001 gallons of liquor and made 74 arrests. The local office also took part in seven firearms cases and one explosive case." But the one explosive case would stand alone in Bryant's career. Of the hundreds of suspects Bryant arrested, Moody had been most memorable, for his ever-calculating personality, his unending complaints about the handling of the case, the calls Bryant got about Moody throughout the remainder of his years with ATF. He remembered the first time he interviewed Moody after his wife, Hazel, was maimed in the explosion. He came off as cordial, happy to help. But as Bryant left the hospital room, he encountered a middle-aged, country-looking man in overalls.

"Mr. Bryant, can I talk to you?" he said. They walked around the corner to a nurses' station. The older man said his son-in-law had something to do with this. "I know he did."

Eventually, Moody became less cooperative, replying to questions by telling the investigators they were smart and could figure the answers for themselves. They did. But Bryant would always believe the case wouldn't have been made if the crime happened a year earlier, even a *month* earlier. As moonshine ebbed, Bryant went to explosives school at the Redstone Arsenal in Huntsville, Alabama, from which

he returned to his post in Macon on a Friday. He entered the Moody
case on Monday. He immediately applied what he'd learned to construct a highly technical case, built—with Erwin's aid—on a trace of
powder here, a toolmark there. Going into court, Bryant knew it was
a touch-and-go, circumstantial case, and Moody was acquitted of
building the bomb. He was convicted of "constructive possession" of
it. Bryant always thought Moody's worst mistake was to take the
stand against his lawyer's advice.

Lloyd Erwin and Chet Bryant had stayed friends; the month before the mail bombings Erwin attended Bryant's retirement ceremony in Washington, D.C. When the lab man called on the
afternoon of December 19, 1989, Bryant, who had moved back to
Georgia, couldn't put his hands on his old case file right away. It was
stored in a miniwarehouse. But he could give his old friend something Erwin didn't have yet, a full name. *Walter Leroy Moody Jr.* Chet
Bryant knew he'd never forget that name. There were no overt
threats. But Moody's menacing mien was the reason he'd told his
wife and children, years before this, never to open a package if they
didn't know who sent it.

————

Brian Hoback glanced at the sketch Rich Rawlins brought from
lunch. "Who drew our bomb?" Hoback asked.

"That's not your bomb," Rawlins replied.

"Bullshit. It's got the square end plates and it's got the rod." The
young agent hadn't noticed there were four threaded rods in this
sketch, rather than a single rod as in the Eleventh Circuit bomb.

Rawlins filled him in on Moody and the 1972 case. "Find out what
you can," he told Hoback. "It originated in Macon."

Maybe a couple hours later, Lloyd Erwin called.

"Brian, I'm tellin' you," Erwin drawled. "You need to look at this
guy."

"Okay," Hoback replied perfunctorily.

"No, no, no, I'm tellin' you, you need to look at him."

Hoback called the resident agent-in-charge at ATF's satellite office in Macon and asked him to quiz some of the old heads about
Moody and look for the case file.

Finally, Hoback found W. L. Moody. In the phone book. The address was in Paulding County, one of those rural areas gradually
evolving into suburb, about thirty-five minutes from downtown At-

lanta. Hoback and another agent drove out to scope the house, but three hundred, maybe four hundred yards of driveway made it tough, even with binoculars, just to get the tag number off the car and avoid notice.

"We'll come back at four o'clock in the morning," Hoback told the other investigator, "and we'll sit on this guy and see what we find out."

And, at Brian Hoback's instigation, in the predawn darkness four agents in two cars rolled into Paulding County. One of them, Gene Richards, an attorney by training, climbed out and headed on foot into a black, moonless pasture hung with a fog so heavy his night-vision goggles wouldn't work. He worked his way along a ridge and through dark thickets. He crossed a creek. Finally about a half mile from the car, Richards, camouflaged and on his belly, reached a clearing near the house. Suddenly somebody came out of the door. Richards froze. The figure from the house headed for a car, climbed in and drove off, but not before the agent got the tag number. Richards found some rocks on a ridge where he could watch the house awhile longer, then he made his way back to the other agents, capping Hoback's first expedition as lead agent on his biggest case. Later, somebody ran the tag. Wrong Moody.

Not that it turned out to be a crucial delay.

Before the week was up, Hoback went to the headquarters of the multiagency mail-bomb task force to which he was assigned and briefed a lower-level supervisor, an FBI agent, on Moody and his 1972 case. Soon after the briefing began, the supervisor held up both hands as if to say he'd heard enough.

"Whatever you guys come up with, you guys handle it," he said in a tone Hoback took to be patronizing and condescending. Lacking confidence and experience, he hid his irritation at what he considered a blow-off.

4

The Faith of Willye Dennis

Willye Dennis was a big woman, eloquent and ebullient, warm and wily, so powerful in presence she seemed bigger than life. As the sixty-four-year-old president of the thousand-member Jacksonville branch of the NAACP, she was chairwoman of the executive committee, chief spokeswoman, public relations person and, usually, opener of the mail.

Early on the afternoon of December 18, Willye Dennis was running late. The press conference was originally set for the seventeenth, but postponed a day so she could attend a memorial service on the seventeenth in Mims, Florida, where a dozen years before two NAACP officials had been killed—in a bombing. She had not known them, but to Willye Dennis, people killed for a cause deserved to be remembered. Now, on the eighteenth, still in the NAACP office with the press conference about to begin elsewhere, she was in a hurry. So, when shortly after noon the mailman brought a parcel neatly wrapped in brown paper, she set it aside on a table. As she did, she thought fleetingly how odd it was to get a package with a return address in Warner Robins, Georgia. NAACP chapters are keenly aware of jurisdictional lines, and Warner Robins, way up in middle Georgia near Macon, was far outside the territory overseen by the Jacksonville branch. Furthermore, the parcel was addressed not to Mrs. Dennis, but to "Legal Counsel, Jacksonville Branch NAACP." Though the branch had used lawyers before, notably in a successful school desegregation case just affirmed by the Eleventh Circuit Court of Appeals in Atlanta, there was no official, full-time "legal counsel." So, as usual, opening the box fell to Willye Dennis. But that had to wait; she planned to come back to the office before the day was done. About eight minutes before one P.M., she locked up and rushed off to the news conference set to begin at one o'clock sharp. The Clanzel T. Brown Community Center was about ten minutes away.

The Clanzel T. Brown Community Center was across the road from some apartments in the vicinity of which a few days earlier a stray bullet from some kind of shoot-out ripped open a teenage girl who happened to be walking nearby. Another wild shoot-out, another killing . . . it was time the people reclaimed their turf . . . such was the message Willye Dennis wanted to send at the community center. She was joined by the Baptist Brotherhood, the Ministerial Alliance, the Urban League and the president of the mostly black Brotherhood of Police Officers, Anthony Rogers. He sat on the executive board of the Jacksonville branch of the NAACP, knew Willye Dennis well, and affectionately called her Boss Lady. She sometimes called him Kangaroo Pouch, an allusion to the big belly beneath the round, clean-cut, oft-smiling face.

"This car feels funny, Anthony," Mrs. Dennis told him before she knocked the gearshift into reverse in her 1987 station wagon after the press conference.

"Aw, Boss Lady . . . ," he replied, laughing, shaking his head side to side, dismissing her automotive intuition.

Close to two P.M., maybe fifteen minutes after the news conference, Willye Dennis was turning off Moncrief onto Edgewood Avenue, into one of the busiest intersections on Jacksonville's north side. Suddenly, the wagon's wheels just seemed to lock up. The engine ran, but the car was inexplicably and inextricably mired. This hit traffic like a brick dropped on a nest of fire ants. A truck driver climbed out of his cab and tried to tell Willye Dennis how to turn her wheels, but they were locked tight as a cross-threaded nut. The second policeman on the scene was Kangaroo Pouch.

"I told you that this car sounded funny," said Willye Dennis.

Officer Rogers walked around the corner to Wiggins Automotive and sent the first tow truck. The tow truck showed up and backed up to her car. Then the tow truck stalled too. Another tow truck rumbled into the glutted intersection. It also broke down. A policewoman on the scene called for a third wrecker. Somehow, Willye's son, Leo, heard his mom was having car trouble and he showed up, parking the wrong way on a one-way street in keeping with the disorder of the day.

Amid all this, it rained. Willye Dennis finally decided to leave and try to rent a car.

At about ten minutes before six P.M., the Dennises arrived at the offices of a car leasing and rental company she'd used before with good results.

The clerk asked wet and weary Willye Dennis if she had a reservation. Mrs. Dennis replied she did not, and the clerk peremptorily announced only one car was available.

"I can only drive one car," came Willye Dennis's reply.

It was a sports car, the clerk warned.

"Look at me," Mrs. Dennis said. "I'm a sporty woman."

She finally got the car, but well after dark, and she still had to close up FAMCO. Willye Dennis was the director of Family Cooperative Learning and Development, Inc., founded in 1978 when she and a few others became distressed that children at their church couldn't even read the Sunday-school lessons. By December 1989, FAMCO provided day care, after-school care, counseling and even computer training for close to two hundred children, from infants to teenagers. One news conference, one breakdown, three tow trucks, one unpleasant rental clerk and one FAMCO stop later, she decided it was too late to return to the NAACP office. The package would have to wait until the morning. Willye Dennis went home.

The phone ring wasn't the only loud noise to jar Willye Dennis into waking close to six o'clock the next morning. Bob Ingram was calling, and he has a voice to match his size, which was about six feet six inches, 350 pounds.

"Leader, you awake?" he boomed without trying.

Ingram was executive director of the Health Center, a sort of halfway house for recovering drug users in Jacksonville. He was also active in the NAACP, and a close friend of Willye Dennis. He told her he normally did not watch TV news in the morning, but this morning he had watched and learned of the mail-bomb death of sometime-NAACP-lawyer Robbie Robinson in Savannah, a couple of hours up I-95 from Jacksonville.

"Well, if you get any funny-looking packages," Ingram told his friend, "you call the authorities."

But if there was a connection between what Bob Ingram told her about Robbie Robinson and anything in her life, it didn't immediately occur to Willye Dennis. She was preoccupied with her children, a busload of them from FAMCO she was scheduled to take downtown that morning for a Christmas program at the Chamber of Commerce.

The next phone call came from Willye Dennis's niece, Martha. Martha was sixty-six, so in age as well as intimacy niece and aunt were more like sisters. They'd grown up together and still talked every day, usually in the morning. Lately, both women had been in, as Willye Dennis called it, "a kinda scriptural mood," and Martha had called to talk about a particular verse of Scripture, Romans 8:28.

> *And we know that all things work together for good to*
> *them that love God, to them that are called according to*
> *His purpose.*

Preoccupied as she was with the field trip, something gnawed at Willye Dennis. That package. . . . She called Lloyd Pearson, treasurer at the NAACP Jacksonville branch, who also had keys to the door, and who'd mentioned he planned to stop by the office. Don't open that package on the table, she warned Pearson. Then she called Jerome Spates, chief of community affairs for the Jacksonville Sheriff's Office—JSO for short—with whom she'd dealt concerning black-on-black crime and police-brutality issues. She trusted him and asked if he could have the package inspected before it was opened. He agreed.

This happened to be the morning John Sheddan came in early, at seven-thirty, just to get a head start on the day. When Chief Spates called, Sheddan was in his office, which was really the sheriff's department electronics room, a jam-packed jumble of surveillance and bugging gadgetry, video cameras and workbenches for maintenance. Chief Spates told the bomb tech Willye Dennis had called him because she didn't want to make a fuss, didn't want patrol cars swarming or anyone unnecessarily alarmed if there was nothing to it. But in light of what had happened elsewhere, he wanted Sheddan to scope out that package. The chief told the bomb man to stand by for a callback when somebody would be at the NAACP to let him in.

If the chief wants it, the chief gets it, Sheddan told himself, expecting his main mission to be reassuring Ms. Dennis, an influential

member of the community. There was nothing, Sheddan thought, to
tie Jacksonville to the bombings in Georgia and Alabama. But Sheddan had been a bomb tech more than a decade, handling hundreds
of calls, dozens involving what turned out to be live devices. And his
professional curiosity was aroused by the Southeastern mail bombings, which by now were all over the news. Now he had an excuse to
call his old buddy in Atlanta, Bob Holland.

In a quarter century with ATF, this wasn't the first time Holland
had been roused out of bed by a ringing phone. He and Sheddan
went back years, largely through their memberships in the International Association of Bomb Technicians and Investigators, and Holland had thought enough of Sheddan to bring him in to teach
budding bomb investigators at ATF's training site in Brunswick,
Georgia. Swapping notes about the latest in bomb-builder chic is a
way of life for a good bomb tech, a way of *prolonging* life.

Sheddan explained he'd refrained from calling the day before,
since public reaction quickly arches into overreaction, and he knew
the Atlanta bomb techs must have been awash in phone calls.

"For the record," Sheddan said with mock officiousness, "I need a
description of what these packages look like."

As Holland spoke, Sheddan took notes on a 3 1/2-inch-by-3 1/2-
inch scratch pad on his gray metal desk. On the first slip he wrote:

> *Brn Paper*
> *String tied in center*
> *Mailing label*
> *Red & white*
> *Typed*
>
> *Postage neat*

Holland told him the box was rigged so the victim could only
open it at one end, that the battery pack had two C-cells, the pipe
was two and one-half inches by eight inches and had a three-
eighths-inch rod down the center, running through the welded end
plates. He described the ignitor and red and gray wires that ex-
tended from it like a pair of legs.

Both sides of the first slip now full, Sheddan grabbed a second to
note aluminum wire, maybe fence ties, had cradled the pipe in the Atlanta box. And on a third scrap he wrote that the Birmingham pipe dif-
fered in that it had one-and-one-quarter-inch or one-inch end caps.

"It's probably gonna be nothing," Sheddan said.

Chief Spates called back and told Sheddan somebody would be at the NAACP office. Sheddan headed out in his Chevy van toward a small strip mall on Soutel Drive. That's where the office was, with brick walls and a weathered white gable. The white paint on the big sign reading NAACP was so faded the grain in the plywood showed up as discernibly as the washed-out NAACP seal. A smaller sign read NO LOITERING. Black metal burglar bars were installed over two front windows and the door, of no account against an intruder who chooses so stealthy a route as the U.S. mail.

Sheddan, a tall man with a shock of black hair, a mustache and hawklike visage, parked seventy-five or eighty feet away and walked to the doorway. Inside, amid paneling and rust-colored carpet of a style popular in the 1960s, were scattered tables and chairs such as you might find in an old school or municipal-government office. Directly in front of Sheddan, maybe a dozen feet away, Lloyd Pearson was on the phone with his back to the door.

"Hello, I'm John Sheddan with the Sheriff's Office. I understand you have a suspicious package."

"Yes. It's right there."

Pearson turned, sort of cradled the receiver under his chin and pointed to a pair of blond wooden tables shoved together to make one long surface, littered by an edition of the *Palatka Daily News*, a large manila envelope, a letter on U.S. Senate letterhead and other items. Amid all this, straddling the seam where the two tabletops met, reposed a package neatly wrapped in brown paper, bound perpendicularly with string tied in the center, a typed, red-and-white mailing label, and a palmful of neatly placed stamps depicting the American flag flying in Yosemite National Park. Sheddan knew instantly what he had.

"Hang up the phone."

By the time Lloyd Pearson said "What?" Sheddan, six foot four, 240 pounds, was upon him. He grabbed the startled older man with both hands and hustled him, half walking, half stumbling, out the door. As they got outside, another officer was coming down the sidewalk and Sheddan steered Pearson toward him. Evacuate the west end of the mall, Sheddan instructed, and he went door-to-door on the east end. The first door he rattled turned out to be padlocked. Good thing nobody's there, he told himself. It was headquarters for a motorcycle "club." He moved on to a barbershop with maybe five barbers and forty customers and ordered everyone out for their own safety. Sheddan was an organizer of the Greater Jacksonville King-fish Tournament for charity, a lobbyist for the Fraternal Order of Police in Tallahassee, a diplomat when the situation called for it. This one did not. The big cop moved quickly to dam up the torrent of questions.

"Everyone has to leave and take your cars from the parking lot or they will be towed."

As the unclipped and partly clipped filed out, an off-duty police officer identified himself. Make sure the parking lot is clear, then close off Soutel Drive, westbound, Sheddan instructed. He spotted two ATF agents arriving. This is the real thing, he called out, and they helped with the evacuation, which included nearby houses as well. The sheriff's department communications center called the gas company to cut off the gas. A mobile command center, a big truck replete with radios, phones, charts, maps and coffeepot, housed administrative types on the scene. Sheddan and other bomb techs from the JSO, the FBI and ATF huddled in a carpet store at the end of the shopping center.

Sheddan wouldn't cross the doorsill of the NAACP office again for three and a half hours. He wanted to work the phones, find out what the crew in Atlanta had learned the hard way, how the bombs were put together and how to take one apart. He called Holland, by now at the ATF offices in downtown Atlanta.

"I've got one of 'em," Sheddan said. "There's no doubt."

Then he got Pete McFarlane on the phone. They talked and Mc-Farlane faxed him the X rays he and Bill Briley had made. Then Sheddan talked to Tom Thurman, a top FBI bomb expert in Washington who told Sheddan he had the Atlanta bomb on the table in front of him. Thurman faxed more X rays.

Typically, the three JSO bomb techs took turns handling call-outs. Sheddan had operated all day thinking this was his turn, but Gary Fussell, another bomb tech, took issue, insisting a minor call he had handled the week before didn't count. It was like fighting for the last cup of Kool-Aid in Jonestown.

"You guys are crazy," said the SWAT team commander before he walked off.

They flipped a coin.

"I told you it was my turn," said Sheddan upon the result.

The other bomb techs pitched in squirelike to clothe Sheddan in his armor, $17,000 worth weighing close to ninety pounds, the key components Kevlar and steel plate. He lumbered like Frankenstein's monster down the sidewalk from the carpet store to the NAACP carrying two cameras. In the bulky suit he couldn't swing either the Polaroid or the 35-mm model up to see through the viewfinder, so he held them at arm's length, pointed toward the package and snapped his photos. He retreated to the command post to fetch a portable X-ray unit, another blue, shoebox-sized model similar to the one Briley and McFarlane had used in Atlanta. He would take four pictures with it, trudging back and forth between the NAACP and the carpet command post between each. The sheriff's department and FBI bomb techs handled developing while the ATF guys helped Sheddan sit down between each trip and take off his headgear, which resembled a motorcycle helmet except it weighed around twenty-two pounds and the Plexiglas-type face shield was about an inch thick. While the wet, chilly weather might have meant misery to the cops on the perimeter, it was a blessing to Sheddan, tempering what might have become a sauna in his suit; still, he lost five pounds in two hours. Mindful the bomb assemblage might include sensors to trip an explosion during the X-ray process, he shot most of the images by remote control. But one X ray, from a particularly important angle, had to be taken by hand, Sheddan holding the machine balanced on the back of a folding metal chair even as he, like McFarlane and Briley in Atlanta, balanced the risk to his safety against the magnitude of the case.

Sheddan, Fussell, JSO bomb tech Art Holton and FBI bomb tech Dennis Durden compared the X rays with the faxes they got earlier in the day. In shades of gray and black according to the density of the metal, the X rays revealed the same components in the same configuration as in the Atlanta bomb. They could make out the presence of batteries, the large pipe, metal strapping that compared to the wire cradling the Atlanta device and on the perimeter of the pipe, small shadows. The nails. They made their plan of attack.

Sheddan hefted his helmet, tightened the straps on his bombsuit and headed back to the package bomb. He carried with him a render-safe device called a disrupter. Durden, the FBI bomb tech, walked behind him unfurling a long wire. Without touching the package, Sheddan aligned the disrupter an eighth of an inch from the bomb. Moving the parcel out of the office to do this was never an option to Sheddan. No plaster, no paneling, nobody's furniture was worth his life. When he taught bomb classes, Sheddan told his students if he were ever called to the Louvre for a bomb by the *Mona Lisa*, somebody better take a picture of the *Mona Lisa*.

Sheddan retreated a safe distance and sat cooling off on a car. The wire Durden had strung led from the disrupter with the bomb to a "hellbox" Fussell held a safe distance away outside. To arm the disrupter, you pull back a toggle switch on the hellbox and watch the meter charge. Once the needle moves all the way to the right, you shove the toggle switch forward.

A final check was made of the perimeter security. "Fire in the hole!" Durden yelled three times. Then Fussell moved the toggle switch forward. The disrupter activated and ripped apart the package, scattering the contents. The steel pipe full of explosive hurtled ten or twelve feet across the room, knocked a hole in the paneling, bounced off the wall, and stopped back under the table upon which it had originally rested. Most of the packaging came to ground near the pipe. The inside of this box too was painted coal black. Elsewhere on the floor were other remnants—paper towels, a paper clip, the string, a battery and, bundled in brown tape, several sheets of photocopy paper.

Guarding against a delayed reaction, Sheddan waited two or three minutes before going back in the office, looking about to make sure no power source remained near the pipe with its volatile filling. He finally spotted the steel cylinder, thick, black, suspended, like the Atlanta bomb, between two square, steel end plates. Wisps of brown paper—part of the cardboard box to which the bomb had been glued—stuck to the face-up side of the device. Rubber bands still held some of the nails in place while others were scattered about the room. Upon the pipe, Sheddan draped a net, roughly thirty inches across with a drawstring that, when pulled, could close the net like a sack. Holding a rope tied to the drawstring, he plodded, still in his bombsuit, into the parking lot, to a place behind the bomb trailer. He threaded the rope through a hook suspended over the trailer on a rotating arm, then pulled the net sack closed and dragged it— bomb inside—along the ground until it lifted and hung suspended from the hook. Sheddan and Fussell used ropes to remotely maneuver the hook until it was over the bomb basket on the trailer. They gently let out the line to lower the bomb into the basket.

Leaving the processing of the other evidence to Fussell, Sheddan and FBI Agent Durden, in a truck pulling the bomb trailer, headed for the JSO range, about twenty miles away. Rain complicated things; rear-ending this rig could bend more than fenders. Against that, a patrol car followed and two motorcycle cops rode in front, and the convoy took the I-295 beltway to avoid populated areas. Darkness neared and folks were tired—a good setup for a bad screwup. Sheddan arranged for an officer to guard the bomb in the trailer overnight, and plans were made to reconvene the next morning.

Leona Sheddan wasn't one of the police wives who flooded with fear every time her husband left for work. John had been a bomb tech for the entirety of their marriage, and he might as well have been heading out the door to sell computers, such confidence did she hold in his abilities. She saw the NAACP case on TV and figured her husband had to be in on it. When he got home, she asked if everything was all right and he said yes and that was enough for her. But her spouse couldn't purge it from his thoughts, knowing people had already died, knowing the Atlanta bomb had caught fire and part of the evidence had burned, knowing it was the biggest case of his career and probably that of every cop who had been on Soutel Drive that day.

At eight A.M., Sheddan, Fussell and Holton—the three locals— met at the office to plot an attack on the pipe that wouldn't ignite the powder. Fussell had made diagrams outlining various strategies. They settled on this one: place the bomb in the big red steel vise bolted to the back of the bomb trailer and use a rope to remotely wrench the nuts loose on the ends of the threaded rod. That would allow them to pour out the powder and remove the detonator. The plan, Sheddan thought, had the best mathematical chance of saving the most evidence. But there was risk. Stray powder in the threads of the rod, friction from the turn of a nut . . . the combination could leave Leona a widow.

At the range, the JSO men met representatives from the FBI, Postal Inspectors, ATF and Florida Department of Law Enforcement. Fussell and Sheddan climbed upon the bomb trailer and pulled off the metal cover to expose the pipe bomb—soaking, they discovered, in about four inches of water; rain, Sheddan figured, had poured in during the trip from Soutel Drive the day before. Jarring as the sight was at first, he decided it shouldn't be a problem and might even make the powder less sensitive to friction. After each agency got a chance to photograph the pipe, Fussell and Sheddan moved everyone back.

The two bomb techs removed the rubber bands binding the remaining nails in place. Fussell took the pipe in hand and Sheddan cranked open the vise.

"Hold it!" said Fussell.

It startled Sheddan, no fan of sudden speech around bombs. One of the nuts, Fussell told him, was loose.

"Are you sure?" Sheddan said.

"Yes, I am."

"Is it loose enough to come off?"

"Yes, it is."

Pause.

Fussell: "Let's go for it."

Sheddan was about to break his own rule, his prime directive. Never, he'd preached, do a hand entry—as opposed to a remote entry—unless going in by hand could save a life, as when, for instance, a bomb is strapped to a human being. Fussell felt the same way. But here Sheddan stood while Fussell, holding the pipe, unscrewed one nut with his fingers. The nut slipped off and the rod slid slightly into the pipe, pushing powder—dry powder—out the opening where the nut had been. Sheddan fetched a clear plastic evidence bag into which they poured the red-flecked granulation, nearly all of it. Most detonators contain highly sensitive explosive, and this detonator was still in the pipe even as Fussell gently tamped on the end to knock loose the last of the powder.

"Gary, hold it," Sheddan blurted.

The detonator had fallen into the hole in the center of the steel end plate and protruded about a quarter inch. Sheddan, the guy who would blow up a da Vinci rather than take a needless risk, slowly tugged at the most volatile part of the deadly assemblage, trying to squeeze it through a tiny opening in the steel plate. When it came free, they had beaten the bomb and, for the moment, the bomber. Fussell set the pipe on the back of the bomb trailer and shook hands with Sheddan. They could congratulate themselves not just on surviving, but in recovering for evidence nearly every piece of a mail bomb, replete with all the powder. Strange about the powder. Later, somebody tried to pour it back into an identically sized pipe and it wouldn't fit. There was too much. The bomber must have *packed* it into the pipe, another indication of the lengths to which he went to heighten the bombs' destructive power.

The package had been mailed to the NAACP and might have

killed people there. But John Sheddan had also been at risk, had his skills not lived up to Leona's expectations. After it was over, he was left feeling as if he were the one the bomber was trying to kill. The bomber, however, had already announced something about his intended victims. In that bundle of copy paper from the bomb package burrowed four messages:

The first, obsolete by the bomber's own doing:

> MR. ROBERT ROBINSON;
>   AMERICANS FOR A COMPETENT FEDERAL
> JUDICIAL SYSTEM SHALL ASSASSINATE YOU BECAUSE
> ATTORNEYS HAVE FAILED TO PROPERLY STRIVE FOR
> A COMPETENT FEDERAL JUDICIAL SYSTEM.
>
>   010187

The second was obsolete, possibly by the bomber's ignorance. The addressee, a prominent Columbus, Georgia, lawyer, was dead already of natural causes.

> MR. MARTELLE LAYFIELD, JR.;
>   YOU ARE ORDERED TO NOTIFY ALL FEDERAL
> JUDGES AND ALL ATTORNEYS IN THE UNITED
> STATES THAT THEY HAVE BECOME TARGETS FOR
> ASSASSINATION BECAUSE OF THE FEDERAL
> COURTS' CALLOUSED DISREGARD FOR THE
> ADMINISTRATION OF JUSTICE.
>   AMERICANS FOR A COMPETENT FEDERAL
> JUDICIAL SYSTEM SHALL INDICATE CREDIT FOR
> EACH ASSASSINATION BY PROVIDING YOU WITH
> THE NAMES OF THE DECEASED FOLLOWED BY THE
> SECRET CODE, 010187. THE CODE SHALL NOT BE
> MADE PUBLIC.
>   FAILURE TO COMPLY WITH ORDERS OF
> AMERICANS FOR A COMPETENT FEDERAL JUDICIAL
> SYSTEM SHALL RESULT IN YOUR ASSASSINATION.
>
>   010187

The third, more ominous for its lack of specificity:

> Judge;
>   AMERICANS FOR A COMPETENT FEDERAL
> JUDICIAL SYSTEM SHALL ASSASSINATE YOU

BECAUSE OF THE FEDERAL COURTS' CALLOUSED
DISREGARD FOR THE ADMINISTRATION OF JUSTICE.

010187

And the fourth, ominously clear:

TO THE OFFICER WHO OPENED OUR SMOKE BOMB;
   YOU ARE HEREBY ORDERED TO NOTIFY ALL
OFFICERS OF THE NAACP THAT THEY HAVE
BECOME TARGETS FOR ASSASSINATION BECAUSE OF
THEIR FAILURE TO PROPERLY STRIVE FOR A
COMPETENT FEDERAL JUDICIAL SYSTEM.
   AMERICANS FOR A COMPETENT FEDERAL
JUDICIAL SYSTEM SHALL INDICATE CREDIT FOR
EACH ASSASSINATION BY PROVIDING YOU WITH
THE NAMES OF THE DECEASED FOLLOWED BY THE
SECRET CODE, 010187. THE CODE SHALL NOT BE
MADE PUBLIC.
   FAILURE TO COMPLY WITH ORDERS OF
AMERICANS FOR A COMPETENT FEDERAL JUDICIAL
SYSTEM SHALL RESULT IN YOUR ASSASSINATION.

010187

The "Americans for a Competent Federal Judicial System" would make a dramatic entry in the lexicon of hate groups, if indeed it was a group. So long as it wasn't leaked, the code, 010187, would enable investigators to know henceforth when they were dealing with the real killer and not some hoaxer, and it allowed the bomber to authenticate his communiqués so no copycat could cut in on his limelight. The code's derivation, whether it signified, for whatever reason, January 1, 1987, or something else, would be the subject of intense forensic scrutiny, like virtually every scintilla of evidence from the Jacksonville device. Even the blank pages from the bundle of copy paper would undergo meticulous inspection in the crime lab. Even the blank pages might say something.

5

Americans for a Competent Federal Judicial System

In a meeting room at the Atlanta FBI's building, mike cords crawled up the podium like kudzu vines naked for the winter. The head postal inspector in Atlanta, Leo Shatzel, made the opening remarks. To his left, wearing somber suits and sober expressions, FBI SAC Bill Hinshaw, Georgia Bureau of Investigation Director Robbie Hamrick and ATF ASAC Rich Rawlins stood in a row, each tall and husky with his hands folded in front of him. Between Shatzel and them was an easel with a large, white poster board, imprinted with, in big, black, sans-serif characters:

PHONE
404-361-1092

Shatzel had a neat, businessman's-type haircut, smooth skin and he came across as solid and sincere. He wore a blue-gray herringbone jacket, button-down shirt and a conservative striped tie of periwinkle, gold and navy. He faced a room jammed with journalists, from newspapers, radio and television, local and network.

"The investigation into these bombings continues at a very accelerated pace by all agencies involved," he said, gently rotating his gaze back and forth from one side of the room to the other as he spoke. "And as part of that investigation we have established a twenty-four-

hour hot-line number to be used as a tip line to furnish any information . . . regarding the mailing of the bomb parcels, or . . . as to the
identity of the sender."

He read off the phone number, then repeated it.

"We are asking public assistance in identifying the perpetrator of
this cowardly crime."

Pause.

"This twenty-four-hour hot-line number will be manned by or
staffed by postal inspectors, but will instantaneously be made available to all the investigative agencies that are investigating this
crime." Pause. "With that, I'll open up to any questions."

First question: "Sir, does this mean that we're not close to arrest in
this case, if you are asking the public to help?"

Shatzel: "No, sir. It simply means that, uh, we're seeking additional, uh, investigative, uh, support in this."

In plain language, he might have answered, *Hey, the guy might
walk in and surrender tomorrow. But obviously, if we knew who he was, we
wouldn't be here talking to you.* But by the standards of law-enforcement-
ese, a dialect spoken mainly at news conferences and in press releases,
Shatzel had given a good answer. He didn't lie. Nor did he reveal
the unvarnished truth that might comfort—even embolden—the
bomber: the conventional wisdom in policeland is that if you have to
appeal to the public, whether through tip line or composite sketch,
you haven't got much.

Next question: "Can you address the quality of the forensic evidence that you're going over . . . good stuff or have you got a long
road ahead?"

Another deft maneuver by Shatzel: "I'll let Bill Hinshaw, the director of the FBI here, address that."

Hinshaw stepped to the microphones. "We have a tremendous
amount of physical evidence, both from the blast scenes where the
two homicides occurred and then also from the devices that were
rendered safe here in Atlanta and down in Jacksonville. It's all under examination. It's a very tedious process. We're getting some results back. We don't have any announcements to make, but we hope
to use that to be able to further identify the person or persons responsible for this."

Translation: *We've got heaps of "evidence." Evidence can be anything
connected to the crime. So far none of it has handed us the bomber.*

Another question: "The other gentleman referred to a perpetrator. Are you reasonably certain that you're looking for a person here or—"

Hinshaw: "Well, we know we're looking at least for one." A masterpiece of cop-speak. He maintained a mostly straight face. "If there are others, they'll get the ride too."

"Sir . . . with all the attention now and the scrutiny being given packages, do you expect the perpetrator or perpetrators to act again? Do you think they may be laying low now?"

"We didn't expect him to do this in the first place. We have no expectation."

Hinshaw managed to get Rawlins to the podium. The ATF supervisor seemed reticent, and when somebody lobbed a question about whether there had been follow-up letters in the aftermath of the bombings, he ducked, deferring to the postal inspectors or FBI.

Leo Shatzel weighed in, and suddenly the news conference was no longer mundane.

"There have been follow-up letters sent," he revealed, "since the receipt of the bomb parcels.

"It appears that these letters may have been sent by the individual who mailed the parcels."

Excitedly, somebody sought clarification: "You mean, you mean, somebody has sent follow-up letters to the NAACP and Judge Vance and the Eleventh Circuit and . . . Robinson?"

"There have been several follow-up letters," Shatzel replied.

Up to this point, the news conference had been uncommonly collegial, questions occasionally even prefaced by "sir." Suddenly it was on fire. "Who received the letters and what did they say?" rose from the back of the room.

"I'm not going to comment on that right now because that is part of the current investigation. I'd rather not disclose the contents of those letters."

The postal man did confirm the letters had been mailed in Georgia, received in the last day or two, and "were threatening additional mailings to other individuals."

In fact, an envelope had turned up the day before addressed to "The Late R. Lanier Anderson, III," a troubling designation since Anderson was alive and an active Eleventh Circuit judge. The envelope contained copies of the same four letters discovered in the Jacksonville bomb package. On the twenty-first, the same day as the news conference, FBI agents from Atlanta, Mobile, Tampa, Jacksonville and Miami reported that eight other Eleventh Circuit judges had received similar letters. (Judges were already moving about with twenty-four-hour security.) Letters identical to Judge Anderson's also turned up at the NAACP office in Atlanta and at the Birmingham post office, the latter addressed to "The Late Robert S. Vance." And similar threat letters were delivered to the home of Carolyn Layfield in Columbus. She didn't think the sender knew her husband was dead and believed he was likely targeted because he had been chairman of the editorial board at the *American Bar Association Journal*. All the letters were postmarked in Atlanta on December 19, the same day the fourth mail bomb turned up, meaning the awful results of his handiwork had not stifled the bomber's urge to continue his campaign.

The press and public knew little, if any, of this.

The news-conference questions continued, rapid-fire. Shatzel's replies came in short bursts.

I can't comment on that either, he said.

I can't comment on that.

I'm sorry. I can't comment on that.

Hinshaw stepped in to deflect heat off Shatzel—and attention away from the letters. When and if a suspect was finally identified, investigators would try to determine if he possessed information only the bomber would know. The more information made public, the less interrogators would have with which to work.

"There's a great deal of interest in these letters," Hinshaw said, assuming a no-big-deal tone. "Those of you who have been around incidents like this know any number of people can claim credit, things like that. All of them are checked out. Situations like this tend to bring out the worst in people."

Someone asked if anybody had claimed responsibility for the bombings.

Hinshaw replied he'd rather not comment. "We don't have anything really definitive to say. . . . Any question we answer would lead to five other questions, which just fuels the frustration—"

One voice lifted above the cacophony. A reporter coolly informed Hinshaw that his "comrade" in Birmingham had already made an announcement. "He said that there have been people who have claimed responsibility. He said that at a press conference at eleven o'clock our time this morning . . . and that y'all are following leads from that. So can you elaborate on that for us?"

"No," Hinshaw replied tersely. "If he's told you that, then I wouldn't need to elaborate."

He paused, and fragments of shouted questions filled the void.

"He's already told you more than I would." The normally genial FBI agent cracked his crooked smile, a wry smile, not a happy one. The exchange was telling. There were four bombs, delivered into the territories of three FBI field offices. Two of them, Birmingham and Atlanta, were in many ways running separate investigations.

Someone fired a question about what was happening where.

"I think it's safe to say that there's more investigation being conducted in Georgia than anywhere else, but that's because we have more leads in Georgia because we had mailings in Georgia," said Hinshaw, politic now. "We had two deliveries in Georgia. We have just more things going on. This person might be in Anchorage, Alaska, for all we know."

Concerning the letters, Hinshaw continued dissembling, managing not to lie, revealing little truth. Eventually a reporter asked Shatzel for clarification. "We're confused," she said.

"Good!" Hinshaw boomed. Shatzel maintained the tone his FBI counterpart set. Finally, somebody elicited a summary of what investigators knew and were willing to share.

"I guess we're fortunate today," Hinshaw said. "We didn't turn up any bombs—knock on wood." Hinshaw rapped on the podium. "Are we expecting any more? We hope not, but we are vigilant for it . . . and other people should be.

"We can't say that this person stopped."

———

The snapshot was turned in by a citizen who found it near an Atlanta shopping mall. Amid what looked like a cluttered workshop, it showed a white guy, a weird white guy, maybe sixty, with glasses, khaki trousers and a windowpane-plaid shirt. Behind him were venetian blinds, and in front of those a cross, perhaps covered in aluminum foil. And he held what seemed some sort of bizarre device.

The picture made a stir around the task force headquarters in the first days. A supervisor asked Hoback to look at it and see if he thought the old man was building a bomb. But Hoback could get nothing of consequence from it. Nobody did. And, in the end, it came to nothing. In that respect, it was no anomaly. Within a few

weeks, at least 149 "potential suspects" emerged, ranging from a na-
tionally prominent feminist to a death-row inmate's brother. Investigators briefly considered an ex–police officer and scrutinized a
litigant who had allegedly threatened to kill a bankruptcy judge.
One man under consideration wore a hat lined with aluminum foil
to his interview—to combat shocks and electronic rays directed toward him by persons unknown, as a report would later note.

While judges remained under twenty-four-hour guard, crime-lab
experts trained FBI agents and others how to look for certain typing
characteristics as they pored over *pro se* documents from Eleventh
Circuit case files. Agents hunted string-tying machines that might
have bundled the bomb boxes. The case was treated as top priority
from Washington on down. The president himself spoke on camera
of bombings and "the baggage of bigotry."

Psycholinguistic analyses had begun even before the December
attacks. The author of the August "Declaration of War" letter was
described as "most likely an intelligent, adult male, who would be
known for his arrogance. In addition, this individual had likely written to the court system previously about this or other issues." He
might be acting out of revenge and feeling "justified in his actions,
since he feels that the system has wronged him and he has a right to
even the score."

There was one prediction later events ended up rebutting: "Con-
sultation with the FBI's outside psycholinguistic expert . . . resulted
in the opinion that the threat is most likely not a valid one." True, he
didn't unleash the deadly gasses the letter threatened. Perhaps the
bombs were plan B.

Linguistic analysis after the December threat letters described a
man who "parrots the language of the courts more as one might expect from a criminal than from a lawyer" and who was criminally sophisticated, dedicated and intelligent.

"But at the same time he demonstrates the sorts of lapses in intellect which might lead him to underestimate his adversaries as in-
competently easy to deceive."

An expert at one point suggested the author was a black man, but
quickly conceded the reasoning "may have been falsely premised."

Indeed, from the beginning, the premise for some was the opposite. On December 20, the day after the fourth bomb turned up in
Jacksonville, an FBI agent showed up at the Atlanta Federal Penitentiary and met with the warden and staff members. The warden was

alerted that suspects in the case would include white-supremacist-type groups and was asked to report anything about such organizations that surfaced. "Mail cover"—a record of first-class mail received—was instituted on about a half dozen Georgians considered proponents of racist or right-wing extremist ideologies.

On the surface, what happened just after Christmas seemed to bolster the racist angle. That's when the Americans for a Competent Federal Judicial System went public in a letter to Brenda Wood, an anchorwoman at WAGA, Atlanta's CBS television affiliate:

> TO: BRENDA WOOD
> FROM: AMERICANS FOR A COMPETENT FEDERAL
> JUDICIAL SYSTEM
>
> ON DECEMBER 19, 1989, OFFICERS OF AMERICANS
> FOR A COMPETENT FEDERAL JUDICIAL SYSTEM
> FROM ALABAMA, FLORIDA AND GEORGIA MET IN
> SECRET SESSION IN MONTGOMERY, ALABAMA TO
> ADOPT NEW ORDERS.
>
> THE FOLLOWING ORDER IS DIRECTED TO YOU.
>
> 1. YOU SHALL CONTACT MARTELLE LAYFIELD JR.
> AT 3301 CATHRYN DR. COLUMBUS, GEORGIA 31906
> AND PROVIDE HIM WITH THE FOLLOWING
> INFORMATION.
> ROBERT S. VANCE, JUDGE 010187
> ROBERT ROBINSON, ATTORNEY 010187
> THE ABOVE INFORMATION SHALL NOT BE MADE
> PUBLIC.
> 2. UPON RECEIPT OF THIS ORDER, YOU SHALL
> PRERECORD A REPORT IN WHICH YOU READ ALL OF
> THE INFORMATION IN SECTION THREE BELOW. A
> COPY OF YOUR REPORT SHALL BE PROVIDED TO
> ALL MAJOR NEWS SERVICES.
> ON DECEMBER 25, 1989, YOU AND ALL MAJOR
> NEWS SERVICES SHALL BROADCAST THE COMPLETE
> REPORT ON THE EVENING NEWS.
> FAILURE TO COMPLY, FOR ANY REASON, SHALL
> RESULT IN YOUR ASSASSINATION.
> 3. THE UNITED STATES COURT OF APPEALS FOR
> THE ELEVENTH CIRCUIT HAS BEEN QUICK TO

STRESS THE IMPORTANCE OF CIVIL RIGHTS FOR
BLACKS BUT SLOW TO STRESS THE IMPORTANCE OF
BLACKS TO DEMONSTRATE CIVIL RESPONSIBILITY.

THIS FAILURE CREATED A CLIMATE THAT HAS
SPAWNED AN ALARMING NUMBER OF SAVAGE ACTS
OF VIOLENCE BY BLACK MEN AGAINST WHITE
WOMEN.

JULIE LOVE, FOR EXAMPLE, A YOUNG INNOCENT
WHITE LADY WAS ROBBED, KIDNAPPED, GANG
RAPED, SODOMIZED, MURDERED AND
DISMEMBERED BY A GROUP OF BLACK MALES. HER
REMAINS WERE CONCEALED FOR AN EXTREMELY
LONG PERIOD OF TIME, LEAVING HER LOVE ONES
IN EXCRUCIATING ANGUISH.

JULIE LOVE WAS AN INNOCENT PERSON, AN
INNOCENT PERSON WHO ALSO HAD CIVIL RIGHTS.
SHE IS ONLY ONE OF THOUSANDS OF INNOCENT
WHITE WOMEN WHO HAVE BEEN RAPED AND
MURDERED BY INHUMAN BLACK BARBARIANS.

PROTECTING THE INNOCENT WARRANTS A
HIGHER COURT PRIORITY THAN GRANTING THE
BLACKS' DEMAND FOR WHITE TEACHERS FOR
THEIR CHILDREN.

THE MESSAGE AMERICANS FOR A COMPETENT
FEDERAL JUDICIAL HAS FOR THE JUDGES IS SIMPLE,
IF YOU WANT TO LIVE, YOU SHALL MAKE
PROTECTING THE CIVIL RIGHTS OF THE INNOCENT
YOUR HIGHEST OBLIGATION AND YOU SHALL
FULFILL THAT OBLIGATION.

THE MESSAGE AMERICANS FOR A COMPETENT
FEDERAL JUDICIAL SYSTEM HAS FOR ATTORNEYS
AND FOR THE BLACK LEADERSHIP IS ALSO SIMPLE,
IF YOU WANT TO LIVE, YOU SHALL TAKE THAT
ACTION REQUIRED TO PREVENT BLACK MEN FROM
RAPING WHITE WOMEN.

AMERICANS FOR A COMPETENT FEDERAL
JUDICIAL SYSTEM ASSASSINATED JUDGE ROBERT S.
VANCE AND ATTORNEY ROBERT ROBINSON IN
REPRISAL FOR THE ATROCITIES INFLICTED UPON
JULIE LOVE.

TWO MORE PROMINENT MEMBERS OF THE
NAACP SHALL BE ASSASSINATED, USING MORE
SOPHISTICATED MEANS, AS PART OF THE SAME
REPRISAL.
    ANYTIME A BLACK MAN RAPES A WHITE WOMAN
IN ALABAMA, FLORIDA OR GEORGIA IN THE
FUTURE, AMERICANS FOR A COMPETENT FEDERAL
JUDICIAL SYSTEM SHALL ASSASSINATE ONE
FEDERAL JUDGE, ONE ATTORNEY AND ONE
OFFICER OF THE NAACP.
4. THE CODE NUMBER 0I0I87 AUTHENTICATES THE
ACTIVITIES OF AMERICANS FOR A COMPETENT
FEDERAL JUDICIAL SYSTEM AND SHALL NOT BE
MADE PUBLIC.

The station consulted with the FBI, aired the story and, as the
sender demanded, dutifully distributed to other news outlets a portion of the letter. Virtually every news organization in Atlanta knew
the Julie Love story. The perky, attractive young woman had disap-
peared from a fashionable Atlanta neighborhood in July 1988, and
the months-long mystery of her whereabouts and the eventual arrests of her killers had been one of Atlanta's biggest stories. But if
the bomber intended to suggest in the Brenda Wood letter that the
Love case had been the impetus for his campaign of terror, he was
probably blowing smoke. Charges in the Love case weren't brought
until days after the NAACP tear-gas incident and the mailing of the
"Declaration of War" letters in August. And until the case was broken, the public did not know of the race of Julie Love's killers.
Notwithstanding his selection of targets, the virulent racism of the
Brenda Wood letter was new to his communiqués, leading Hinshaw,
Hoback and others to suspect the bomber was simply playing to
speculation in the media.

Furthermore, the linguistic expert who analyzed the Wood message said, "I do not . . . find the message's avowal of large, tri-state
membership to be at all credible."

The analyst found the style consistent with that of a high-school-
educated, Southern white between thirty-five and fifty years old.

"Although the ideation is both masculinely assertive and violent
in character," the analyst wrote, "the rendition is nearly prissy in its
fussiness. These anomalies suggest the sort of pattern more typical

of the secretarially trained female rendering a typescript from the draft (or) dictation of another."

The passage in the Wood letter concerning "the blacks' demand for white teachers for their children" presented interesting possibilities. Robbie Robinson had been involved in a Savannah school-desegregation case. And the Jacksonville NAACP had been involved in a school-desegregation case, in which Judge Vance authored an important opinion. But a third desegregation case was recently before the Eleventh Circuit, involving schools in DeKalb County, in metropolitan Atlanta. Federal agents began interviewing DeKalb County school-system employees, focusing on the recent involuntary transfer of more than one hundred senior teachers. It remained an emotionally charged issue.

"I've been in personnel nineteen years. It's the most traumatic thing that I have been involved with, for sure," said a school-system official.

Eleventh Circuit records showed teachers were to report to their new schools on August 21, 1989—the same day the tear-gas bomb arrived at the Atlanta regional NAACP office and the day the "Declaration of War" letters were postmarked. Could a teacher—or a teacher's husband—have been moved to murder? Racing against the return of students from Christmas vacation, more than one hundred agents fanned out into every school in the sprawling DeKalb system. They looked at shop classrooms where pipes might have been welded and the end plates fabricated. They took exemplars from every manual typewriter they could find, samples that could be checked against the typing in the threat letters and bomb-package address labels. It was a clever theory, ambitiously pursued, but a dead end.

———

Decked in riot gear, Hoback was on the street before sunup on Saturday, January 6, 1990. So was another investigator on the mail-bomb task force, Terry Pelfrey from the Georgia Bureau of Investigation. In the darkness, they moved carefully around a bag discovered in the bushes near the state Capitol. Hoback helped Pelfrey into his bombsuit. When it was over, they'd rendered safe a sack of clothes. But it wasn't a time to take chances, especially considering what was supposed to happen in a few hours. Hoback and Pelfrey were not alone. Indeed, 144 of Pelfrey's GBI colleagues joined him. And 184 from the Georgia State Patrol. From the Department of Corrections, 85. Another 75 from the Georgia Building Authority. About 300 from Atlanta Police. Even 28 from the Georgia Department of Natural Resources. And 1,594 from the Georgia National Guard.

Nearly 2,400 cops and troops were called out to keep the peace so a handful of Klan types could rally by the Capitol steps. It was not unusual for authorities to outnumber the demonstrators at such events, and this time the robed ones could probably have fit on a little yellow school bus, with room left to stack their Confederate battle flags.

Hoback was there to look for leads, and indeed the bombings came up when a pale young Klan leader in a red satin robe and matching pointy hat bellowed into a microphone, his voice resounding in the canyon between the Capitol building and a church across the street.

"We don't advocate what the bomber or bombers are doing—" He paused as if to hear his own echo, then added with emphasis, "But—" Another pause.

"I myself salute you, brothers!"

He thrust his hand in the air, Nazi style. "White power!"

"White power!" came the guttural response.

"White power!"

"White power!"

From an evidentiary standpoint Hoback's day was a waste. And when a violent clash erupted between police and counterdemonstrators, it melted into a surreal nightmare. All this underscored, however, a key point about the KKK theories: the Klan was riddled with people who talk too much. And the braggarts and informants just weren't talking as they would if these were Klan bombings.

By Christmas, Hinshaw, for one, had concluded the bombings weren't the work of any group but of a loner driven by enough hate and obsession to so meticulously craft the bombs. The SAC harkened back years to his research for the FBI bomb manual, when somebody told him that the complexity and workmanship in a bomb was directly proportionate to the length of time the hatred had been building in the bomber. But as early as the first week, Hinshaw had felt pressure from the Justice Department to focus on white-supremacist angles. If officials from Washington simply harbored preconceptions about Southern-fried crime, they risked playing into a killer's plans. But knowing the arrest of a race-hater would be a victory to trumpet to a black constituency long courted but so far unwon, Hinshaw was troubled by a remark one official made about a "political agenda." He was frustrated, wanting to keep the investigation wide open until there was reason to narrow it. Hinshaw's point man on the day-to-day conduct of the case, Harold Jones, had also concluded early that the bomber had injected race into the case as a smoke screen, that his real gripe was with the courts. Jones warned of the lesson learned near the start of the decade in Atlanta's missing-and-murdered-children case, when many might have expected the killer of young black men to be a redneck in a pickup truck. And the prime suspect turned out to be a young black man.

So far as anybody knew, Roy Moody did not belong to the Ku Klux Klan or any group more radical than an experimental-aircraft association. The terrain of his psyche may have been littered with bizarre formations, and to believe a couple of old girlfriends it included a rocky outcropping or two of racial discomfort, but Moody's record on race seemed no worse than that of millions of Southerners who grew up in the forties and fifties.

Not long after the mail bombs turned up in Alabama, Georgia, and Florida, Moody and his young wife Susan were together when they watched an evening-news story about another pipe bomb, which exploded in a Maryland judge's apartment. *This* one, Roy told Susan, wasn't his.

Maybe two days later, Roy loaded a chair into his pickup truck from a front bedroom, which had been sealed off from Susan for weeks. Susan drove them to a nearby car wash where Roy abandoned the chair and they carefully cleaned the truck bed, bed liner and camper shell.

6

Joe Gordon

Litigious paranoids often utilize the legal
system as a vehicle to act out their fantasies
and delusional preoccupations. Imaginary
grievances, accusations based on delusional
ideation and irrational vindictiveness toward
imagined persecutors may find full expression in any number of legal contexts. They
can defeat the rational and legitimate objec-
tives of the legal system, enmesh innocent
and unsuspecting victims in nightmarish legal
entanglements and subvert the process of justice.

—Robert L. Goldstein, M.D., J.D.
Journal of Forensic Sciences
July 1987

Black hair piled high and swept back like a Hollywood werewolf's,
piercing eyes—everybody remembered the eyes—pale and bright
like a glacier in the sun, Walter Leroy Moody Jr. was either often
wronged and in search of righteous redress, or he was lupine not
just in look but life approach, prowling the legal system, a litigious
lobo who went to court more than many lawyers. He sued his

brother and sister. He sued the county where he lived. He sued a bank, allegedly using phony documents and close to a dozen lawyers over the course of the case or related proceedings. Accused of abandoning three employees at sea in the Florida Keys, he won a dismissal of attempted-murder charges when the jury couldn't reach a verdict. Then he sued the police. And the alleged victims. He sued a man in a breach-of-contract dispute, then tried to prosecute him on extortion charges and later for poisoning his dog, though a veterinarian reported no evidence of poison. Attending law school for close to two years, keeping a small law library in his study, often representing himself, Moody occasionally won in court; sometimes he lost and appealed. In one of his cases, a psychiatrist would testify about Roy's take on the Golden Rule:

"Do unto others before they do unto you; or do unto others what they have done to you."

And the psychiatrist was a witness for Moody's side.

Joe Gordon knew none of this when he reported to work the day after Christmas, 1989.

Like Hoback the week before, Gordon was filling in for a vacationing agent at ATF district headquarters in Atlanta. Gordon had grown up around Atlanta, been a suburban cop there, a state trooper there. This was the city where he'd been hit in that shoot-out on the MARTA bus. But now he lived in Macon, assigned to a satellite office, where from the moment he'd heard about the bombings he'd itched and angled to be assigned to the case. A deputy marshal had called him first on December 16, asked by a Macon-based federal judge to check a rumor that a judge had been killed in Alabama. Gordon called Tom Stokes, his boss in Atlanta, confirmed the information was true, then passed what Stokes told him back to the deputy. Gordon couldn't sleep that night, and at eleven-thirty P.M. he called his marshal's service buddy on his beeper to see what else he'd learned. The deputy marshal called back on a cell phone from a judge's house, having already been dispatched for security.

The bomb case was the biggest thing to happen in the two and a half years he'd been with ATF, and Gordon didn't want to watch from the stands. He'd thought he found an opening a few days later as a handful of agents talked casually in the Macon ATF office, a place of old fluorescent lights, old venetian blinds, old acoustical tile and a view of a roof and Interstate 75. Gordon listened as an office veteran recalled the Moody case, which had unfolded in Macon years before. Gordon didn't know about the threaded rod and the square end plates. He didn't know, as Chet Bryant did, about Moody's mind-set. He simply knew Moody, like anybody else in Georgia with a bomb case on his rap sheet, needed checking out. And he knew Moody might be the crowbar with which he could wedge his way into the bomb case. But on December 20, when he called the Atlanta office to offer Moody's name, he was disappointed to learn Hoback already had it.

Gordon's stint in Atlanta beginning six days later gave him a second shot. The bomb case was *the* case at the district office when he got there. Gordon was filling in as operations officer, an administrative slot that quickly bored him, so he took the chance to freelance. He wandered over to the task force offices in the FBI's cavernous command center, compartmentalized by portable workspace dividers and packed with modular office furniture and computer terminals. Computer printouts of agency names hung horizontally over corresponding work areas. Colored pins poked a map marking significant developments. Potential suspects decorated a "wall of shame," photos on poster paper with ID data. Moody was among them, but hardly prominent. Gordon's impression was that most of the energy was focused toward hate groups. Moody was Gordon's hook, however, and Moody was the name he stuck with back at the ATF office, when he set out on a paper safari in search of the 1972 case file.

Nancy Peek, the salty secretary to the SAC, knew how the place worked, having hired on with ATF's predecessor in 1963. She told Gordon how the former filing system functioned, that a case this old was in the archives if anywhere, and that she doubted it could be found. Gordon got a computer run of Moody's criminal history and spotted what he recognized from Nancy Peek's description as the old case number. She steered him next to an almond-colored file cabinet about six feet wide and chin high to the tall agent with thick hair, carefully coiffed and prematurely streaked in the hues of a weathered barn. For about thirty minutes, he sifted through the roster of cases sent off for warehousing, listed with no names, only numbers. Finally he found the number matching Moody in the computer. With it were also a batch number, a box number and the date the case file had gone to the archives in East Point, a small city just south of Atlanta. Gordon's problem was that what he was doing had little connection to what he was supposed to be doing as acting operations officer, which was chiefly reviewing case reports—*contempo-rary* case reports. So he called upstairs where most of the investiga-tors had their desks and asked for help. A young agent volunteered to fetch the file from East Point, a chore that took about two hours.

Gordon opened the folder to find the case report, including typed statements from Chet Bryant, Erwin, other key investigators and witnesses. The file included, too, a chilling story:

> Moody, Walter Leroy, Jr.
> Address: 1360 Dublin Avenue, Macon, Bibb County, Georgia.
> Description: White; Male; American born citizen (born 3/24/34, Peach County, Georgia); 71 inches; 160 pounds; green eyes; black hair; ruddy complex-ion; medium build; married.
> Criminal record: No record known with this office.
> Defendant claims: several cases for bad checks . . .
> Financial responsibility: Defendant claims no property, no cash, no assets.

Hazel Moody found a pair of boxes in the bottom drawer of a file cabinet in the room her husband used as an office. She placed the smaller box on a makeshift desk, pulled off the brown wrapping pa-per and removed the top. She looked inside at, she thought, an air-plane part on which her husband had been working. She replaced the top. A loud explosion . . . a scream . . . covered in blood, her hair afire, Hazel ran from her carport across the front yard toward her next-door neighbor's home, where Dale Stewart was visiting his sis-ter Myra.

"Dale," Hazel said, "please don't let me die."

Dale Stewart put out the flames with his hands and tried to make Hazel comfortable in the driveway. Roy Moody, seen leaving with his child shortly before the blast, returned a couple hours or so afterward.

"Is it true my wife has been hurt?" he asked.

A doctor reported Hazel had suffered first- and second-degree burns on her face, neck, and left arm, that her right hand was badly mangled and that he had spent considerable time removing gun-powder from her eyes. The left eye was badly injured.

Macon Police Detective Victor Heinzelman got to the house and found a trail of blood inside, along with pieces of cardboard and metal, including a piece of aluminum with the ends of four bolts attached, and a similar piece of aluminum with the other end of the bolts. At City Hall, Moody urged the detective to look around the house and find out what happened and said there were still packages at the house he was afraid to open. The next morning, Moody presented one, which Heinzelman took outside, accompanied by Chet Bryant. The detective opened the package. It contained not a bomb but a binder, a notebook. Moody told Bryant and Heinzelman he knew nothing of the explosion or of the package's being in the file cabinet, that someone must have put the bomb in the house while he and Hazel were out.

But when the package wrapper was reassembled, most of an address emerged. "To Tom Downin-, 486 West ——htree Street N.W., Atlan-a- Georgia." An extortion note was partly burned but partly legible: "Warning . . . or get 43 stic . . . of dynamite you will see friends and relatives go first- $65,000."

An investigator in Atlanta confirmed that in 1969 Moody bought a '67 MGB roadster from Downing Motor Company. Its president: Thomas N. Downing. In March 1971, more than a year before the explosion in the Moody bungalow, the car was repossessed. Moody owed about $350 on the MGB and sent a check for $357, but Downing had added $100 for the cost of the repo job. Both Downing and Moody said they'd never met each other.

Bryant, Erwin, Heinzelman and ATF Agent Herman Higginbotham hit Moody's house with a search warrant on May 16, 1972. They took wire from a model airplane and powder traces from a workbench in the kitchen and the floor nearby. The lab determined the wire matched that in the bomb and had been cut with the same tool. The powder from the floor and workbench also matched that in the bomb. A week after the search, Bryant and Higginbotham returned to Moody's house with an arrest warrant. Higginbotham read Roy his rights.

A textbook case, Gordon told himself. He called a contact in the federal probation office in Macon, told him he was in Atlanta and that, if the file on Moody could be found, he wanted to read it. The probation man found and faxed it.

April 1974. A "Special Progress Report" for inmate Moody, Walter Leroy, who did his time at the Atlanta Federal Penitentiary. Under the heading "Current Offense" was synopsized the Official Version of the case, consistent with the case report Gordon had already perused; beneath it was the Offender's Explanation: "Moody still says he can prove that he is innocent and he is expecting to be released eventually."

Under Prior Record: "It was learned by presentence investigation that Moody's father had picked up numerous bad checks given by his son then finally refused to pick up any more. Chief Cochran of the Macon Police Force said the defendant became very antagonistic toward his father and caused considerable family trouble with his threats." The document revealed Moody had married Hazel Strickland about seven years before the report was written. "He states that he and Hazel got a little excited one time and ran off to Tennessee and married. He thought it was humorous.

"Mrs. Moody said that she and her husband always got along fine although he never told her much about his business or what he was thinking about or doing. She has been working since age 16 and apparently has carried the burden on the financial end while her husband worked at his get-rich-quick schemes and attended school."

Gordon read a 1972 report from the chief psychologist at the federal penitentiary. "It is likely he expresses hostility in indirect ways," he said of Moody.

A prison psychiatrist noted: "When he first arrived he was in a big hurry to get back to Macon, Georgia to stand trial. At one time he threatened to write to a radio or TV station if his psychiatric evaluation was not completed by a time limit he set."

Gordon tried to tell himself he was looking for something to rule out Moody so he could get on with his business. He couldn't find it. He called his buddy with the Marshals Service in Macon and asked him to find the court file and hold it for him. And he took Gordon P. "Gus" Gary to dinner in Underground Atlanta, named for a section of downtown that years ago had been paved over, streets, buildings and all, then disinterred to become a cobblestoned commercial complex replete with restaurants and nightclubs. Gus Gary, an ATF agent in the midst of a fellowship at the National Center for the Analysis of Violent Crime, listened and encouraged Gordon to keep digging into the Moody angle, and he concurred with Gordon's belief the bomber's writings showed too much sophistication and not enough racial invective to match the Klan clatter he'd come to expect over a lifetime in Georgia. Gary grew up in York, Alabama, near the Mississippi line.

Terry Pelfrey knew the Klan too. The Southern White Knights, the Invisible Empire, the Christian Knights—he knew the factions, the who's who, the who's not. He was a member of the GBI's Anti-Terrorist Squad, and knowing the Klan's plans was part of Pelfrey's job. The GBI watched the Klan and the Klan knew they were watching. "Turn right and look for the G.B.I. entry point," read the directions in the Klan flyer promoting the rally at the state Capitol. And, in the first days, providing intelligence on the white-supremacist angle was a big part of Pelfrey's official role on the task force. Though he didn't think the Georgia Klansmen he knew of were capable of these bombings, or of keeping their mouths shut, he did his duty. He went to the rally. He put his informants out. But it was, after all, a bomb task force, and Pelfrey felt obliged to throw out the name of the only convicted bomber he knew of in Georgia, somebody who hadn't come up in his work on extremist groups. He wasn't sure exactly when it was, but it had been a while back, when somebody in law enforcement called from Florida. Something about an attempted-murder case in the Keys. Pelfrey had sent what information the GBI had on hand, mainly old newspaper clippings about an old case. And he'd gone out to take a picture of the guy's house. Maybe that's why it stuck with him, because of the location of the house. Pelfrey lived in Ellenwood and this guy only lived about four miles away, in Rex. It was Roy Moody.

During the week he was in Atlanta, Gordon hooked up with Pelfrey and Dave Kirkland, a U.S. postal inspector. Postal inspectors knew Moody well; his mail-order business, a sort of vanity press for aspiring short-story writers, had been the subject of a lengthy investigation by postal authorities, and of a consent decree. The three men divvied up leads. Postal planned to start watching the mail to Superior Sail Drives, another business with which Moody was affiliated, and on a couple of female associates. The postal folks would also check out that Florida case. Among other things, the GBI would open a surveillance of Moody's trash. Pelfrey had learned the lesson mainly from his Klan work: to know somebody's life story, get their garbage. He'd arrange with the waste-disposal people simply to put Moody's trash bags aside when they picked them up. Gordon volunteered to track down Hazel Moody and more old files.

Once back in Macon, Gordon picked up the court file from his Marshals Service contact the day after New Year's. The yellowed onionskin paper on which the trial and a hearing were transcribed reeked of mildew. But he stayed up until three A.M. reading.

Surprisingly, considering Hazel Moody was the victim, Moody's defense lawyer, Tommy Mann, noted in his opening statement, "His wife and his family sits back here with him—behind him." Not surprisingly, Mann continued, "He is a rather, as the evidence will show to you, at this point, a frustrated young man, because, as you will see throughout this trial, he maintains his innocence."

Gordon noted the testimony of an assistant registrar from Mercer University, where Moody attended off and on between 1956 and 1971. Moody took eight chemistry courses, one as recently as 1970, and three physics courses. Whoever built the '89 bombs had some aptitude for both disciplines.

But it was Lloyd Erwin's testimony that grabbed Gordon and shook him hard. Erwin described the bomb that had injured Hazel Moody. The pipe ends cut off smooth. The square, metal end plates held in place by bolts running lengthwise. The battery. All of these were similar to the components of the 1989 mail bombs, but were not surprises to Gordon by now. The flashlight bulb was a different story. In the 1972 trial, Erwin described an ignition system keyed by the filaments of a flashlight bulb. Gordon, in his week in the district office, had been in on enough briefings about the bomb case to know flashlight filaments triggered the '89 bombs too.

The defense started strangely. Moody's lawyer prompted the judge to advise Moody on his rights concerning whether to testify in his own behalf—or, perhaps more to the point, on his right not to testify.

"Do you understand, Mr. Moody?" Mann asked his client. "Is it your understanding that you want to testify?"

"Yes, that is correct," Moody replied.

He testified that the day of the explosion Hazel, he and his young son had dinner with Hazel's parents. The plan was to head south to Fort Valley to visit Roy's mom, but the embers reignited from a day-old argument about how Hazel fixed her hair. Roy and the boy ended up in Fort Valley without Hazel. There his mother called him to the phone where someone told him his wife had had an accident. Roy borrowed his mother's car—his tires were no good—and drove to Macon as fast as he could. He went first to the house, then to the hospital.

Eventually, Moody described in his testimony cleaning up after the accident:

"Just to look at the room, you would think that it was just blood-stains on the wall, but when you started cleaning it off, you see that there are thousands [of] tiny pieces of flesh blown all over the wall, and you couldn't wash it off. I had to get a bucket with soapy water and I had to get a brush and I had to scrub it.

"It got to be such a job I realized the best way to do it was to get everything out of there, so I moved everything that was in the room."

He added, "The only place left that would accommodate all this stuff was the workbench that I had in the kitchen."

He was trying to lay down an alibi, Gordon thought, an explanation for the powder found by his workbench. An investigator had already testified there was powder throughout the room where the blast occurred. Now Roy had laid the groundwork to suggest the powder the feds found by his workbench had simply fallen off items that had been in the home office when the explosion occurred there.

"What was the physical condition of the articles that you moved?" his lawyer queried.

"Some of them—well, everything in there had gunpowder," Roy answered. And, he suggested, he brushed off a number of the items from the blast room in the kitchen. Somehow, he never did get around to cleaning the kitchen.

"Have you got any idea how that package got in there?" his lawyer asked.

Moody explained he and Hazel seldom locked the house. "And it would be no problem for them to put it anywhere in the house they wanted to put it, because there was nothing there that had a lock on it."

Moody claimed to have an idea who had placed the bomb in his house, but he suggested his family might be in danger if he revealed the name. He launched a long, roundabout explanation beginning with the $100 that Downing had tacked on to his arrearage in order for Moody to get his repossessed MGB back.

"I didn't think I was required under contract to pay that money," Moody said—bolstering, Gordon noticed, the prosecution's motive theory.

"Now the thing in my mind was this," Roy continued. "Was Tom Downing going to hold that car for a while to see if I was going to pay them that additional one hundred dollars that I didn't think he could collect, based on the contract, or was he going to really sell the car? . . . I drove up there to look around just to find out whether or not he had my car on the used-car lot."

Moody said he drove by and didn't see his car, then stopped at a restaurant where he ran into someone he knew, whom he asked to go to the car dealership and check out the situation further.

The judge cut to the point: "Who is the man you are talking about?"

Moody: "Do you want me to name him?"

Judge: "Why certainly. We are seeking the truth in this case. Who are you talking about and what connection did he have with it, if you know?"

"The man's name is Gene Wallace."

Moody suggested Wallace and a friend of his, by secretly placing the bomb package in Moody's house, might have been trying to intimidate him or seek revenge for Roy's refusal to go along with an extortion plot Wallace proposed involving the mailing of a bomb to Tom Downing.

In cross-examination, the prosecutor elicited from Moody that he had never told investigators about the mysterious Gene Wallace.

"I think I was interested in determining if they had the professional ability that I thought they needed to have to protect my wife, myself and my child in the event I revealed to them this extortion plot," Moody explained. "And they indicated to me that they did not have that ability. . . . If they had determined that I had not made the bomb, then I would have told them everything I knew."

Gordon believed he now knew the identity of the mail bomber and found nothing to dissuade him from his suspicions in the transcript of a pretrial proceeding.

"I do believe that without further help this young man will wind up on the rolls of the State handout permanently unless some change can be wrought in him." Dr. Thomas M. Hall, a psychiatrist, rendered that diagnosis in 1967, as he began a series of more than forty sessions with Moody in connection with some sort of vocational program. He read it aloud in an August 1972 deposition.

Moody, Dr. Hall reported, gave him a long, involved history of inadequate behavior and "unjust accusations, which could have legally taken place like Mr. Moody described, but somehow it seemed highly unlikely." According to Hall, Moody was self-destructive but not suicidal. Moody's lawyer asked if Moody would have been destructive to society.

"It is a difficult judgment," the doctor replied. "I was constantly afraid that he would get into some embroilment . . . some sort of destruction toward society. He never did at that time, but there was always the constant threat hanging over his head. You know, 'I am going to do this. I am going to do that,' that sort of thing, when somebody disappointed him, when somebody crossed him in any way. He thought violently about other people."

Moody was, however, charming—or at least manipulative. Hall likened him to "the type of individual who could sell you the Brooklyn Bridge with you looking at him and it and knowing that he couldn't do it, but he could still do it anyway. Very persuasive." And he was very bright. "He has a great deal of potential," Hall offered. "But he was the kind of person that was going to blow that damn potential to a cocked hat."

Hall recalled Moody was attending Marshall Law School in Atlanta and hoped to join the bar.

"And he probably would have made a good lawyer."

———

Hoback had been out of town when Gordon started digging, then had trouble running him down to find out exactly what he had. But within hours of Gordon's late-night reading binge, they talked and Hoback told him to get up to Atlanta.

The Richard Russell Federal Building was the hub of the federal government's presence in Atlanta. Getting in a courtroom or the clerk's office there after the bombings meant going through one metal detector by the door run by one group of security guards, then through another one by the elevators handled by a second outfit. That is, unless you came from the mail-bomb task force headquarters in the annex across the street, in which case you simply took the tunnel running under Spring Street and you wound up by the cafeteria and the auditorium. The auditorium was where Hoback had to be, along with investigators from virtually every agency working the mail-bomb case from all four cities where the bombs had been delivered. It was the first such meeting and the first time, two weeks into the case, that Hoback heard such a detailed description of the devices.

The meeting was compartmentalized into a series of briefings, the first on crime-lab findings.

"496 items of evidence," he wrote on his pad. "End caps welded in Savannah, Jacksonville, Atlanta . . . Birmingham end caps screw on . . . welding is bad, not professional . . . pipes in Jacksonville, Atlanta, same length and size, abnormally thick . . . wire is telephone type . . . white silicon adhesive . . . aluminum pie plates."

He started a new page. "Pipe nipples scored to boost fragmentation . . . detonators the same in all four, made from part of a ballpoint pen, Faber-Castell, manufactured in Tennessee, June 1989 . . . the high explosive inside the detonators came from small-arms ammo, painstakingly removed from twenty-five, maybe thirty-five bullets just to get one detonator . . . tests still running for DNA from the stamps and labels . . . no fingerprints found so far, except for one belonging to a bomb tech."

The next briefing was on data systems, how leads would be processed and kept up with, something called "tactical case management." Then the postal inspectors were up. The hot line had netted 228 calls so far. Mail screening was in place for judges, dozens of NAACP offices and Brenda Wood, the news anchor. Pelfrey dutifully delivered his briefing updating intelligence on white-supremacist groups. "Klan is quiet," Hoback noted on his fourth page.

Then Bill Hagmaier took the floor. Tall and angular with longish, red-brown hair, Hagmaier was from the FBI's storied behavioral-science unit. He was widely respected by rank-and-file investigators, considered communicative and unpretentious. He presented the profile pieced together from what was known of the bomber so far.

He would be a white male, working alone, though there might be one other person in whom he would confide. Hagmaier estimated his age between forty-five and fifty. He lives alone or with another adult. Disciplined, neat, clean, self-structured, attentive to detail, sort of feminine in personality. He wants people to know why he did it, but might be a coward. If somebody says the wrong thing, there could be more bombings. Hagmaier gave the impression the Wood letter was written in a hurry, spurred by the bomber's dissatisfaction with what he'd read and heard about the case so far, that he threw in the mention of the Julie Love case in a bid for positive public reaction.

He'd been to college, maybe beyond. He believes his vocation beneath him. A social outcast. Has his own morality. Probably not a Klan member. Profiling predicted even characteristics of the bomber's vehicle: dark, a four-door or pickup.

There were differences here and there, but still Terry Pelfrey had chills up his back. Outside the Russell Building cafeteria he told Hagmaier he didn't know if Roy Moody was the bomber, "but you just wrote his life story."

Nonetheless, Moody wasn't mentioned by name during the big meeting, nor at the smaller confab that followed, among the case agents. Hoback considered it, having with him information Gordon had driven up from Macon, but factoring in what he considered to be his earlier blow-off, and hearing no one else ask about the ex-con whose name had been hanging in the task-force office for several days now, he kept his own counsel. Instead, when Hoback's turn came, he detailed developments on another suspect whom he also considered viable. A Midwestern ATF office turned up information about a Klansman boasting of "dirty deeds" done in Atlanta the same week as the bombings. Travel records confirmed his presence in town. Still, Hoback considered him not a target on which to lock, but somebody to eliminate in the constant winnowing of the field of possibles.

In Macon, not every document Gordon turned up was moldy, not every document sixteen or seventeen years old. *Walter Leroy Moody, Jr. versus United States of America* was the heading on the transcript of a February 1988 hearing before a federal judge in Macon. An extraordinary hearing. Nearly a dozen years after he finished his prison sentence for the 1972 conviction, Moody was still fighting it. A woman named Julie Ann Linn testified. She was in a wheelchair, the result, she explained, of a spine-severing car wreck in 1970. Two years later, by her account, she was staying with her mother and stepfather in a hotel in Sandy Springs, a suburb of Atlanta, when a young man helped her mother get her wheelchair into a restaurant.

His name, she said, was Gene Wallace.

As Julie Linn told it, her acquaintance with Wallace developed until she accompanied him on a trip to Macon, where they had lunch, after which Wallace said he wanted to see somebody before he left Macon.

"We went to this person's house that he wanted to see, and he got out of the car and knocked on the front door," she testified. "There was no answer, and he knocked on the side door and there was no answer. So we got back in the car and we drove around."

They returned to the house again, she said, but still there was no answer at the door, as there was none on the third visit. But supposedly this time he found the door was open, returned to the car, reached in and said, "I want to leave this package. I'm going to make him get rid of it."

She described, of course, a package wrapped in brown paper with stamps and writing on it, then quoted the elusive, if not illusory, Gene Wallace: "I'm going to put this in the house and I'll call him when I get back home."

Julie Linn continued: "About twenty minutes out of Macon, he explained, 'Damn, I forgot that he doesn't have a phone and I can't call him. I need to go back.'

"So we turned back around and went back into Macon, and as he was driving the car onto the road, turning into the road that . . . the house was on where he left the package at, he explained, 'Oh, my God, it blew up,' and there was a bunch of people in the yard of the house . . . and several other people were running down the road and there was a police car in front of the house.

"He didn't bother to stop and got back onto the highway to Atlanta, and all the while I kept asking him questions like, 'Why did it blow up?' and 'What did you leave that package in his house for?' and so then when I kept asking these questions, I guess it made him really angry because he seemed really nervous then anyway, and so he started telling me to shut up and I just kept asking him questions, and all of a sudden he just backhanded me and hit my jaw and then pulled the car over on the side of the highway and just started freaking out and yelling, 'I told you to shut up,' and he was beating on me and hitting me and I didn't know what to do because, I was in the car and I couldn't get out very well, and so I just leaned forward and he was beating on my back and just yelling at me, 'I told you to shut up,' and then I couldn't do anything because he was bigger than I was.

"So then he finally calmed down for a few minutes and then he threatened me and said, 'If you ever say anything about today, you're going to live to regret it.' "

When she got back to Atlanta, she was too afraid of Wallace even to tell her mother, and the next day, they left for Wisconsin, she said.

Julie Linn testified she finally did move to Atlanta in 1976 and, a decade later, had a nightmare—apparently about the Wallace episode—so bad "it woke my son up because I woke up crying and I must have been yelling in my sleep."

Finally, she related, she had to tell somebody, so she told her mother and they went to the Macon library, where they found newspaper articles on microfilm about "a mysterious blast on Dublin Avenue."

Ms. Linn said they used a map to find Dublin Avenue, and sure enough, she recognized 1360 Dublin Avenue as the house where Wallace left the package so long ago.

"Oh, and the articles also had stated that Mrs. Moody had been injured and that Mr. Walter Leroy Moody Jr. had been later sentenced to five years in prison for a homemade bomb."

That, of course, would explain how she could have tracked him down to give him his long-lost alibi.

Gordon recognized the name of one of the lawyers representing the government at the hearing and headed to her office in the stately old federal courthouse in downtown Macon. She was a short woman with short hair, petite and neat, one of the best prosecutors he knew. She gave him the clear impression hardly anyone believed Moody's new witness, and she helped him navigate the byzantine byways of Moody's appeals file. The 1973 motions were to be expected. The 1986 and 1987 developments stemmed from Julie Linn's supposed "revelations." But it didn't end there.

In June 1989—roughly two months before the "Declaration of War" letters and the NAACP tear-gas package—the Eleventh Circuit Court of Appeals ruled on the case. Against Moody.

———

Bibb County Probate Judge Bill Self had been at a bar function when news came of the Vance bombing. A domestic-relations lawyer who remembered a case from Self's days in private practice came up to him and said, "So who does this bombing bring to mind?"

"Well, who do you reckon?" Self replied rhetorically. As soon as he heard about the bombing, Roy Moody came to mind. Self had been a green, twenty-five-year-old lawyer in 1974 when Hazel Moody walked in his office and told him she wanted a divorce. The young attorney figured serving the case on the husband of this shy, quiet woman would be easy; he was in the penitentiary. So the fee he quoted her was small. And he began what would become the most involved, hard-fought, costly and emotionally draining legal battle of his career.

Self remembered what an assistant DA had told him soon after he took the case: "I wonder what a man who would send a bomb to the man that would repossess his car would do to a lawyer who represents his wife in a divorce?"

The probate judge's office was just down the street from the federal courthouse in Macon, the Bibb County seat. On January 10, Gordon showed up there with Dave Kirkland, an affable but intense, white-haired postal inspector who had joined Gordon and Pelfrey in Atlanta at that meeting on the Moody leads. Judge Self told them his representation of Hazel in divorce and child-support proceedings lasted several years, during which Roy repeatedly hired and fired lawyers and seemingly ignored child-support orders from the court. Roy was twice charged with child abandonment; one was later reversed.

According to Judge Self, Roy occasionally represented himself in local courts and on appeals as high as the U.S. Supreme Court. Self opined that Moody was "highly intelligent" and had he finished law school and passed the bar, he would have been a formidable lawyer.

The investigators wanted correspondence from Moody, to compare the typing in it to the typed bomb-package labels and the threat letters. Self had plenty and said they could come back and review it.

———

In Atlanta, Hoback worked until midnight in the hours following Gordon's first meeting with Judge Self. Something told Hoback it was time to crank up a notch the scrutiny of Roy Moody. Maybe it was learning about Moody's legal training, or maybe the details of his Eleventh Circuit appeal, maybe a combination of everything, including that the Midwestern Klansman no longer looked good as a bomb suspect. Hoback drew up plans for a surveillance on Moody and asked Gordon to come up from Macon to run it. Hoback didn't sleep much. The surveillance started at five A.M. in Rex, about an hour's drive from Hoback's house on the northern fringe of Atlanta's suburbs. Hoback instructed the assembled agents Moody might be the suspect, he might not. The idea was to watch Moody from the time he got up until he went to bed, to get his daily routine, places frequented, his associates. Anyplace he went into, he was to be followed—especially post offices. But the surveillance should still be loose.

"I'd rather lose the guy than get burned," Hoback said.

When Moody emerged, near noon, a woman was with him, a woman much younger than he. Later as a hidden investigator photographed them, the young woman, earthy in tight blue jeans and a long brown ponytail, threw her arms around Roy and kissed him, and that is how they were captured on film. The desultory surveillance lasted two more days, during which Moody did unremarkable things such as visiting a small airport, a flooring store and Lake Lanier, a huge hydroelectric reservoir made by damming the Chattahoochee River about an hour north of Atlanta. On January 13, the surveillance went on hold, lest Moody catch on. They'd resume on the eighteenth.

In Macon, Judge Self made good on his pledge about the documents. Among the copies he provided Gordon was a letter wherein Moody invited—almost challenged—a judge involved in his child-custody case to appear on a TV program in Atlanta.

"Since I plan to call public attention to this matter," the letter read, "I think I should be candid and advise you that if my right to appeal is not respected, I shall seek injunctive relief in the Federal District Court. If that becomes necessary I intend to hold the functionaries that were responsible for the denial of due process accountable in a civil rights action."

Gordon was no psycholinguistics expert. But he believed he saw distinct similarities between the prose in Moody's old letters and the threatening missives from the bomber. And the involvement of the TV station . . . in his rooting about in official files Gordon had also seen a letter Moody had copied to all three major TV networks. It brought to mind the letter the mail bomber had sent to Brenda Wood, the TV news anchor.

Judge Self also helped lead Gordon to Roy Moody's ex-wife.

Gordon and another ATF agent drove into a modern, well-landscaped apartment complex in a small town in south Georgia. Inside, the apartment they visited was similarly neat and contemporary. The former Hazel Moody looked to be in her late forties, maybe fifties. She had frosted hair, a thin frame and thick glasses over red, glassy eyes. She said she'd just gotten over a cold. She smoked. Gordon could see no scars of the type an explosion would leave, not outwardly.

She shook as if chilled. Her voice cracked and her eyes watered, and she pleaded for assurances Roy would never be able to find her. Nonetheless, she said she never saw Moody angry. Their only argu-

ments grew out of her requests he get a job, which she'd only
known him to have once in their marriage, at a tile plant from
which Roy later told her he had a leave of absence to attend school.
She said she discovered he was drawing unemployment. She described him as very private and speculated his current wife or girlfriend wouldn't know his business in detail. Moody, his ex-wife told
investigators, used to work in their kitchen while she was at her job,
but returned things to a locked bedroom before she got home each
day. Moody, she related, never allowed her or their son in that bedroom and told her he was building a model airplane. The room,
one day, happened to be unlocked. When she went in, she related
to the investigators, she found the package that eventually blew up
and injured her.

She did not tag Roy for racial hatred. He didn't drink too much
or abuse drugs. Every evening, she said, Moody watched the TV
news, religiously. He hated the ground on which her lawyer, Bill Self,
walked. And she seemed terrified of Roy. She announced she would
not cooperate with the government in any way if her location, or her
son's, got out.

Gordon met with Hazel on January 17. On the eighteenth, the
Moody surveillance resumed. About eleven-fifteen at night, the
evening shift picked up Moody and the young woman leaving his
bungalow in Rex. The woman was driving as they headed out in
Moody's black Ford pickup, which made its way to Interstate 75,
then north to an exit near Hartsfield International Airport. The
dark pickup pulled onto the grounds of metro Atlanta's main post
office. Young ATF Agent Sonny Fields could see the woman drop
several letters in one mailbox, then several more in another. Fields,
who stayed behind while the rest of the team followed the truck back
to Moody's house, used a car phone to call Hoback, who in turn
called Postal Inspector Jim Garrett, an early believer in Moody as a
bomb suspect, at home. They met at the post office and removed the
mail from the boxes. And more than ever before, Hoback was convinced of Moody's viability as a suspect. Garrett pointed out to him
an anomaly in the postmark at the main post office, a tiny dash or
minus sign in front of the PM characters. Investigators had seen that
postmark already: on the letter to TV anchor Brenda Wood.

By the next day, January 19—one month after the delivery of the
fourth bomb—Hoback was able to gather enough resolve and Gordon had gathered enough of Moody's papers for Hoback to seek out

an FBI documents expert to examine them. But he was quickly deflated. That's when he found out the FBI had already scored a big break on the documents front that very day, maybe the biggest break of the investigation. A typewriter match turned up between the mailing labels on the bomb packages and legal papers in an Eleventh Circuit case. And none of it seemed to have anything to do with Roy Moody. Instead the key figure in the mail-bomb case was suddenly a man named Wayne O'Ferrell, who ran a salvage shop in Enterprise, a small town in south Alabama heretofore distinguished by its town square, which had as its centerpiece a monument to the boll weevil, the insect that dethroned King Cotton and ushered in agricultural diversity. Enterprise was about to see a swarm of federal agents, followed quickly by an infestation of newspeople.

7

Wayne O'Ferrell

One look at the cavernous, metal-walled warehouse crammed with dented cans, old clothes, shoes in which you wouldn't mow your lawn and a zillion other odds and ends of limited appeal, and you realized the stark contrast between the persona manifest in the Old and New Surplus Salvage store on one hand, and on the other, the meticulous, precise craftsman who built the mail bombs. One walk through the dim light and January chill to the cash register next to which Wayne O'Ferrell reposed on a stool, and one listen to his affable, twangy conversation, and a gaping chasm opened up between him and the image of the mail bomber conjured up by the grandiloquent rhetoric in the threatening letters. The tall junk dealer with yellowish gray, wavy hair, glasses and an Alabama Crimson Tide sweatshirt seemed at odds with the role of mail-bomb suspect in many ways, but on January 19, 1990, no cop knew what motivated the bomber, let alone what he should look like or talk like.

And the FBI had something solid. On January 19, the payoff came from the careful combing of court papers from cases in which litigants acted for themselves, without a lawyer, before the Eleventh Circuit. In a case called *O'Ferrell versus Gulf Life Insurance Co.*, something turned up so compelling supervisory Special Agent Bob Thompson raced to the airport under lights and siren and hand-carried some of the typewritten documents in the file to the FBI lab in Washington, D.C. They included a typewritten envelope return-addressed from Robert Wayne O'Ferrell of New Brockton, Alabama. Other papers in the same case were gathered from a federal courthouse in Montgomery, Alabama, and from a lawyer's office in Birmingham.

By the end of the day the lab had determined that the envelope and two notices of appeal—signed by Robert Wayne O'Ferrell—had come from the same typewriter as the labels on the four mail bombs. The typing on the O'Ferrell filings also matched threatening letters mailed to the Eleventh Circuit judges in December. Moreover, Gulf Life, O'Ferrell's adversary in the case, was headquartered in Jacksonville, Florida, one of the four cities where bombs had arrived. An FBI agent contacted the Coffee County, Alabama, sheriff and his chief deputy. The chief told him O'Ferrell operated Old and New Surplus Salvage in Enterprise. Sheriff Brice Paul told the FBI that about a year earlier, he had seen seven to ten typewriters at an address on Main Street—an address that, the feds were informed, O'Ferrell had occupied.

The next day, an agent from the Birmingham division entered O'Ferrell's salvage store and eyeballed the man rapidly emerging as the central figure in the mail-bomb case, observing while there a number of typewriters on display. As he reached for the door to leave, the agent noticed that in place of a knob there was a long bolt through the door with a flat square of metal held on by nuts, prompting a comparison with the boltlike threaded rods, square end plates and nuts used to construct the Atlanta, Savannah and Jacksonville bombs. An FBI surveillance team parked across the street from the store thought someone from within peered back at them with binoculars. Much of this was folded into a sworn statement by a Birmingham-based FBI agent, to be used as a basis to obtain search warrants for O'Ferrell's home and business. Some, such as Hinshaw, advocated a low-key approach, such as undercover purchases of the typewriters in the shop. But by two P.M. on January 20, a Saturday, a U.S. magistrate in Montgomery had signed a search warrant for O'Ferrell's house.

Tall, lanky, with a distinctive white thatch luminescent amid his otherwise brown hair, Todd Letcher was the kind of agent the public might have expected when Efrem Zimbalist Jr. played a G-man on TV: smart not smug, a Wharton business grad willing to work for wages paid by the government, a member of both the white-collar-crime squad and the SWAT team. He was already home for the weekend when the ASAC beeped him with orders to head to Enterprise with another agent from the Atlanta office, to act as liaison to the Alabama division and keep the Georgia end of the investigation posted on what was happening. Letcher got to south Alabama by Saturday night and surveillance was already in place. Sunday came and the searches still didn't come off; the salvage shop would take more people than first figured. More Atlanta agents arrived among the reinforcements.

Monday, January 22, two days after the first warrant had been signed, the troops massed in a field in Enterprise, dozens of agents, each with an assignment. Letcher and Robert E. Lee, from the Mobile office and also SWAT-trained, moved out in a Chevy Blazer following a car carrying Steve Brannan, out of the Birmingham FBI division, and Bill Hagmaier of the behavioral-science unit. The latter pair parked and went inside the salvage shop. Nearby, in the Blazer, Letcher had his MP-5, a fearsome assault-style carbine. Lee had a shotgun. Brannan and Hagmaier had a deadline, and if they didn't meet it by coming out with O'Ferrell or signaling everything was okay, Letcher and Lee would lead the backup through the front door. Finally, Brannan came out and said everything was all right, then headed back in. More waiting; Letcher learned later O'Ferrell was concerned somebody be there to run the store. Finally, the foursome of feds and the junkman headed across town to Enterprise Police headquarters. As soon as they got there, the searches of O'Ferrell's store and his home in nearby New Brockton commenced. Lee and Letcher stayed around as security so Brannan and Hagmaier could dance O'Ferrell through a carefully choreographed course of questions meant to elicit not only information but a sense of veracity.

That same day in Washington, D.C., key leaders of the NAACP met at the White House with President Bush and Atty. Gen. Richard Thornburgh. The president expressed his concern and made clear he would do everything he could to put an end to the mail bombings. The Atlanta newspapers would report that Thornburgh went beyond that, telling top NAACP officials that day a "major development" was imminent.

When the assignment desk got a call saying something was up on the mail-bomb case, Michael Marsh jumped on it. Marsh was a reporter at WSB, Atlanta's most watched and most venerated TV station, and the bombings, for a month, had been the biggest story in town. He called a source in law enforcement who confirmed he was correct, that something was indeed up. They started the word games that are almost ritual in such situations, to leave room for plausible deniability should anyone later look for the leaker of information.

"Is it here in Atlanta?" Marsh asked. No, came the reply. The newsman thought of Savannah, where Robbie Robinson had been killed. "Is it on the coast?"

Wrong again. Other direction, the source prompted.

"Can you get there by helicopter?"

"Well, you probably could, but you'd want a fast plane."

Marsh rattled off Southern cities. Jacksonville . . . Columbus . . . Birmingham. The last got a response.

"Go south."

"Hang on." Marsh put his contact on hold while he hurried to a big map that pulled down like a color-splashed window shade behind the assignment desk. He picked up a phone, took the call off hold and started naming towns south of Birmingham. Montgomery . . . Mobile. You're cold, the source said.

"Dothan?"

"That's extremely hot."

"Well, is it Dothan?" Marsh spotted a city just west of Dothan. "Is it Enterprise?"

Silence.

"*Is it Enterprise?*"

"You didn't hear it from me."

Marsh informed the desk. Then he leafed through the affiliate directory to find the nearest ABC station, since WSB was an ABC affiliate. He found one in Dothan, called and found out somebody there had picked up rumblings about federal agents up in Enterprise. Then he called the Enterprise Police Department and found out the feds were in town all right, an *army* of agents. The station chartered a twin-engine plane. Marsh and a photographer took off for Enterprise. A woman from the local Ford dealership, contacted by the station while Marsh was airborne, was waiting with a car when they landed. Marsh had no travel money, no spare clothes, no satellite

truck to get his story back, no names, no idea of where to start, and
he was about an hour and a half from the six-o'clock news. But the
Ford lady told him there were plenty of federal agents at Wayne
O'Ferrell's store, and she gave him directions.

A yellow posterboard sign on the front door advertised work
pants at $3 a pair, five pairs for $12.50. A blue-and-orange WARE-
HOUSE SALE banner hung over a porch roofed by a blue tarp. Marsh
arrived to find only a handful of other journalists. The Dothan station had somebody there, as did the local newspaper and radio station. WBRC, the ABC affiliate in Birmingham, had a crew in town
and a satellite truck on the way, from which Marsh could feed tape
to Atlanta for the six-o'clock show. But by the time the feds finished
for the day with the junkman, nearly fourteen hours after they
started, the media landscape had changed. The world was there—
all three TV networks, CNN, local crews from Atlanta, Birmingham
and Savannah, newspaper and wire-service reporters. Unfortunately, hard information wasn't as plentiful as the people trying to
gather it. Marsh was well traveled; by the age of thirty-five he'd
worked in TV in San Antonio, Salt Lake City, San Francisco, Denver
and Baton Rouge—twice. He had anchor looks, with smooth, tan
skin and thick, dark hair, neatly trimmed. But he knew how to report too. And with agents on the scene and official spokespeople in
Washington giving away little, he had to scrape for a decent story.

His best pictures were of the salvage store in daylight, crime-
scene tape stretched across the front, investigators in suits and blue-
with-yellow-print FBI raid jackets huddled outside.

"Neighbors say it's operated by the Reverend Wayne O'Ferrell of
nearby New Brockton, Alabama," Marsh intoned in his voice-over.
"And the agents wanted to know about O'Ferrell too."

He cut to a sound bite with a local woman who told him she'd
been interviewed by investigators. She had a broad, honest-looking
face, brown hair, big glasses and an earnest manner on camera.

"They wanted to know if he had a violent temper," she said with
emphasis on the first syllable of *violent*. "Or if I'd ever seen him talk
bad about anybody or if I'd ever seen him be rude. And I have never
seen any of those. All I know about him, he's a nice man."

He butted against that a second sound bite from another woman:

" 'Have you ever known him to have a violent nature? How well
do you know him? Have you ever seen anybody over there as far as

unusual activities, a lot of cars, a lot of vehicles? How does he talk to you when you go in there, how does he act?' And I told them, he's always been a very polite gentleman."

Marsh resumed his narration. "Agents also searched O'Ferrell's house . . . the FBI has confirmed that search warrants are the first to be exercised in the ongoing and ever-broadening investigation of bombings in the Southeast . . . and agents did confirm they are looking for materials used to build bombs."

But, Marsh added, if the FBI found anything, they weren't saying.

The story was big enough for the station to send the satellite truck and a second reporter. That night, Tom Regan arrived to double-team Enterprise. He tracked a quick profile on O'Ferrell:

"Authorities have released little information on the background of the self-proclaimed preacher, who acquaintances describe as quiet and reserved," Regan reported. "A woman who handles advertising for the local newspaper says she talked to O'Ferrell on Friday about reserving advertising space for his warehouse. She described him as religious."

Cut to interview with woman: "When you first arrived, what was he doing?"

"He was reading the Bible. And we started talking about the Bible, doing our daily Bible reading. And he was telling—sharing some experiences with some things in his Sunday-school class."

Regan shot a stand-up—the part of a news story where the reporter is speaking directly into the camera—in front of a Phillips 66 station. "In a town like Enterprise, Alabama," he observed, "burglary is considered a serious crime. So you can imagine the reaction most folks had on hearing that the FBI was looking for evidence connected to two fatal mail bombings."

Regan followed that with a sound bite from a woman who looked to be standing behind a counter: "Everybody who's walked through this door has had something to say about it. Everybody. . . . They just cannot believe that anybody from Enterprise would be involved in something like that."

O'Ferrell himself freshened follow-up stories. Marsh's package featured the junk dealer entering his store in the company of Hagmaier, Brannan and Todd Letcher, among others. He reported agents continued to search the place, and he used a piece of an interview with O'Ferrell to explain what they were looking for.

"A typewriter," said O'Ferrell, "we *supposedly* have had, have sold. We don't have any idea who it was sold to, when it was sold. You know, you don't keep a record of that kind of stuff."

A Regan report used still more of O'Ferrell, opening with video of the sudden celebrity walking a dog along a red dirt road and waving amiably toward the camera.

"There's nothing to worry about. I'm not guilty, don't have anything to hide," he drawled.

Regan tossed in a couple more community-reaction sound bites. "It's hard for me to believe that he would be connected with anything like that," said a middle-aged, bespectacled woman in a bakery.

But events in Enterprise only got stranger. Investigators looking like bright yellow spacemen in protective suits made for a graphic spectacle on the news after search warrants were issued for O'Ferrell's septic tanks. O'Ferrell nailed up a NO TRESPASSING sign and publicly pleaded for privacy, but a troop of journalists staked him out anyway. He suddenly roared off in his pickup truck and hit the highway. Panic engulfed the press corps, which took off after him in a speeding caravan. "This is ridiculous," Regan thought, fearing someone would get hurt. But if O'Ferrell was on his way to a confession, it wasn't to the FBI. The news folks wound up tailing him to Bible study at church.

Stories out of Enterprise continued to feature accounts from locals about their encounters with investigators, who had been asking about welding, gunpowder, nails and more. One report said hundreds had been interviewed. And then there were the typewriters. Typewriters tested. Typewriters taken. T-shirts turned up for sale featuring the Columbia-like statue that held the giant boll weevil overhead on the town square. In the cartoon on the shirt the bug was replaced by a typewriter.

And the probe pushed far beyond Enterprise. In Savannah, for instance, Robbie Robinson's secretary was asked about a July 1987 mention of Gulf Life Insurance of Jacksonville, Florida, in Robinson's office mail log. Gulf Life was O'Ferrell's opponent in his Eleventh Circuit case. But she said she had no idea what the correspondence was about, and the name Robert Wayne O'Ferrell meant nothing to her. Elsewhere in Georgia, the reverend whose name had been used in the return address on the Savannah bomb was reinterviewed. He said, so far as he knew, he wasn't acquainted with anyone in Enterprise or New Brockton. The retired evangelistic preacher pointed out, however, that he had preached revivals in Alabama.

Michael Marsh found himself kneeling in front of a church. It was Sunday, January 28, nearly a week after his arrival in Alabama. Amid a cluster of TV people, he aimed a microphone at O'Ferrell, who that morning had delivered a testimonial to the congregation in which, Marsh would report, he denied guilt in the bombings and asked for prayers to help the FBI find those responsible.

"Somewheres another there is somebody who's guilty,"he said on camera. "And if people would pray like I'm askin' 'em to do right now, they'll be led to the right person."

It made him feel good, O'Ferrell suggested, somebody thought he was bright enough to build the bombs.

"I wished I was smart enough to know how to do something like that. But I tell you one thing, hey, I ain't gonna hold one in these hands, 'cause, hey, I wanna use 'em. And if I had one in these hands, it might blow 'em off!"

Marsh believed him. His skepticism had mounted for days, but now he felt certain this wasn't the guy. He was not alone in his doubts.

Frank Lee was dispatched to Enterprise as ATF-Georgia's representative the day before the searches started. He arrived close to nine P.M. to join a meeting of investigators in progress in Dothan. He estimated 150 agents had been brought in, two FBI SACs, four assistant U.S. attorneys. His job, essentially, would be to check out local firearms dealers, searching for the source of the powder in the bombs. But he'd been there only about a day and a half when, shortly before noon, he called the ATF office in Atlanta and left a detailed message for his bosses, Tom Stokes and Rich Rawlins:

> He and Ron Patterson have been asked to re-interview firearms dealers in the area (9 of them).
> Search still going on at O'Ferrell's business (new one)—2 ATF agents there.
> Man talked to them 14 hours yesterday; did not tell them anything. . . .
> Lee and others there do not think this man is capable of making the bombs.
> They still have not been able to locate the typewriter—the man's wife is trying to help them find it.

> *Frank Lee will probably be turned loose in the morning
> to go back to Savannah unless Stokes wants him to go
> somewhere else. . . .*
>
> *In essence, what he is saying is that the Alabama thing
> was a bust!*
>
> *He still thinks we need to keep Moody as a viable candi-
> date.*

Hoback had done his part to see Moody wasn't forgotten. On the nineteenth, the day the typewriter match had been made, he went to see Stokes and briefed him on O'Ferrell. Then he argued for keeping the surveillance on Moody until results were in from Alabama. Stokes, after some hard questions, agreed. At task-force headquarters, Hoback volunteered to work Saturday—so he could be the one to shuttle two FBI document examiners between Hartsfield International and the smaller airport where they would catch a government plane to Enterprise. When he had them captive in his car, he urgently told them as much as he could about Moody. Then he handed over some of the Moody papers Joe Gordon had collected in Macon. The experts told him none of the documents he had matched the typing they were looking for in the bomb case. Hoback tried not to show emotion, but told himself these were old specimens anyway. And he knew, somewhere, there were newer, better ones with Moody's name on them.

———

There had been other interrogations of Wayne O'Ferrell after the first on January 22. He spoke with agents the next day as well, and again on the twenty-fifth. Todd Letcher had come to town expecting someone clever and meticulous, and that wasn't how the junk dealer came across to him. Maybe it's an act, the FBI agent considered. Maybe he is slick enough to pull it off. The typewriter match was a big piece of evidence, almost like a fingerprint. He waited, at first, for O'Ferrell to snap. But the longer Letcher, Hagmaier, Brannan and Robert E. Lee were around the salvage seller, the less sense it made that this could be the bomber.

But Wayne talked about somebody else. Two somebodys, Brian and Georgia Fleming, who had a business called the Printing Press directly across the street from the erstwhile bank building agents had converted into a temporary base of operations while they carried out their investigation in Enterprise. The FBI learned Brian Fleming had gotten an award certificate from the president of the Enterprise NAACP chapter for his civic contribution.

"010187." If it was a cryptogram, investigators couldn't decipher it, but they knew what it meant. When it appeared at the bottom of a letter purporting to be from the mail bomber, the letter was for real. An early theory linked the code to the January 1, 1987—1/1/87— edition of the *American Bar Association Journal*, which featured a racially tinged Georgia death-penalty case, but that never proved out and the numerical puzzle remained one more frustrating taunt from the killer. Imagine, then, how it was when more than a month after the bombings, the FBI found out about Fleming's certificate, dated January 1, 1987.

About the same time as this discovery, O'Ferrell said he'd done some photocopying at the Printing Press involving his Eleventh Circuit court case. The photocopier the bomber used to duplicate threatening letters was, of course, one of the items agents were hunting. The feds also discovered other mundane business dealings between the Flemings and O'Ferrell.

Brian Fleming was tall and lanky, with a brown mop of hair and a boyish face incongruously interrupted by a heavy mustache. His wife was slight and fair-complected with straight, gray-brown hair and glasses. To a reporter visiting the printshop in early 1990, they seemed reticent but otherwise exceedingly polite, oddly European in their manner. That the young couple did business with O'Ferrell was not unusual; Enterprise is a small town. What was unusual is for a young couple in the piney plains of lower Alabama to be allegedly active supporters of the Irish Republican Army, among the world's best-known terrorist bombers. Indeed, when federal agents swooped in on Enterprise and Wayne O'Ferrell, the Flemings were already known to federal agents from ATF and U.S. Customs, and Brian Fleming was already under indictment for an alleged conspiracy to export firearms out of the United States without a license and for the illegal transfer of a firearm to an out-of-state resident.

According to documents, Fleming told an undercover Customs agent he wanted a legitimate business relationship as a front for illegal activities, and in 1988, the year before the mail bombings, a confidential government informant supposedly supplied Fleming with a "booby trap" manual. Furthermore, a wiretap in the ATF-Customs investigation had allegedly caught a phone call between Georgia

Fleming and a known IRA supporter, a call involving Georgia's suggestion of using booby traps in English cemetery plots.[*]

Wayne O'Ferrell, accompanied by a lawyer, spoke to the FBI for at
least the fourth time. The focus, at least in part, was on the unrecov-
ered typewriter used to type the bomb labels and threatening letters. In a sworn affidavit two days later, an FBI agent described the
conversation: "It was determined during this interview that O'Ferrell had not shared information during previous interviews concerning his thoughts and realizations of whom he might have sold his
typewriter to."

O'Ferrell named two men. One denied the next day he ever
bought, got or hauled any typewriter of O'Ferrell's. The other man
was Brian Fleming, and the FBI obtained search warrants for the
Flemings' home and business. The plate-glass storefront afforded
the TV crews outside great shots of the action when agents hit the
Printing Press office. Cameras were there as each of the Flemings
was taken to the building housing Enterprise Police headquarters,
but each was shortly taken home.

"If it does anything from Wayne O'Ferrell's position, it helps,"
said O'Ferrell's lawyer concerning the developments around the
Flemings.

The Flemings seemed out of place in a small town on the coastal
plain of south Alabama. But that didn't make them mailers of the
bombs that killed Judge Vance and Robbie Robinson. And nothing
surfaced in the searches, or anyplace else, that did.

As for O'Ferrell, his home, store and septic tanks had turned up
no proof he was the mail bomber. And the search for evidence went
even further than that. One dreary day lawmen escorted him from
his store into a waiting car, which arrived soon after at a local hospital. By the hospital door, his lawyer told reporters he had had his
blood drawn for testing.

"Was that for the purpose of DNA testing?" a TV reporter asked
the attorney.

"I have not been told that, but it would be my opinion that it . . .
will be some sort of DNA testing."

---

[*]Ms. Fleming says she has a vague recollection of such a conversation and if anything
like that was said, it was in a joking manner. She disavows the use of violence and calls
herself a pacifist. Brian Fleming also says he renounces all violence. He maintains the
search warrants were unnecessary since he was already cooperating with the investigation.

8

Stokes and Rukstele

I've been appalled at the recent mail bombings across this country. Every one of us must confront and condemn racism, anti-Semitism, bigotry and hate. Not next week, not tomorrow, but right now. Every single one of us.
—Pres. George Bush
State of the Union address
January 31, 1990

The trip from Atlanta to Savannah takes about four hours by car, with just one turn, in Macon, where you veer off Interstate 75 and onto Interstate 16. Frank Lee made a slight detour when he hit the middle-sized, middle-Georgia crossroads city on his way back to the coast from a meeting in Atlanta. He'd hoped to pick up the '72 trial transcript and take it on to Savannah for perusal, but Joe Gordon wouldn't let his hook into the mail-bomb investigation leave Macon, so Lee got pizza, beer and a hotel room and started reading. He started a list, the bolt . . . the battery . . . the smokeless powder. He called his boss in Atlanta, Tom Stokes. This is the guy, he told him. He called Brian Hoback too. Don't let up, he said. The next day, instead of heading immediately on to Savannah, Lee backtracked to

Atlanta. At some point, he got a look at the surveillance logs. What he saw bothered him, and he wasn't alone.

There were a thousand reasons a do-it-yourselfer like Roy Moody might have visited Wickes Lumber, Home Depot, Wheeler's Building Materials, Builder's Square and other hardware-type stores while being surreptitiously shadowed by a small cadre of maverick mail-bomb investigators in January 1990. He might have needed material for the outbuilding under construction in his backyard or sealant for the sailboat in the driveway or nuts for an airplane. But another possibility fueled the urgency welling up in Lee, Hoback and other investigators. An ATF agent checked the inventory at Home Depot, which, not surprisingly, included black latex paint, two-inch-wide brown wrapping tape, brown wrapping paper, galvanized pipe, small flashlight bulbs and three-eighths-inch by thirty-six-inch threaded rods. He checked Wheeler's and it carried most of the same items. At Builder's Square an agent spotted Moody looking at specialized screws and bolts. Whoever built the mail bombs built them clean; so far, some of the top forensic experts in the world had failed to find any fingerprint, DNA or other physical evidence to directly implicate the bomber. Adding to the frustration, he built them, in large part, from material that might be found in almost any American household. So while the chances were that Roy Moody's shopping was entirely innocent, the possibility that it wasn't spurred the investigation of him forward.

On January 25, Hoback reported to a requisite, six-hour, on-the-job training class. He was so distracted by thoughts of the bomb case and got so many phone calls or beeps on his pager about problems with the Moody surveillance, on the ground and now in the air, he was getting nothing out of the class. He left, hooked up with Terry Pelfrey from the GBI, and they brainstormed on how to push things ahead. That afternoon Hoback snuck Pelfrey onto the line in an ATF teleconference involving Tom Stokes, several other ranking ATF officials from around the country and the case agents from the four bomb cities. The conversation meandered along the still-unresolved white-supremacist avenue of investigation. Suddenly Pelfrey, a clean-cut ex-Marine, piped up and announced plans to get a search warrant for Moody's house. Conversation halted.

"We got some things breaking," Pelfrey added.

After the call, Hoback, as surprised as anyone else, hurriedly took the GBI agent aside and asked him what he had.

Nothing more than what Hoback already knew, he replied. But it was time to take a shot and see what happened.

Hoback knew Pelfrey was right. The ATF agent spent the weekend collating everything he had on Moody. On Monday, January 29, a small group of investigators pursuing Moody from ATF, the GBI, the Marshals Service and the U.S. Postal Inspectors set up their own base of operations to focus on Moody—away from task-force headquarters. They picked the U.S. Postal Inspection Service offices near Hartsfield International Airport, which happened to be not far from Moody's house in Rex. They quickly reached a consensus to go after the search warrant, and word spread fast. Near the end of the day, Hoback fielded a call from a federal prosecutor in Birmingham who said he had heard about the warrant and wanted to lend assistance. That night, Ray Rukstele, the prosecutor spearheading the case in Atlanta, got a call from the Department of Justice. No search warrants, Rukstele was informed, without the Department's approval.

Before a U.S. magistrate would issue a search warrant for Moody's house, the agents would need to come up with an affidavit describing the probable cause. Such sworn statements are typically signed by one investigator, as this one would be, but to speed things up, the following day the drafting process was parceled out among several agents. Pelfrey's portion pieced together the reports on Moody's psychological makeup. Deputy Marshal Bill Grom would cover Moody's prison records. Postal inspectors would analyze Moody's correspondence. Hoback's job was to synopsize the surveillance. Frank Lee would detail the identifying features of the bombs and sign the completed document. Meanwhile, the investigation kept moving.

———

Mike Ford was licensed both as a pilot and ground instructor, even trained in the military as an aircraft mechanic. Roy Moody was into airplanes. Ford was a lawyer, in practice with his wife, Diane, as Ford and Ford, with offices in the well-to-do suburb of Dunwoody, just north of Atlanta. Moody, of course, had not only studied the law, but often seemed obsessed with the law and lawyering. Ford had his roots in small-town middle Georgia. So did Roy. It was easy to see the affinity Moody found for Ford, even easy to imagine Mike Ford was what Roy Moody wanted to be, might have been. Roy was already tangled in litigation against a local bank when he came to

Ford as a referral from another lawyer. Later, Ford helped him with his Eleventh Circuit appeal concerning Julie Linn and the 1972 case. Ford believed Moody, who convincingly played the underdog who was repeatedly in the wrong place at the wrong time. Moody once told Ford if a meteorite was about to fall in the Arizona desert, and Roy was walking somewhere in the vastness, the space rock would choose to land where Roy happened to be standing.

It was decided an agent would set up over the phone an interview with Mike Ford, avoiding specifics. The inquiries would be general, about Eleventh Circuit cases the lawyer might be handling, as if investigators were also contacting other attorneys with Eleventh Circuit cases pending. But it was clear to Ford the investigator who called wanted to talk about Roy Moody. It was a bomb investigation and Roy Moody had been convicted in a bomb case. So, mindful of the bounds of attorney-client confidentiality, he called his client to get permission to discuss the case, which Moody gave.

Ford had sleepy eyes but an alert manner. He was in his early forties, smooth-complected, with dark, neat hair, slightly receded. His law library featured kelly green wall-to-wall carpet and a teak conference table. Postal Inspector Jim Rushwin and ATF Agent Gene Ford sat on one side, across from the lawyer, whose tape recorder was positioned between them and was rolling.

"Am I a target or a suspect in some of this? Because, if so, this is going to be a very short conversation," Ford said.

Rushwin told him he was not and indicated they were simply checking on any cases he might have had before the Eleventh Circuit. Ford brought up Roy Moody. He said they might already know about him because of his 1972 conviction involving a bomb. Moody, the lawyer said, had had a lot of hard luck. Ford wouldn't say how long Moody had been a client or give up any correspondence; that intruded too far on the attorney-client relationship. But Ford told them Moody would probably make available the papers they wanted to see if they would call him. Ford mentioned three more cases before the Eleventh Circuit. He also mentioned he'd clerked, back in 1972, in a law firm in Warner Robins—the locale in the return addresses for two of the mail bombs. And he mentioned Robbie Robinson. Perhaps ten to twelve years earlier, Ford revealed, he worked for the firm of Hill, Jones and Farrington in its Atlanta office. Robinson was in the Savannah office. The two young lawyers encountered each other about three times in Atlanta. Once Ford may have taken

Robinson to the airport. Moody was now the first major suspect with a link, tenuous as it was, to Robbie Robinson.

At nine o'clock that night, the agents working on the search warrant affidavit finished the rough draft. Hoback called Rukstele at the Atlanta U.S. attorney's office, and at ten-thirty A.M. the next day, they went over the document. Ray Rukstele was solidly and squarely built, forty-seven, wore glasses and spoke in a soft monotone, part Jack Webb and part Peter Lorre. He was unfailingly polite, almost formal. His boss, U.S. Attorney Bob Barr, was leaving, and Rukstele already knew he'd be the interim office chief. He also already knew about Moody, owing to a visit several days earlier from Tom Stokes, seemingly beside himself, frustrated in his belief that no one at the controls of the investigation seemed willing even to consider Moody seriously as a suspect. He'd spent close to an hour and a half, maybe longer, persuading Rukstele that Moody was indeed a viable possibility.

The prosecutor gave Hoback suggestions about the affidavit and asked to get the revised version the next day. Then, he said, he would fax the document to his Department of Justice superiors. Hoback left believing he would have an answer from Justice by the next afternoon.

The night of Hoback's meeting with Rukstele, George Bush delivered his State of the Union address about Operation Just Cause in Panama, about Solidarity in Poland, about the fall of the Berlin Wall. And about mail bombs.

"The state of government does indeed depend on many of us in this very chamber," the president told the joint session of Congress. "But the state of the Union depends on all Americans. We must maintain the democratic decency that makes us a nation out of millions of individuals. And I've been appalled at the recent mail bombings across this country. Every one of us must confront and condemn racism, anti-Semitism, bigotry and hate. Not next week, not tomorrow, but right now."

But right now the search warrant wasn't ready. The morning of February 1, Hoback delivered the corrected package back to Rukstele, who offered more suggestions and sent it back again. The next day at eight-thirty A.M. Hoback delivered a third version. A career prosecutor, Ray Rukstele considered himself a team player, and his team was the Department of Justice, of which the U.S. attorneys' offices around the country were a part. But that day Rukstele engaged in a terrible row with a superior at the Department, as the Washington headquarters is known to prosecutors out in the trenches. Rukstele was furious to find out an assistant U.S. attorney in Birmingham had been reviewing the warrant and had a laundry list of things he contended needed to be done before the document was approved. He had apparently cited a legal precedent Ray Rukstele flatly believed did not apply here. All of this was set against the backdrop of a building battle over turf. Still unannounced by Washington was whether, when it was time to arrest someone, the formal charges would come from a grand jury in Birmingham, who had jurisdiction because Judge Vance was killed nearby, or in Atlanta, where bombs and threat letters had been postmarked, and where the Eleventh Circuit bomb and NAACP tear-gas device had been delivered.

Hoback got word it was still no go with the Department of Justice and the U.S. Attorney's Office in Birmingham. He knew the decision wasn't simple. Unless a connection surfaced between Moody and O'Ferrell, a search of Moody's house could amount to a public admission that the Enterprise adventure was a mistake. And investigators—and news crews—were still in Enterprise.

Somebody in Birmingham relayed a list of additional checks wanted for the Moody warrant. One was find out more about Susan Moody. Get a list of magazine subscriptions. And most burdensome of all, return to the hardware stores Roy had visited, purchase the kinds of items used to build the bombs, then send that material to the lab for comparison to the actual bomb components.

"Well, Tommy, it sounds like there's a problem down there," said an ATF official in Washington during another teleconference.

The remark was tossed to Tom Stokes, but Hoback intercepted.

"The fuckin' problem is in Washington, and we're getting screwed," spat Hoback, who, along with Frank Lee, was taking part in the conversation from the postal inspectors' offices. Lee rushed toward the younger agent and tried to wrest the phone away. When Hoback placed his hand over the receiver, Lee rebuked him.

"That's the chief of the explosive division in Washington, you dumb ass!"

But this was a different Hoback. He was on a tirade and knew the top of his bald head was turning red. He tuned back into the conversation in time to hear Stokes say, "Well, actually, the boy's right."

That night, Stokes called his newly impetuous charge and re-minded him it was the SAC's job to fight those battles.

"What you did was wrong," Stokes said. "But it got their atten-tion."

The bottom line was the wish list would have to be addressed. Hoback and Lee did most of the shopping. Hoback hit a Hallmark in search of Faber-Castell pens, an auto-parts store, a pair of Home Depots. He visited the Griffin Servistar Hardware, where Moody had also been seen, and the young agent was able to purchase there most of the generic components in the mail bombs. On Sunday, Feb-ruary 4, he prepared the paperwork to go with the gathered goods, and on the fifth he met Lloyd Erwin at the airport so the lab man could hand-deliver the stuff to the FBI in Washington. On the sixth near five P.M., the latest version of the search warrant affidavit went to the U.S. Attorney's office.

On the seventh, Hoback met with his counterparts from the GBI and the postal inspectors to draw up a plan for executing the search warrant, whenever it might happen. He took part in another ATF tele-conference, and he got word from Ray Rukstele the Department of Justice still would not approve the warrant, though the changes re-quested this time seemed minor. The prosecutor had resisted talking directly to his counterparts in Birmingham, but continued talking to Justice daily, without the high decibels of the first flare-up. It wasn't Rukstele's style to stay angry, but he was uncomfortable telling the agents they still lacked Justice Department approval. He was dis-turbed to have to listen to the investigators' vituperation. But he felt compelled to just sit there and take it. While his heart was with them, while he thought the agents were right, he wasn't the type to criticize his employer to them. And he believed it only a question of time before things would sink in and the right thing would happen.

The surveillance team on Moody was short an agent or two, and Hoback headed over to help out. Near nine P.M., Moody was on the move in his black pickup truck, heading along a main thoroughfare near his house, then left past a grocery store and a gas station.

"Hey, he's going in a big circle," Hoback radioed to the rest of the team. "Let's be real loose on 'em right now."

The key to a good tail job is frequently changing the car closest to the quarry, so he doesn't see the same one again and again in his rearview mirror. So when Moody turned into a subdivision in Riverdale, another suburb south of Atlanta, the first two or three cars drove straight on by, then the next in the procession peeled in after him. But Moody headed straight for a cul-de-sac. Over the radio, the lead car warned the rest of the team not to come in. It was too late. Hoback was one of the drivers caught in the neighborhood as Moody swung his truck around at the end of the asphalt diverticulum and headed back out the way he came. Hoback veered quickly into somebody's driveway, parked and started walking toward the door as if he lived there. The suspect passed two more government cars and continued on. As the investigators hustled to catch up, Moody turned down a highway entrance ramp, then suddenly whipped the truck to the shoulder and slammed on the brakes. Virtually the entire surveillance team was left naked and exposed, with little choice but to file on by in plain view.

That's it, Hoback said. It's over. The team regrouped at a shopping center the agents had used as a mustering point to change shifts during the days of stakeout. The mood was an odd blend of anger, frustration and—because their blown cover would almost certainly force things to a new stage—excitement.

"Stokes is gonna go crazy," Hoback worried aloud.

"I'm glad you're making the call and not me," someone offered.

Tom Stokes was of average height and build, with dark hair parted on the side and a boyishly mischievous grin usually perforated by a cigarette. The Atlanta job had about doubled his pack-a-day addiction. There's no way to know if that's why his voice had the timbre of mixing cement; the first time his parents caught him smoking he was ten. After a kidney-stone operation he tried to quit and got down to three cigarettes—for one day. His assistant special agent-in-charge told him he was turning into an asshole. He also wore neckties about two inches above his navel, worked long hours and could be counted on to raise hell when he saw the need.

Hoback called Stokes and told him Moody had made the surveillance. The investigator expected the smoking volcano to erupt. Instead, Stokes was almost placid.

"You can't sit out there three or four weeks and not expect to get burned," he said. "We've been telling them this and telling them this."

Stokes hung up and called Ray Rukstele at home. It was a pivotal moment not just in the case but in the life of Tom Stokes, who long before had made a conscious decision to forsake the street for the managerial ladder. In a move many might think inconsistent with that agenda, he threw a hardball at the Department of Justice. He told Rukstele if he didn't have a federal search warrant by the next day, the Georgia Bureau of Investigation would go to a state judge and get a state search warrant, potentially leaving the Department of Justice out of the loop on its biggest case. Rukstele told Stokes to stand by, then called back and told him to have the agents at his office at midnight.

Rukstele realized once Moody burned the stakeout, they had to move immediately. When he called a Department of Justice official in suburban Washington and got him out of bed, Rukstele didn't offer a choice, but a fait accompli. Moody made the surveillance, we're going to proceed with the search warrant and it has to be now. It's incumbent upon you to notify whoever has to be notified. Fortunately the man in Washington was in full agreement.

Rukstele wore a suit and tie when he met the investigators on the eighteenth floor of the Russell Federal Building in the middle of the night. Frank Lee, summoned from his hotel room, settled in to work with Rukstele and his secretary. Stokes went to the ATF offices a couple blocks away, to wait and smoke.

———

Moody left his bungalow in Rex and climbed into a sky-blue Volkswagen Bug, carrying a white box. Susan was with him. Hoback's heart raced. *He's gonna do something right in front of us*, he thought. There was no dearth of experience on the stakeout team this night. Jim Arey, Bob Finke and Gene Ford had more than a half century on the job between them. But the call was Hoback's, and the rest were waiting for him to make it. "Bumper-lock him," he radioed.

"If he drops the package off, take him down."

Stokes was listening at the office base station and cut in on the radio.

"Why do you want to take him down? Why don't we just sit on the package and follow him?"

The boss was right. Hoback realized he'd been carried away and passed the plan on to the rest of the crew. Moody led them back to that big post office he'd visited before, the main one on Crown Road. This time, he drove around to the loading dock at the back. He left his package there. It turned out to be a corrugated-plastic

U.S. Mail bin full of letters pertaining to Moody's vanity-press operation, the Associated Writers Guild of America. *He's messing with us,*
Hoback told himself.

The surveillance team stuck with Moody the rest of the night.
Hoback headed to the postal office and met with Postal Inspector
Jim Garrett and a secretary. They made corrections to the affidavit
as required and faxed them to Rukstele and Lee at the U.S. Attorney's Office. By about four A.M. they thought they had a finished
product. At that point there were actually six search warrants, all using the same affidavit: for the house, a miniwarehouse rental storage
area, a sailboat in the driveway and three cars. Frank Lee's affidavit
laid out the basics of the crimes under investigation. He recounted
his review of the 1972 trial transcript and Lloyd Erwin's recollection
of that case. Lee itemized ten similarities Erwin and FBI bomb expert Tom Thurman had identified between the December bombs
and the '72 device, including the metal end plates, the threaded
rods, the flashlight-bulb initiator, the booby-trap-style box lids, the
smokeless powder and the absence of "safety mechanisms used for
bomb builder safety." Lee reported a computer search of ATF
records dating back to 1975 had turned up not another pipe bomb
with square, metal end plates and the threaded-rod-and-nut construction anywhere in the United States. Thurman had told him the
explosive unit at the FBI lab hadn't seen another one either. The
physics and chemistry courses, the old psychological and psychiatric
analyses and the interview with Mike Ford all found their way into
the sworn statement. Lee had also conducted his own interview with
the former Hazel Moody.

"She stated that she feels threatened by Moody, whom she says
she has not seen in 13 years," he wrote.

Postal Inspector Dave Kirkland contributed a startling comparison of the language in the mail bomber's threatening letters with
the verbiage in a series of documents Moody authored in connection with his Associated Writers Guild in the early eighties. From the
latter, Kirkland noted these phrases:

> *I shall*
> *Incompetent*
> *Cause us to pay for your incompetence*
> *Failure of the U.S. Postal Service*
> *Has been wrongfully sent*

Due to the incompetence of
Wrongfully accusing
Failed to do something
We shall
Disregard

The mail detective extracted these phrases out of the 1989 threat letters:

Wrongfully refuse to fulfill
Protect the innocent
Court's failure to render
You shall
Failure to comply
Shall result
Protecting the innocent
You shall make
Callous disregard

Making all the necessary copies of the thick document commenced near five A.M. Stokes called Hoback at the postal offices and said a U.S. magistrate was standing by at home. After about a quarter case of copying paper, the discovery of a mistake in the affidavit caused the copying to start over. Near eight A.M., Stokes called, reminded Hoback again about the waiting magistrate and asked what the problem was. The conversation degenerated into yelling. Finally, close to nine A.M., the copying was finished. Hoback asked another ATF agent to pick up a suit at Hoback's house and bring it down to the postal offices, where he'd clean up and change. Frank Lee called and said Ray Rukstele had decided on two more search warrants, for the Moodys' persons. It was a good idea, but meant another delay. Meanwhile, the surveillance team, out since the night before, persevered.

About lunchtime, Moody strode into a Best Western motel in Stockbridge, not far from his house. So far as Joe Gordon knew, Moody hadn't made him yet, so he was the one who followed the suspect inside. He heard a voice, followed it and found Moody talking on a pay phone in an alcove near the men's room. Gordon walked into the bathroom, held the door shut with his foot and put his ear up to the door. He heard Roy mention his appeal at the Eleventh Circuit. Then Moody seemed to be listening.

"I'm not a member of any racial group or organization, and they're not going to find that I ever had been," Moody continued. "The only thing I belong to is a pilots' association."

He mentioned his 1972 conviction for "constructive possession" of a bomb.

"They tried to prove that I made the bomb but were unable to do that."

Moody said he was being followed. "They have a plane on me," he noted, which was true. He told the other party he would "FedEx" him some materials and sought an address. The conversation ended close to twelve-forty P.M., and Moody headed out. Another car picked him up. Gordon rushed to his car and hurriedly wrote down everything he remembered, including exact quotes.

That afternoon, investigators from the FBI, ATF, the Postal Inspectors, U.S. Marshals Service and GBI gathered in the annex of a church Terry Pelfrey had found not far from Moody's house. The Enterprise investigation had drawn heavily on the Atlanta FBI office's mail-bomb resources. But case agent John Behnke and one or two other Atlanta-based agents would be in on the search operations, along with FBI bomb-expert Thurman, who was key finally to bringing around officials in Washington. Standing before the assembly: Brian Hoback, a lowly grade 9 in the civil-service ranks, three years earlier ensconced in a promising career in heavy machinery, now keenly aware of how far he had come in hardly more than a month. Jim Garrett and Frank Lee had been processing the estimated thirty pounds of paperwork at the courthouse. Lee told Hoback to start the briefing without him. The young agent distributed photocopies of the game plan and began the briefing on the biggest current criminal case in the country. Sometimes serving a search warrant, especially in drug and fugitive cases when fast entry is key, involves smashing through the door with a battering ram or a swift kick, but Hoback explained this wouldn't be a door-kicking search. He went over the shooting policy, routine before such an operation. He announced there would be no raid jackets, referring to the midnight blue windbreakers emblazoned with a police agency's name or acronym in big yellow letters to let criminal suspects know the folks crashing through the door are police. The jackets also garner exposure for each agency when the TV cameras show up, but the plan today didn't include TV. This would not turn into the circus Enterprise did, Hoback said bluntly. Hence there would be tight control on the number of vehicles at Moody's house. A van would take most of the investigators in and drop them off. There would be no telltale cluster of Fords and Chryslers with blackwall tires, so easily recognizable to the press as "unmarked" cars they might as well have blue lights on the roofs and emblems on the doors. There would be little on the outside to betray what was going on inside. Hoback introduced ATF bomb expert Terry Byer, who used a mock-up he had built of one of the bombs to discourse on the components for which searchers should look. Lee arrived with the warrants and Hoback went over a few more logistical details. The plan called for catching Roy and Susan together at home. Sometimes plans change. Word came from the surveillance team: Susan was on the move.

———

By late afternoon, a sober-faced Frank Lee perched on a stool next to Roy Moody, who reclined, feet up, in an easy chair the color of boiled lobster shell. Moody wore jeans, a white pullover, white socks with brown shoes and what looked to be reading glasses, wire-framed, through which he assiduously inspected the search warrant with an air one might expect more from a professor grading a term paper than an ex-con reading about a raid on his house. Lee and Postal Inspector Dave Kirkland had driven up to the house alone. The other agents had been prepared to wait if Moody would talk to the pair, but he declined, and Kirkland radioed in the rest of the troops in the van. Lee asked Moody if he had any guns in the house, a standard question. Moody told him no, and he said they were welcome to search—if there was a proper search warrant. Kirkland read him his rights. To Lee, Roy seemed as if he'd been expecting them. The veteran lawman thought Moody was taking this thing very coolly, almost amused at what was happening. Eventually, he wanted to call his attorney. Lee arranged it. Afterward Moody told him the only thing the lawyer wanted him to do was make sure he got a copy of the warrant.

Lloyd Erwin didn't think Roy recognized him. In 1972, Lloyd's hair was in a tight crew cut. Now it was slightly high on the forehead instead of high on the sides. Moody, on the other hand, hadn't changed much. And neither, Erwin noticed, had the way he lived. Reminiscent of the kitchen workbench where Erwin gathered crucial evidence in the first case, the kitchen in the Rex house looked almost as much a woodshop as a food-preparation area. What would in most houses serve as a bedroom was in the Rex residence a cluttered home office, with a door placed across a pair of mustard-yellow file cabinets for a makeshift desk, much like the one in the room where the bomb blew up on Hazel Moody in 1972. Architectural convention obviously did not constrain Roy Moody; he used few rooms in the house as most occupants would. The living room, where Roy read the warrant in his recliner, was dominated by a large bed. A bathroom was used to store word-processing equipment. But in contrast to the tools, building materials, papers and other clutter pervading the rest of the dwelling, an erstwhile bedroom in a front corner was virtually empty, but for a few clothes in the closet and fuchsia wall-to-wall carpeting that appeared to be new. The room was also freshly painted.

The surveillance had split up when Susan departed just before the raid. The team that stayed with her was able to radio Hoback and Postal Inspector Jim Rushwin into position to confront her at an Amoco station where she was pumping gas into the Volkswagen Beetle. She walked toward the car after paying the clerk. Both investigators held up their badges. Rushwin identified himself to Susan and asked if she would talk to him. She walked quietly, obliviously between the pair of startled agents and robotically climbed into the Bug. Hoback hurriedly grabbed the top of her car door and asked whether she was aware of some problems her husband was having. Talk to her husband, she suggested. He asked if she wasn't curious what he was talking about. No. She had some errands to take care of. She closed the door, started her engine and drove off. Hoback was stunned. He'd considered a lot of possibilities, but not that she would simply ignore them. It was as if, he thought, she was on a mission and was fixed on completing it. He and Rushwin rushed to their car to follow. Hoback decided she'd made him look like an idiot. The agents tailed her, first to the drive-in teller window at a bank, then to Southlake Mall, where she stopped at an eyeglass store. Hoback dispatched ATF Agent Bill Bass into the store to watch her, then he radioed the command center and asked for a female agent and copies of the search warrants. They're on the way, came the reply. Hoback parked his car, portable blue light displayed, behind the Volkswagen so she couldn't get out of the parking lot. Susan came out and Hoback told her he had search warrants for the car and her person. The soft-spoken young woman asked to see the warrants. Hoback told her they were en route. She replied she was leaving and they couldn't search her or the car. Hoback explained they didn't need warrants in hand to begin the searches and he asked her to sit on the curb, which she did, but a couple of minutes later she abruptly got up and headed back toward the eyeglass store. Hoback was determined she wouldn't get away again, not until he was ready, but he suggested to Rushwin they let her enter the store. When he asked where she was going, she answered she was making a phone call. Hoback and Rushwin listened to her end of it.

Hoback heard her ask for Roy, then she waited a few seconds.

"They say they have search warrants for me." Pause. "They do?"

She paused again, as if listening.

"You'll have to take care of that package yourself. They've detained me."

FBI Agent Sally Heintz and Deputy Marshal Bill Grom arrived. Susan was shown the warrants. The searches turned up two compelling items. In the car Hoback found a Federal Express overnight-letter envelope, addressed to Jeffrey Weiner, attorney-at-law, in Miami, Florida. And in Susan's purse were seventeen twenty-five-cent stamps depicting the American flag flying over Yosemite National Park.

Hoback explained to her what was being kept and left her copies of the warrants and the inventories of items seized. He asked the young woman if she would be willing to talk with them. She wouldn't answer, unless her silence was her answer. Hoback told her she was free to go. When Susan arrived back at the house, she seemed to Frank Lee panicky and upset, unsure of herself. Roy looked at her, talked softly to her, and she settled down almost immediately. The oddness of it stuck with Lee. When one's home is crawling with men and women carrying badges and guns during the service of a criminal search warrant, it is routine for an occupant to ask permission even to go to the bathroom—routine, that is, to ask one of the law enforcement officers for permission. Susan asked Roy.

———

A WSB-TV news helicopter crisscrossed the skies over the corner of Clayton County where Rex was. The crew on board had somehow gotten wind something was happening on the mail-bomb case, but they weren't sure exactly where and what. They were looking for the

telltale cluster of unmarked cars that typically tipped off a major police action, but the only bunching of vehicles they saw was at a
church. Having run out of options, if not fuel, the chopper crew set
down in a vacant dirt lot to meet a photo truck, which then headed
to the small country chapel. It took just one look in a car window, at
the portable blue light inside, for the news crew to know they were
on to something. One of the newsmen walked around the corner
and recognized, framed in a window, John Behnke, the FBI case
agent for the bombings out of the Atlanta office.

A narrow porch with wrought-iron railings and brick stanchions
ran across half the front of the cedar-sided, ranch-style Moody
house. Bamboo-looking shades had been hung on the front of the
porch, so from the front when the news arrived, they could get little
in the way of pictures at first. But from a neighbor's backyard they
found a clear shot into a pair of side-by-side windows in the back of
Moody's house, a clear shot of the crowd of investigators scrutiniz-
ing the interior. Eventually Charles McMichen, a jovial GBI supervisor with wavy brown hair and a mustache, came out front and
delivered a bare-minimum statement that sounded as if it had been
arrived at by committee.

"All I can tell you at this time is some search warrants are being
served, and beyond that, I can't make any comments."

But the newspeople had seen Behnke and recognized Pelfrey, Lee
and Hoback as investigators assigned to the mail-bomb probe. They
had their story in time for the eleven-o'clock news. The focus of the
mail-bomb case had shifted from Enterprise, Alabama, to Rex,
Georgia.

———

Rushwin and Hoback had headed for the house once they finished with Susan at the shopping mall. The ATF agent noticed her
now cuddling and caressing her much-older spouse. Seeing Roy
close-up, Brian Hoback thought him smug and self-assured, as if
certain his uninvited guests would find nothing of consequence.
Moody was right if he thought they would find no hard physical evidence; but they wouldn't leave empty-handed. Pelfrey took samples
of wire from the crawl space and pipe from the backyard. A postal
inspector took samples from a copy machine. Erwin located glue,
string, rubber bands, nails and metal plates. In papers at the house
concerning the '72 case, passages about investigative techniques

had been highlighted. In the pickup truck, ATF agents found a spiral notebook with names, addresses and phone numbers, and they found two .38-caliber bullets. At the warehouse, a GBI agent came up with a welder's handbook. Among the most intriguing finds was an article Birmingham-based ATF Agent Reynold Hoover turned up at the house. It concerned the FBI investigation in Enterprise. Hoover also found a letter to Jeffrey Weiner, dated that very day.

The Moodys sat together as Frank Lee explained the inventory of items that would be retained from the house. Nothing taken from the house seemed to upset Roy. But the Federal Express envelope from the Volkswagen was different. Moody told Lee the agents had taken both the original and a copy of a letter to a Florida lawyer, and he wanted one of them back. Lee told Moody if he had a problem, he could have his lawyer call the U.S. Attorney's office. The Moodys looked in the office, kitchen and living room, and finally Susan found something handwritten in a mail tray. She told Roy she'd found the rough draft and would begin typing right away. She started before the last agent was out of the house. Again, Hoback noticed, she seemed determined to carry out the instructions she had been given. The young wife's subservience made an impression on the young agent.

———

After the search, Roy and Susan headed to the small airport in Griffin, about half an hour south of their home in Rex. The couple strolled along the runway.

"If they find any evidence," Roy said, "it would be DNA."

9

Roy Moody Talks

On February 9, 1990, the morning after the service of the search warrants on the Moodys, the investigators who had been meeting for two weeks at the postal inspectors' offices were no longer outcasts, no longer alone. Close to a dozen FBI agents showed up to start poring over the items seized the night before. Among them was a supervisor whom earlier both Hoback and Lee had perceived to be sympathetic but unable to divert resources from the Enterprise angle. He sidled up and put his arm around Hoback.

"Nobody liked you yesterday," the supervisor said. "Everybody wants to be your friend today."

As the FBI agents began talking up their new plans for Moody, as they read every document they could get their hands on, Hoback found himself intimidated by the sheer numbers, by the whole experience. At one point he called for more ATF agents to come down; he felt outnumbered. True, they were all on the same team. It had just been so long since they'd used the same playbook. Hoback made an entry in his diary: "FBI now believes in Moody, wants to take over."

A few miles south of the postal inspectors' offices, the microwave masts of television live trucks jutted into the steel-dust sky. News vehicles parked bumper to bumper nearly the entire length of Skyline Drive, Roy Moody's street. Roy and Susan managed to slip out and make their way to Mike Ford's office. Roy wanted to take his case to the media, but on his terms. First, there was a typed press release, which criticized supposed government leaks about the case, mentioned his 1972 case was now on appeal to the U.S. Supreme Court, and said, "I do not think I am a serious suspect in the bombings related to Federal Judge Vance and the lawyer in Savannah."

Second, Ford called WSB-TV to offer an interview to anchorwoman Monica Kaufman, an attractive, effusive black woman who blended savvy, intellect and the ability to deliver the news on camera as if she were sitting across the viewer's kitchen table. She was a local institution and easily the most potent audience draw of any television personality in Atlanta. That afternoon Ms. Kaufman and the reporter who had covered the search warrant the night before jointly interviewed Ford on camera in his law library. Roy was out of sight, in another room.

"You asked, I'm here," Monica Kaufman said as the tape started to roll. "I guess the first question is, what did they seize?"

"Well, they seized a number of things. One of the more bizarre things is they appear to have seized all of Mr. Moody's personal papers relating to his Eleventh Circuit and United States Supreme Court appeal, which is currently ongoing."

"You were telling me there is really no connection to Judge Vance that way?"

"Not that we can comprehend." Ford reached across the table. "This is the slip decision* in Mr. Moody's case, and as you can see, Mr. Vance was not on the panel."

Ford said other items taken included a shopping list, common things like string, paper clips and rubber bands, and some construction supplies. He said he was sure they looked for a typewriter, but didn't seem to think they took one. Ford discussed Julie Linn, his own distant connection to Robbie Robinson and the visit to his office by the two federal investigators. The lawyer said all the evidence he had seen showed Moody was wrongfully convicted in the 1972 case. Toward the end of the interview, Ford consented to bring Roy in for some cutaway shots—but not for questioning. Moody walked in wearing a blue coat and maroon tie, his thick black hair neatly combed. He seemed subdued but not at all ill at ease. He smiled almost bashfully.

Shortly before six P.M., Roy and Susan stopped by Rozene Ledbet-

---

*The form in which appeals-court opinions are initially published.

ter's place.* Ms. Ledbetter went out to her porch and asked if Susan was okay. Roy gave her his attorney's card and said she didn't have to talk to federal agents if they showed up.

"People need to stand up to them," he said.

Ms. Ledbetter had known the couple since she managed a barbecue restaurant where Roy and Susan were daily customers. The Moodys ate out often. Later Susan had invited her to do some part-time clerical work for the Associated Writers Guild of America. She had heard on the radio something about a Rex couple and the mail-bomb case, and though the report didn't name him, she immediately thought of Roy.

Her television was tuned to WSB, and the lead story on the news, of course, was about the mail-bomb investigation. Susan said she didn't want to watch and went to a back bedroom where cartoons were on the TV. But Roy smiled the whole time he watched the report.

The station ran several stories about the case that night. The reporter who covered the search warrant opened one segment with a shot of Roy.

"At his lawyer's office today, we found out what Walter Leroy Moody looks like, and we found out more about what federal agents may have found in a search of Moody's home last night," he said, shifting to the video from the search the night before. He paraphrased Ford about what was seized, recounted the 1972 conviction and Moody's appeal, and quoted from a copy of Moody's petition to the U.S. Supreme Court, in which Moody philosophized that when a person lives his life inside the law, he earns a right to have that known to society.

"Whether this court elects to protect that right will have profound social consequences; for in the absence of such protection, not only are citizens subjected to wrongful loss of freedom but also one of the main incentives for them to be law abiding, the protection of their reputations is removed."

Monica Kaufman did a piece built around the Ford interview.

"Ford feels the government is treating his client shabbily," she said in her voice-over.

Another story, by WSB's weekend anchorman, John Alston, covered reaction in Rex.

"Action News has learned this neighborhood has been under sur-

*The description of this visit is according to an account Ms. Ledbetter later gave federal agents, as reflected in documents.

veillance for the past few weeks," he said in his stand-up. "On occasion neighbors have even called Clayton County Police to report suspicious cars that turned out to be surveillance vehicles."

Alston cut to a neighborhood resident: "Anytime a strange vehicle sets out here and nobody moves in it and I know somebody's in it, they're up to something."

"What did police say when they came here?" Alston asked.

"They just said it was police business, not to worry about it. They'd handle it."

Michael Marsh reported from Enterprise—he was back there for his second stint—that O'Ferrell and the Flemings denied knowing Moody. But a story Marsh fed back later may have told more about the situation in Enterprise. In that piece, he said the FBI had not talked to O'Ferrell in two weeks, and in the meantime, O'Ferrell had become "sort of a folk hero." Marsh made liberal use of snatches of a country song about the junkman, under video of somebody pushing a button on a cassette player and then Wayne O'Ferrell gently rocking his chin up and down as if keeping time to the twangy tune.

"Some of the supporters have called, sent letters and even money to O'Ferrell," said Marsh. "But O'Ferrell says he still hasn't gotten what he wants most, an apology. . . ."

"I believe they will," Wayne said. "Because they're gonna realize one day what a big boo-boo they made."

A little more music:

> Well, Wayne, we love you and we pray from our hearts
> That you'll prove to them
> You were innocent, r-i-g-h-t   f-r-o-m   t-h-e   s-t-a-r-t!

––––––

The public had yet to hear an interview with Roy Moody, but that would change the next day. When Moody had agreed to rendezvous near the courthouse with the WSB reporter who had covered the raid on his house, the newsman was hoping to get copies of the legal motions Moody was about to file, and some video of Roy filing them. When Roy agreed to say something on camera, he hoped maybe for a single decent sound bite. But Roy kept talking, calmly, even serenely, in patrician Southern tones. He wore a pressed white shirt with thick sky-blue stripes, a red silk tie with a gold diamond print, a blue blazer and creased gray slacks.

The TV reporter asked for the gist of the papers Moody would be filing in court that day.

"We are filing papers relative to the search that was conducted at my house Thursday, last Thursday, I think it was," he said. "We are under the impression that the search and seizures were in fact illegal searches and seizures for numerous reasons. We are in the process of addressing that issue in court."

Next question: "Do you have any connection to the mail bombings in December?"

Moody's gaze, for the most part, stayed fixed on his interviewer. "I have absolutely no connection with them whatever, and I'm not concerned about anybody finding any connections regarding those or any bombings—ever. There is no connection." His voice stayed steady and deliberate. "My concern is that evidence might be fabricated or might be misconstrued. Of course that would have to be a concern to anybody, I think."

When the 1972 case came up, Moody pointed out he was convicted of "constructive" possession of a destructive device. He asked, almost patronizingly, if the interviewer knew the ramifications of *constructive*.

"Close to eighteen years after that incident, after the explosion, you're still appealing the conviction. Why?"

"Well—" Moody shifted, gazed to the side, then back, and as he continued, his upper lip seemed to tighten and curl underneath. "The main reason is, I was convicted of a crime that I didn't commit. And that's hard to take. But years after this occurred, the girlfriend of the individual that actually placed the bomb in my house found me while searching for my former wife, and . . . we finally got this girl to tell us the facts and circumstances after I agreed to sign a release not to take any kind of legal action against her.

"She witnessed the crime occur at a period in time when nobody was home. In other words the bomb was placed there while I was gone, it blew up before I came back, and she has direct information."

Moody said both he and the new witness passed polygraph tests and indicated nobody had asked him to take one in this latest case.

"The people that are looking at me now probably are not aware of the facts and circumstances that led to my arrest," he continued. "If they knew that they were looking at an individual that they had previously convicted on fabricated evidence, then I don't think that they would be as interested as they are."

Moody seemed particularly pleased, touched even, when the questioner complimented him on the craftsmanship of his self-prepared legal motions. Moody was not, however, complimentary about the government's legal papers.

"The search warrant itself read like an intent to go in and search a military compound in Beirut. It had indicated on there that they were looking for declarations of war, nerve gas"—he paused to chuckle, then resumed—"and in reading it, it was so absurd it bordered on the ridiculous to me. But of course they know a lot more about it than I do, so from their point of view it may not be ridiculous at all."

He called the seizure of his legal papers concerning the case he currently had before the Supreme Court "grossly improper" and noted it had been ATF that got him convicted in 1972.

"This gets before the Supreme Court, and then all of a sudden they come in under the pretense of looking for nerve gas and take all my court records!"

The reporter had seen the Supreme Court petition. Mike Ford had given him a copy at the office interview. In it, Moody called the courts "Masters of Deceit," not exactly the kind of language to exculpate the writer from suspicions he has a vendetta against judges. The interviewer inquired into whether Moody believed such criticism helped make him a target.

"The criticisms that I have made of the court system I think were healthy criticisms. In any kind of a free society, if we all are not free—and you being in the press know this very well—if we are not free to criticize each other, then we are headed towards a totalitarian state. So criticizing the court is not an unhealthy practice. . . . I think it's unhealthy when you start saying if you don't rule my way, then I'm gonna send you a bomb. That's ridiculous."

Asked about his views on race relations, Moody replied he had spoken earlier in the day with a black attorney who had represented him a number of times.

"He called me and said, 'This is a social call. I just want you to know that you've got a friend. If you need anything, let me know.' And I appreciated that." Roy supplied the lawyer's name.

"My mother and father were not bigots, and they didn't raise me to be a bigot and I've never belonged to any organizations. The only organization that I've ever joined, I think, is the Experimental Aircraft Association, a bunch of nuts that make and fly their own airplanes."

Moody said he'd never had any dealings with the NAACP or Robbie Robinson.

"I'd never heard of any of these people until the news appeared in the press . . . but I have no history of violence whatsoever. I think I was in a fight when I was six years old and I got beat up and I decided that wasn't for me."

He smiled.

In contrast, the ubiquitous press around the mail-bomb case had Hoback scared he'd get blamed for a leak. But watching his adversary on television, Hoback told himself Moody wasn't as smart as he thought he was; this was exactly what the agent had expected the bomber to do. "He's going to take us on," Hoback concluded.

———

The day after the interview, a postal inspector showed up at the federal building in Newnan, where Mike Ford was taking part in the trial of a drug case. During an afternoon recess, the inspector asked Ford to make the Moodys available for fingerprinting. It could be done in Ford's office, the investigator suggested. He assured Ford the Postal Inspection Service wanted to keep the matter low-key.

"I told your compatriots I would make Roy Moody available and they answered with a search warrant," Ford said. "All Roy Moody wants is to receive his property back into his custody."

Hoback was right about Moody taking them on. Most criminal suspects who go to court do so on the government's timetable, typically after arrest. Roy Moody turned the tables. He yanked the government into court much faster than they could do the same to him. The Moody camp fired a fusillade of motions attacking the conduct of the investigation. He wanted his property back. Then there was the debate over whether that Federal Express envelope taken from Susan's car—and still unopened—was protected by attorney-client privilege. And Moody moved for more control of the coverage of the case, which had been massive, and often unflattering, in the week since the search warrant. A hearing was set before U.S. District Judge Richard Freeman, a passionately independent thinker who was consequently sometimes unpredictable. Roy arrived at the Russell Federal Building nattily attired in a muted glen-plaid sports jacket with the look of raw silk, a pressed white button-down, necktie and navy blue trousers. But it wasn't Mike Ford at his side as he moved first through the metal detector manned by a uniformed security guard at the entrance to the courthouse, then through a second one by the elevators leading to the courtrooms and judicial offices. Ford was still tied up in Newnan with that drug case, in which another defendant was represented by a lawyer named Bruce Harvey. Harvey's man had been severed from the others, meaning he would be tried later. Harvey suddenly had an unexpected opening on his calendar, and Ford had a way to fill it. He knew Harvey, and he knew this was the kind of high-profile case he would go for. When Harvey agreed to help, they didn't even discuss fees.

Harvey was nothing if not high profile. Outrageous but a good lawyer—that was Harvey's image, and it was precisely the image he wanted. People remembered him if they saw him in court or on television. Tall, lean and broad shouldered, he wore European-cut suits, film-noir ties, an earring in his left ear, a tattoo on his hand and his prematurely gray hair in a long ponytail. For assistance, or for fun, he called in another counterculture counselor, Michael Hauptman, who resembled the actor Danny DeVito, was married to a noted prostitution-rights activist, and like Harvey, was active in the American Civil Liberties Union. Harvey liked Hauptman for his creativity, his legal ability and his kindred spirit. And Hauptman was the only other male member of the federal bar for the Northern District of Georgia Harvey knew who wore a ponytail.

Said Hauptman to the judge: "When the court looks at the newspaper articles that suggest the investigation of Mr. Moody is chugging right along, but an unnamed federal source said we haven't found anything that would eliminate him as a suspect, that type of writing irreparably harms Mr. Moody's reputation. . . . As a result of the search of his home, his life has never been the same.

"The news media has hounded him day and night. The leaks to the news media have destroyed his right to privacy. He cannot live as a free human being in our society and pursue his livelihood."

Hauptman asked the judge to seal all the records filed with the court concerning Moody, which consisted largely of the motions he and his legal team had filed. And he asked for a gag order on the government, though the Moody lawyers volunteered to submit as well. The judge seemed sympathetic.

"There are too many agencies on board, is part of the problem. Who's doing the talking, I don't know. But somebody is certainly shooting off his or her mouth," the judge lectured. "And it shouldn't be done. I think it's already hurt the investigation."

All this put Ray Rukstele in a tough position. Already, senior Justice Department officials were upset about what they believed to be leaks. There had even been serious consideration given to the *government* seeking a gag order. But the prevailing opinion was that it was a bad idea. It might set a precedent to muzzle authorities in other ongoing investigations.

"I am very disturbed about that, Judge Freeman, regarding the allegations of leaks," the prosecutor said. "And I am professionally embarrassed. However—"

"Well, do you know where it's coming from?" interrupted Judge Freeman.

"No, I have no idea, Judge. I have no idea who it is, where it's coming from, or who's involved."

Judge: "Do you think you could talk to the FBI agent-in-charge? Of course, as I understand, they've got three or four FBI agents-in-charge. They have one here, one in Alabama, one in Timbuktu, and one in some other place. And they've got several ATF people in charge of the investigation.

"And postal inspectors. They've got everybody involved."

Rukstele: ". . . Your Honor, I would respectfully urge that before this honorable court considers such extraordinary relief as a gag order, that the court consider some less drastic measure, and I'd like to propose something to the court."

He proposed, essentially, that the Department of Justice get a chance to clean up its own mess.

"I can indicate to this court that the headquarters at the Department of Justice have spoken to senior officials at headquarters of the Federal Bureau of Investigation, who will again be reiterating to agents of the FBI the Bureau's previous position. That no one is to speak to the press, except through sanctioned channels."

Judge Freeman seemed inclined to go along: "Speak with the attorney general, or whoever it may be, to impress upon the various agencies involved in this investigation the importance of keeping quiet. I think it's already hurt the investigation.

"I thought at the time, you know, about all the things in the newspaper and on television about the typewriter. I couldn't believe all the things that I heard. And I said to my wife, 'Well, if anybody's got that typewriter, you can be assured that it's now going to be in the bottom of somebody's ocean somewhere.' Plus the fact that it does terrible damage to the reputation of innocent people. And that's even worse."

The judge agreed to hold off for the time being. Nonetheless, Moody had won. He was the criminal suspect, but it was the investigators who suffered an unusual public rebuke from a federal judge, almost certain to provoke internal repercussions from Washington on down. Furthermore, over the protests of lawyers from several local news organizations, the judge ordered all records in the case would be kept sealed from the public, at least for the time being. And that too was what Moody had asked. He was smiling as he strode briskly out of the Russell Building, Harvey, Hauptman and a gaggle of photographers moving with him.

That night WSB-TV broadcast excerpts from the letter in the Federal Express envelope over which there had been such haggling. The envelope remained sealed pending a decision by Judge Freeman, but the station attributed the excerpts to "a source."

The letter, to a lawyer in Miami, made clear Moody had known he was under surveillance before the raid on his house and suggested the FBI considered him "a likely scapegoat." But the most compelling text concerned DNA:

"The government has repeatedly leaked information to the effect that they have found DNA material, a chemical fingerprint. The prospective jurors are being conditioned to believe it.

"What worries me is so little is generally known about forensic DNA techniques. Consequently, the government could easily exploit this pervasive ignorance of technique to fool a jury."

Moody said he was convinced that was precisely what the government planned to do. Ironically, though there had been stories mentioning DNA, notably when tissue samples were taken from O'Ferrell, crime-lab experts had yet to find any shred of DNA that could identify the mail bomber.

Meanwhile, agents kept digging into Moody's background. His sister, Delores, elected not to be interviewed. Joe Gordon and Dave Kirkland traveled out of state to interview Roy's younger brother, Bobby, who expressed fear for his family's safety. But he talked with the investigators anyway. He added flesh to the expanding body of knowledge about Roy's litigiousness. He told them about the suit Roy had filed against his siblings after a dispute concerning their mother's inheritance. He said he got notice Roy had appealed a ruling in the case to the Eleventh Circuit Court of Appeals. He fleshed out too the relationship between Roy and Susan. Bobby told investigators Roy met her at a Waffle House in about 1980, and suggested the writers guild was never much more than one of Roy's failed plans until Susan came along.

On the fifteenth, the same day as the court hearing in Atlanta, Hoback, Frank Lee and Terry Pelfrey were in Birmingham, invited by Atlanta FBI SAC Bill Hinshaw to brief FBI agents from around the South about Moody. Near the end of the meeting, Frank Lee took a call from Atlanta. Something was happening. He told the Atlanta contingent about it and they hit the road, Hoback driving through the rain doing about ninety, Frank Lee telling him he was gonna get them killed.

———

Somebody had seen Moody on TV and called the FBI. In response, FBI Agent Jeff Holmes, ATF Agent David Hyche and Postal Inspector Jim Rushwin showed up in Chamblee, just north of Atlanta. A thin, pleasant, older man there said the house next door belonged to his mother-in-law, who was in a nursing home. Now his sister-in-law lived in the cottage with the fieldstone front, metal window overhangs and stone walk near the DeKalb County airport. The man knew Roy Moody, knew that years ago he had rented a basement bedroom from his mother-in-law, and knew Moody continued to rent storage space in the basement. He took the agents into the basement through an outside door, which wasn't locked. They followed a dimly lit path through clutter piled almost to the ceiling, and the older man showed them Moody's stuff. Several boxes and a partly exposed pipe nipple were loose on a wooden pallet. The foursome returned upstairs, where Holmes interviewed the woman who lived there and established something important, that the Moodys were up-to-date on the rent. Rushwin and Hyche, meanwhile, talked about that piece of pipe and decided they needed a better look.

David Hyche had been with ATF just five months and hadn't even completed new-agent training yet. But after he knelt to look at the pipe more closely he got excited. The pipe, which he estimated to be fourteen inches long, four inches in diameter, had caps screwed on both ends. Through each cap was drilled a hole, and fastened over one of the holes was a nut. Through these holes, Hyche decided, one could place a threaded rod.

He fetched his camera from the car, took pictures, then dropped them off at a drugstore with same-day developing. A team was dispatched to keep a watch on the place, and the next day investigators returned with a search warrant and retrieved the odd assemblage. It went straight to the ATF lab, which happened to be about five minutes from the house in Chamblee. Terry Byer examined it. The holes in the end caps, where a threaded rod could fit, the welded nut that could hold the rod in place . . .

"This," pronounced Byer, "is the signature of the bomber."

10

Susan

The sealing of the records at the February 15 hearing had been only a temporary measure, pending Judge Freeman's final decision the next week. On the twenty-first he came down with it: the records would remain closed.

"The Supreme Court has repeatedly recognized that extraordinary cases require extraordinary measures," the judge declared. "This case is extraordinary in the intensity of publicity that has dogged every stage of the investigation and in the number of news leaks that have occurred. . . . The public's interest in hearing the day-to-day developments of this investigation is outweighed by the public's interest in having the perpetrator or perpetrators brought to justice."

The ruling was not likely to withstand the appeal media lawyers were certain to file. But for the moment that did not matter. Moody had gotten the ruling his lawyers sought. Because the proceedings were divided into two hearings, he had now tasted victory twice. As he walked out of the Russell Building that day, Moody smiled yet again. As before, TV, newspaper and radio reporters and photographers with video or still cameras swarmed as Harvey, at the lead of the entourage, wisecracked his way to the car. But someone else was along this time. Perhaps a step or a half step behind her husband, but close enough to clutch his hand, walked Susan, primly attired in a silky, high-necked paisley dress, white hose on long, shapely calves visible from beneath a tan trenchcoat with maroon lining and sashed about the waist. Her expression was at best demure, at worst doleful.

Roy wasn't ready to throttle back. He wrote a letter and stuck a draft in front of Mike Ford at the federal courthouse in Newnan, where Ford was still tied up with the drug trial. Roy's presence clearly upset the deputy marshals there, and one asked Ford if he could get Moody to leave because of the security problems he was creating. Run the letter by Harvey, Ford told Roy. He didn't, but sent it anyway.

February 22, 1990

Mr. Walter Leroy Moody, Jr.
6414 Skyline Drive
Rex, Georgia 30273
404-474-6673

The President of the United States
The White House
Washington, D.C. 20500

Dear Mr. President,

I have contacted you in an effort to minimize the improper dissemination of this information which might negate its usefulness.

When I first learned I was the subject of a government investigation relative to the "mail bombs', [sic] I was concerned I was to be made a scapegoat of an improperly conducted investigation. My attorneys and I assumed a posture calculated to make said contact more difficult. Yesterday, the Honorable Judge Freeman noted sufficient improprieties to warrant incorporating various safeguards to protect the integrity of the investigation.

In preparing to respond to the government's action, information was unexpectedly uncovered which my attorneys and I feel could lead to the arrest and conviction of the per-petrator of these crimes.

After the government investigation of me has run its nor-mal course, I expect the results to show I had no involve-ment in these crimes. When that expectation is realized, I will make the above information available under the fol-lowing circumstances.

1. *If the person or persons named in the information is ar-rested and convicted relative to the mail bombs investi-gation, I will be promptly paid the maximum award provided under Sections 3071 and 3072 F.R.C.P.*
2. *Said payment will be kept secret as provided by Section 3073 F.R.C.P.*

Please have any response directed to my attorneys, Mr. Michael C. Ford and Mr. Bruce S. Harvey.

Respectfully,
Roy Moody

The FBI knew about the letter, sent by Federal Express to the White House, by the end of the day it was dated. John Behnke noted Moody had used a similar strategy in the '72 case.

The letter to the president, the media blitz, the court motions—Ray Rukstele knew Moody was trying to put the government on the defensive and that he was doing a fair job of it. The prosecutor sus-pected that among some people Moody was beginning to garner sympathy. Similarly, FBI SAC Bill Hinshaw believed at times Moody was putting more pressure on the investigators than they were putting on him. In twenty-three years as an agent, Hinshaw had never seen anything like it.

If the government's agents and prosecutors felt defensive, it was part of the plan, as far as Bruce Harvey was concerned. Make the government respond to you before you have to respond to them. That's the style he cultivated—creative, in-your-face, balls-to-the-wall. And Moody seemed to love it. From the start, he was in almost daily contact with the long-haired lawyer, frequently to brainstorm about the next move.

Mike Ford's method was less theatrical but no less direct, as somebody found out the hard way one day when Roy visited Ford's office
in an L-shaped cluster of seven two-story, yellow-trimmed, pink-
brick neo-Georgian buildings, each with twin staircases curving from
left and right to meet at a roofed balcony on the second level.
Moody told Ford he believed himself followed. Ford wanted to know
if his client was paranoid or perspicacious. So he shepherded Roy
out the front door of his office on the bottom floor of the building at
the top of the L. They climbed into the old Cadillac Ford had recently driven up from Florida after inheriting it from his stepfather.
The lawyer drove across the rectangular black-top parking lot, went
right on Peeler Road, then steered suddenly left into another brick
office park catercorner to his. He hit the first driveway, then, barely
into it, braked and threw the gearshift into reverse and headed out
the way he had come. There had been a car behind him, but Ford's
three-corner maneuver forced it to drive on by, farther into the office park.

This time Ford went back the other way on Peeler Road, past his office. He made a left at the next light, onto Shallowford Road. Behind
him, he could see the car he'd momentarily ditched in the office complex, and a second car too. Ford had the advantage of knowing
Dunwoody, the upscale suburb where his office was. He turned off
Shallowford and soon veered into a condo complex where he knew
the main drive made a big loop. He went around one corner, then a
second, and quickly backed the Caddy in between two parked cars.
One of the two trailing cars made the corner, the driver craning as if
looking for someone. When his gaze hit Ford and Moody, he
snapped his head away and kept going. Ford pulled out and continued the loop. As he came back near the front of the complex, the
other car that had been following him was stopped on a side drive,
pointed in the direction that would enable him to pull in behind the
Cadillac once it got on the main road. But it also enabled Ford to pull
crossways in front and block his way. The driver looked to be talking
on the radio. Moody stayed seated, but the lawyer got out.

As Ford moved toward him, the other driver opened his door
and stood up too. Ford asked if he could help him with something.
If the other man replied, it was inaudible. He seemed uncomfortable, agitated.

"You're following me," said the attorney.

The other man denied it.

Of course he was, countered Ford, who recounted the course they'd just taken.

"You're not the only person in the car," the driver said.

Ford asked who he was, what he wanted, whether he was with the FBI. He didn't answer, but Ford was by now convinced Moody was right. The man was a cop.

Some days later, Moody reported the surveillance had gotten tighter. People were following him in the grocery store, seizing mail he dropped off. Make pictures of it, Ford told him. Document it. Moody complied, with relish it seemed. He accumulated a thick stack of snapshots of what he believed to be government surveillance vehicles. A blurry photo that looked to be a T-bird at a stop sign. A dark GM sedan. A maroon Honda. A Mercedes on the Downtown Connector. A white panel van. An indistinct shot of a windshield, another of a bronze hood and a headlight. At least one pickup truck Ford recognized. There were photos too of the suspected surveillance airplane; Moody was correct in his belief the feds were watching him from the air. And there were shots of tire tracks in reddish brown soil, some of which might have been from the thicket at the end of Moody's street.

A videotape held more images of cars and a plane, tremulously photographed as if from a moving car or truck, or by someone afoot and in a rush.

"We're shaking too much. Can you stop?" says a voice sounding like Roy's. The picture, a rear angle on a gold Oldsmobile or Pontiac with tinted back window and an antenna, momentarily stabilizes.

"We can go by him, you can get him too," says a voice sounding like Susan's. The idea apparently is to try to get the driver's face by pulling up from behind him.

"Okay."

"You ready?" It sounds like an engine cranks up, then accelerates. There are noises and wild camera moves. Apparently the gold car has driven off, eluding the photographer.

Life for the Moodys, however, wasn't all one grand adventure, not for Susan at least. Along with the snapshots and video, the Moodys kept a handwritten journal.

March 10, 1990

About 9 P.M., Susan, Max [the Moodys's Great Dane] and I were driving to Bear Creek Airport. Susan tried to lose the FBI tail. After we got on Tara Blvd., we were stoped [sic] by a cop who "claimed" Susan was "weaving." After he checked her ID he let us go. From then on, we were followed by the FBI plane and cars. Both to the airport and back home.

March 12, 1990

Susan got a ticket. P'man also stopped fed car following Susan for speeding. P'man let fed go. Susan got ticket.

Three days later, she was stopped by cops again, but this time was different. The plan was to wait until Roy wasn't with her, which happened midafternoon. The FBI surveillance unit followed the young woman until they had reached a spot where a mobile home could be parked and she could be approached without attracting much notice. After Susan emerged from an office-supplies store, Brian Hoback, accompanied by two female agents, flashed his badge and told her to follow them into the mobile home, where he would serve her with a federal search warrant for her fingerprints. Once inside, he read Susan her rights. She waived none of them.

Sassy and savvy, Theresa Stoop had a Florida tan and a New York accent. Tom Stokes considered her one of his most promising agents. Assigned to the Atlanta ATF firearms group, she'd made lots of arrests, so she had experience taking fingerprints. As a safeguard, a print specialist from the crime lab was in the mobile home to supervise, but Stoop would do the hands-on work; Ray Rukstele had decreed no man would place a hand on Susan. The investigator took one finger at a time, rolled on ink from the base to the tip and then on the sides, then pressed it onto a fingerprint card. She extracted palm prints similarly, explaining to Susan what she was doing at each step. These were what are known as "major-case prints," far more extensive and time-consuming than the normal print job done at jail book-ins. But no matter how long it went, no matter that they were two young women of nearly the same age, Susan offered Theresa Stoop no conversation. None. Stoop was spooked by that, coupled with the vacancy she saw in Susan's eyes, like someone possessed, she imagined.

Hoback noticed Susan's quietude and that she looked no one in the eye. He thought she behaved as if she'd expected something like this. But she struck him as more meek than defiant, as if carrying out instructions instead of standing on principle. About a half hour into the process, he asked Mrs. Moody how she was doing. Okay, she nodded. Eventually, he handed her the warrant. The investigators wanted to get a good picture, to use in photo line-ups. But she wouldn't pose, so FBI Agent Jeff Holmes stepped outside the mobile home to get her picture as she exited. Hoback handed her his business card. She could call him or Stoop if she changed her mind and wanted to talk.

Susan was with Roy in a restaurant parking lot the next day after lunch when Hoback again held up his credentials, identified himself and announced there was a warrant for prints. Follow us to the mobile home, he instructed Roy, who asked to see the warrant. No, Hoback said. He'd show it to him in the mobile home. Moody complied, but once inside refused to sign his fingerprint cards. The courts, he said, did not require him to sign. Tension was building between the young investigator and the government's audacious adversary.

FBI Agent Flo Davis was printing Moody. Hoback asked him to stop, then told Roy he'd forgotten to ask him a question concerning the safety of the agents in the mobile home. He asked Moody if he had AIDS.

"I told you," Moody said, "I'm not going to answer any of your questions."

Hoback told Davis it was up to him whether he continued printing Moody. Davis did. A half hour after the process started, the prints were done. About ten minutes later, as Moody finished cleaning his hands, Hoback told him he'd give him one more chance to sign the fingerprint cards. Moody told him he'd sign if his lawyer or a court order told him to.

"The bottom line is that you will not sign the cards today?"

"Yes," answered Roy.

The exchanges between the two men had been tart, but the climax came when Hoback moved in close, held up his credentials like a TV cop and told Roy he wanted him to know who he was. If Moody was cowed, he didn't show it. He asked Hoback for a business card. The agent told him he'd given one to Susan. She threw it away, Roy retorted. Hoback gave him a card and Moody left. Afterward, Hoback knew how out of character this brazen display had been, in front of a suspect he ought to treat strictly by the book. He was surprised at himself. And he liked it.

The next day brought another entry in the Moodys' diary. Susan learned her brother had decided not to go to a friend's wedding after federal agents showed up at the bride-to-be's house and asked to open a wedding gift from Susan. Said the journal entry: "Girlfriend's family is very upset."

———

Even if they lacked the verve of face-to-face confrontation, dramatic developments were unfolding on other stages in the investigation, including the search for the sources of the bomb components. A woman at a steel company near Rex told them Moody had made purchases from the company and that the Moodys had seemed secretive about what they were doing. She related how she'd figured Moody was "up to something," and how, after seeing news coverage of the investigation, she'd dug into her records and discovered Moody had purchased, in December of 1988, ten three-eighths-inch threaded rods. Three of the mail bombs sent a year later contained three-eighths-inch threaded rods. She picked out both Roy and Susan Moody from photo spreads, as did the manager of a second business in Stockbridge. Shown a receipt taken during the search of the Moody house, he indicated it showed the sale of thirteen feet of two-inch pipe. Three of the bombs were built with pipe two inches in diameter. The information was tantalizing, but its promise went unfulfilled. Nothing surfaced to trace any parts of the bombs to either of those stores. Indeed, no direct physical evidence of any kind had turned up to prove Moody was the mail bomber.

11

The Two Julies

Increasingly, it looked as if high tech would not meet the high hopes of the investigators out to prove whether Roy Moody was their man. If he was, he had stymied a stunning array of forensic science's best tools and techniques. What progress had been made owed to the human element—an old revenuer's recollection, the grit of a handful of determined detectives. And in late March there began an avenue of investigation the success of which depended on whether a young woman in a wheelchair would tell the truth.

Her name was Julie Linn in the transcript Joe Gordon had reviewed among the Macon court files two and a half months earlier. Now she went by Julie Linn-West, but under any name, her story—which purported to exonerate Moody for the '72 bomb while implicating Gene Wallace—still sounded phony. On March 20, Terry Pelfrey and Bill Grom, a deputy U.S. marshal who had also been in that first group to pursue Moody in January, set out to interview Julie Linn-West. They tracked her to Smyrna, a northwest Atlanta suburb. But at her door she said she had to get to work and could talk at ten o'clock the next morning. Meanwhile, Brian Hoback and FBI Agent Sally Heintz had gone to the home of JoAnn Ekstrom. Her testimony had apparently been intended to corroborate Linn-West's in the 1988 federal court hearing in which Moody sought to clear his name with the supposedly new information. A woman in her early twenties answered the door and identified herself as the girlfriend of Ekstrom's son, Shawn. Shawn *Ekstrom?* one of the agents asked. No, Shawn Linn. JoAnn Ekstrom, they discovered, was Julie Linn-West's mother. And she wasn't home. The four agents rendezvoused at a nearby police station and compared results.

With court permission, the task force had placed devices on Moody's, Linn-West's and Ekstrom's phones to record the numbers of outgoing and incoming calls. The numbers printed out instantaneously at the Atlanta FBI office. And at 4:04 P.M.—soon after her visit from Pelfrey and Grom—Julie Linn-West was on the phone to Roy Moody. Almost immediately, a call was placed from Moody's phone to Mike Ford's office. Within minutes, Linn-West called Ekstrom. And those telephone devices at the FBI office kept singing, registering fifteen more calls in the next fifteen minutes or so.

"You guys gotta get your ass back over there," said Harold Jones, the FBI supervisor on the task force who had beeped Hoback.

This time they were insistent. Heintz, Pelfrey and Grom got in to talk to the young woman in the wheelchair while Hoback and a fifth agent talked to her half brother, Shawn, outside the apartment. Shawn related a phone message he'd taken from Roy Moody in February, to the effect that if the police called JoAnn or Julie, the women were not to talk but to refer the cops to a lawyer. Hoback thought he was getting good material, but it paled beside what was happening inside the apartment.

Julie Linn-West, a fair-skinned blonde in her thirties, at first parroted the story about Gene Wallace, that in 1972 she and her mother were in Atlanta when she met Wallace, that on a lunch date she and Wallace went to Macon and he took a package into someone's home and left it, and that a short time later Wallace went back and saw police working a crime scene. But as she told the tale, the agents pointed out implausible elements. They could tell she was nervous, that something was bothering her, and Grom told her so. They were convinced she was lying, but their tone remained low-key. Pelfrey, seated directly in front of her, eye to eye, handled most of the questions. They wanted Julie on their side and they wanted her to know it. Finally, she said the whole thing was a hoax. And she looked suddenly relieved.

Linn-West related how she had met Roy and his then-girlfriend, Susan McBride, in early 1986. Moody told her about his '72 conviction, that he needed someone to testify about Gene Wallace and that he would pay her. For the next several months, Susan coached her on the story so Julie could memorize names, dates and places. Susan, she said, delivered $100 a month. After Linn-West testified in court, she got the balance of her $1,500 bribe. Julie handwrote a statement, which Pelfrey, Grom and Heintz witnessed. After the interview, Hoback showed her photo spreads from which she picked the pictures of Roy and Susan. The agents had found, at last, a crowbar they might use to pry an opening in Roy Moody's armor plate, and most of them stopped by a bar on the town square in nearby Marietta to celebrate. Hoback called Stokes and filled him in. Hoback called his wife, Kathy, too. But Julie Linn-West wasn't on board yet.

Late that night, Roy called her. She didn't have to talk to the police, he said. And he gave her the home number for an attorney named Kehir. By about noon the next day, Moody had called twice more and claimed that Susan wanted to meet with her. She agreed to meet Susan the next day. While Heintz, Hoback and ATF Agent Reynold Hoover were at Linn-West's apartment to put a recording hookup on her phone, Julie agreed to wear a wire for the meeting.

FBI agents also caught up with JoAnn Ekstrom at the mall where she worked in a hair salon. She confirmed what the investigators already knew, that her testimony in the Macon hearing was a lie. She said Moody was furious with her botched performance on the stand and didn't pay her. Ekstrom also revealed she'd been involved in another Moody stunt, concerning the lawsuit Moody brought against a law enforcement officer, the three would-be victims, and others after a jury failed to reach a verdict against Moody in a Florida attempted-murder case. Roy had paid her to pose as a movie researcher to extract information from one of the key players.

———

Julie Linn-West's meeting with Susan was set for lunchtime at a Picadilly Cafeteria near Julie's apartment. Beforehand, Sally Heintz wired Julie for sound.

"Can you see it?" asked Julie.

"No," Heintz assured.

"Okay, okay," said Linn-West. "Let's boogie."

The agents surveilling Susan on the trip up from Rex backed off so she wouldn't get suspicious and fail to show up for the meeting.

"She's here," Julie intoned. She had both a body recorder and a transmitter so investigators could monitor what was happening. "Hi . . . I got here before you for once."

There was small talk about errands, allergies and appearances. The two women went through the serving line in the cafeteria, part of a chain that serves up meats, vegetables, salads and desserts with Southern-style, plentiful portions and reasonable prices.

"How's Roy doing?"

"Fine."

"Is he?"

"Yeah."

When they got to a table, Julie pulled out a subpoena she'd been given for her testimony before a federal grand jury.

"Ha," Susan exclaimed, apparently recognizing something in the paperwork. "The bald-headed guy served it on you."

"Hoback?"

"Yeah."

"Yeah, yeah. They came yesterday."

"I wonder," said Susan, "if we're gonna get one. Well . . . did Kehir or one of those attorneys tell you that even then you don't have to say anything?"

"Uh-huh. He said I could plead the Fifth."

Susan said not to worry, Julie was just a witness, not a subject of the investigation.

"I can't tell you what to do," Mrs. Moody said. "Roy would know best, better anyway."

There was more talk, about the feds and the food.

"Things cool down at your household?" Julie asked. "Is it more like home now?"

"Not really. Trying though."

"I mean, I'm just getting a taste of it and I had a sleepless night last night. I can't imagine how you're feeling."

Susan spoke as if the investigation were a temporary inconvenience, something to be worked through or worked around.

"I chased one yesterday that was following me," Susan said. "I turned around and chased him."

Julie laughed.

"Just make fun of it," Susan advised. "I have to."

"You make light of it sometime, huh?"

"Yeah. See, the whole bottom line is they want to solve this bombing case . . . and I know we're innocent so I can't help but feel like it's, everything's gonna be okay."

In a sense, Susan believed what she was saying. On one level, she kept telling herself Roy *was* innocent, just so she could keep going day to day, because she couldn't accept the alternative, that Roy, the center of her life, was a monster.

When they left the restaurant, both women climbed into Julie's car. Agents were startled; this wasn't part of the plan. But they could figure out from what they heard over the transmitter that Susan intended to make a copy of the subpoena to bring back to Roy. Before she did, she handed Julie a business-sized envelope.

"Be careful opening it," Susan said. "It's something Roy wrote."

The envelope contained a newspaper article about a lawsuit Moody had won in Florida, and a typed letter, which Julie read silently. The first sentence commanded her not to read it aloud to Susan.

According to Julie's later recollections of the letter, Moody claimed he'd met some Miami mafiosi while in the federal pen, and that they gave him financial help when he got out. Now, Roy wrote, he was worried about Julie's mother, JoAnn, who wouldn't return his calls or see him. Roy warned that, if she talked about anything having to do with the Florida case, both Roy and JoAnn would be murdered by mobsters. "Murdered" was underlined. The letter urged Julie to talk to her mother. She had to keep her mouth shut.

Neither the agents nor Susan knew at that moment what Julie Linn-West had just absorbed. But after Susan left the car, apparently to try to copy the subpoena and cash a money order, Julie started sobbing.

"Things are not good," she told the agents over the transmitter. Julie was scared and confused.

After she bid good-bye to Susan, Julie drove her car, specially fitted to accommodate her disability, back to the apartment where she met the agents.

"You did good, gal," one of the agents said.

"I won't fuckin' do it again, I'll tell you that," came the reply. The investigators exchanged worried looks and followed her into the apartment.

"You know the fuckin' Mafia's involved in this!" The agents had to remove the recording equipment from the young woman. "Get this shit off me!"

"Julie, Julie—" Hoback started.

"And I don't want anything else to do with this shit."

"Julie, Julie, settle down," Hoback continued. "You're doing fine."

Julie cried some more. The agents calmed her, Hoback gave her all his phone numbers, and they left.

The next morning at a briefing at the FBI office, the question was whether to hold Julie's hand or give her air. Somebody should have asked Julie. Only later would Hoback discover she'd been trying to call him, and others, without success. She was scared. She felt like a Ping-Pong ball. Moody wanted her to work for him again. The government wanted her to work for them. Moody . . . the government . . . She erased a phone call she'd recorded from Roy the night before. Then she took the equipment off her phone and put it in a brown paper sack. She wanted nothing else to do with cooperating. Midmorning, Susan Moody knocked at her window.

"I'm not answering the door right now because I'm asleep," Julie told her. Susan left.

When Sally Heintz and another female FBI agent came by the apartment, Julie told them she was returning the phone-monitoring equipment, feared for her life and her family's lives, and wanted nothing else to do with it. At some point that day, she called Roy and apologized for the way she'd spoken to Susan. Given that opening, Susan returned to Smyrna with another missive from her husband, several pages long. Moody wanted some revisions concerning her earlier testimony, and he wanted JoAnn to profess being under the influence of drugs when she testified, which might plausibly explain why it was so screwed up. The letter was like the tapes at the top of *Mission: Impossible* episodes; it had a self-destruct message. It instructed Julie to return it to Susan so she could burn it. Julie lit it up herself, and when only ashes remained, Susan put her hands in the kitchen sink and crushed them.

"This is what I usually do," Susan explained, "just like this. Just wash it down the sink."

Hoback, like the other investigators, had been working incredibly grueling hours and hoped to get home early for once. It was his thirty-first birthday and his wife, Kathy, told him their two children were excited. Moments later, Harold Jones tracked down Hoback, told him about the crisis with Julie Linn-West and dispatched him to see what he could do. Hoback hooked up with Bill Grom, the deputy marshal, who looked like Dirty Harry with a Billy Idol haircut. On the way to Smyrna, Hoback was still thinking he could get home in time to go out to eat or do *something* with the family. They found Julie a tearful, nervous wreck. It got worse when JoAnn showed up. It was clear Julie feared prosecution. The two agents worked at winning her trust, assuring her they would watch out for her. But the investigators couldn't make promises on their own. Hoback called Harold Jones and told him they needed immunity. Jones told him somebody was already talking to Ray Rukstele about it. Hoback also called Kathy, to say he couldn't come home after all. She relayed the dismal news to their four-year-old son, who tossed into the trash the birthday card he'd made for his dad. Then he walked off crying.

Jones called back to say Rukstele had confirmed both Julie and JoAnn could have immunity. The agents explained it to the two women, but JoAnn said she didn't believe them.

"You're too excited," she said.

"This is the assurance that y'all been asking for," Hoback replied.

"You're too excited."

Hoback: "Well, I've never been in a position where I could give somebody immunity."

They were toying with the hook. It was time to let out some line and let them run with it for a while. Eat some dinner and think it over, the agents urged. Hoback and Grom left to eat pizza. Hoback got beeped by the task force. Bill Hinshaw, the FBI SAC, got on the phone and Hoback explained the problem. Hinshaw had an uncommon feel for people and a knack for whacking red tape.

"I tell you what," he told the ATF agent. "We'll provide the money. Take 'em to a hotel for a weekend."

"Really?"

"Yeah. Let 'em get out from all the pressure, let 'em feel safe and secure."

The agents went back to the women, explained about the hotel, and said it would give them a chance to make some security improvements to the apartment, and to install audiovisual equipment. Julie Linn-West seemed all for it, and now she joined the efforts to convince her mother, who still seemed afraid of getting arrested and had questions about the U.S. Attorney's role in all of this.

"Well, do you want to talk to him?" Grom asked.

"Yeah."

Grom dialed the phone. "Ray? Hold on. Ms. Ekstrom wants to talk to you."

She agreed to cooperate. Both women cried. The agents helped pack up Julie and her young son, then went to Ekstrom's for her things, then to the U.S. Attorney's Office. Debbie Puerifoy, Rukstele's secretary, who had come in the middle of the night in early February to get the search warrants ready, was there late again, this time doing valuable service by spending time with the little boy.

Rukstele met first with Julie, whom he immediately perceived as gentle and warm and whom he was convinced would do what was right. He sized up her mother differently and talked tougher to her. You've got to decide what you want to do, he told her, play ball with Roy or play ball with the government. Their statements, he assured them, would not be used against them. So long as they were truthful, they wouldn't get prosecuted for what they did for Roy. The government would provide protection. Once the immunity papers were signed, Grom waited in the car with the women and the boy while Hoback picked up money from the FBI office, which was across the street from the U.S. Attorney's space. The FBI had already made arrangements at the French Quarter, an upscale hostelry just north of the city with wheelchair access. Hoback and Grom got home near three A.M. Hoback's birthday was over. Roy Moody's had just begun.

> Guess what,
> Today is my birthday. Where is my present? Susan told me the people who served you with a subpoena had threatened you in some way. I wasn't really sure what went on.
> How about giving me a call as soon as you can, and I will come over to talk to you about it. If they have done anything that is improper I want to pass it on to my attorneys.
> I know these people can be abusive. I had a run-in with one of them yesterday. . . .

Moody probably had no idea Julie Linn-West had finally picked sides only hours before he dropped off his handwritten note. The FBI was installing equipment in the apartment that day, but the surveillance team trailing Moody had given the installers plenty of warning to avoid discovery. On Monday the twenty-sixth, Hoback picked up Julie's son from the hotel and took him to school. He'd stayed in touch with the boy's mother and grandmother over the weekend, and they were fine. He spent much of the rest of the day trying to find furniture for the apartment across the way from Julie's in Smyrna. She was getting some new neighbors who carried badges and guns.

Roy would get his meeting with Julie all right, but this time, at last, the investigators would have something to say about the timing. The plan, on March 27, was for Julie to smooth things over with Roy, to invite him to come by on the pretense that she needed further instruction on how to testify before the grand jury.

"Happy belated birthday," she told Moody on the phone.

Roy indicated he'd tried to bring her some cake, but his truck broke down.

"You know, I'd like to see ya," she said.

Moody made small talk, then asked where she'd been.

"Well, my mom and I had to kinda get ourselves together. So we went to go see family in Alabama."

More small talk.

"Well, can I be expectin' ya?"

"Yeah, I think so," Roy replied.

In less than an hour, there was a knock at Julie's door.

"Who is it?"

"Roy."

Roy was careful, whispering and writing notes. "Your house is probably bugged," he warned. He was right. And hidden-camera videotape was rolling too as he stressed the importance of JoAnn's saying she was doped up when she testified, which, Moody opined, would help herself, help Julie and help Roy. He painted government promises of immunity as practically worthless, and he suggested taking the Fifth would have drawbacks too. He seemed anxious for her to talk to the lawyer named Kehir about the situation. Near the end of the meeting, Roy burned his notes.

Grom, Hoback and three other investigators were in the apartment across the street. They could see the windows were open in Julie's apartment, and both planes and trains could be heard nearby. Moreover, somebody was cutting grass for the apartment complex. Fearing problems with audio recordings that could later prove crucial, Grom ran down the way to the apartment complex office. The manager got the mower noise stopped. Then an ice cream man showed up, banging away on his bell. The investigators decided to take their chances.

Two days later, Roy and Susan Moody both showed up at Julie

Linn-West's place. Susan took a letter from her boot and gave it to Roy, who gave it to Julie. It was five pages, handwritten.

"You don't wear glasses, do you?" Roy inquired.

"No, I don't, but I think after this I might."

> *. . . What we must do is clear;*
>
> *First, you can not ever admit that you gave false testimony.*
>
> *Equally important you can not take the 5th regarding any issue involving me.*
>
> *You must know the material i.e. the affidavit and transcript backwards and forwards so they can not trick you on any thing you have already said.*
>
> *Regarding all other questions; if you don't want to answer them say you don't know.*
>
> *[An]other area of concern is your mother since she has done two things for me. Let's cover each.*
>
> *The first was the thing in Florida—she interviewed the deputy sheriff who arrested me in the keys and made notes on their conversation. Later those notes were put into the form of an affidavit which she signed. That was it nothing more.*
>
> *The only problem that we must deal with is to explain how I happen to get your mother to do that. Both your mother and I have previously testified that I placed an ad in the paper and she answered the ad. We both have said we had not met before.*
>
> *This is how we should deal with it; its very simple. . . .*
>
> *Regarding questions they may ask her about Wallace. The only thing that is important is that you both say what is necessary for it to agree with your testimony. Her admission about drugs will completely knock out her previous testimony about Wallace.*

The note also suggested a news interview done under the right circumstances might put the government on the defensive. Roy wanted Julie to convey that government agents had behaved improperly in their dealings with her.

The Moodys took the letter back and Susan returned it to her boot. Then they took Julie for a ride in the Moodys' pickup truck, and the trailing agents thought Roy was trying to shake them. Only later would Julie say they were simply lost. They were on their way to meet that lawyer Moody had been urging Julie to see.

———

Roy had told Mike Ford that Julie Linn wanted to talk with him. Ford spoke with her on the phone, but told her he couldn't give her legal advice; it could create a conflict of interest because he represented Moody. Still she had a federal grand jury subpoena and sounded as if she needed a lawyer. So Ford referred the case to Paul Kehir, an old friend with whom he'd handled a number of cases. Both lawyers arrived in Ford's car at a law office they were borrowing as a convenient meeting place. They'd spoken about the case once before, so Kehir had some background. And Kehir had earlier represented the Associated Writers Guild of America, Inc., of which both Moodys had been officers, so he was familiar with Roy.

The lawyers found Julie in her wheelchair and in the company of Roy and Susan Moody. Kehir understood they wanted to talk to Julie after he'd had a chance to advise her. Ford and the Moodys went to a conference room. Kehir and Linn-West stayed in the reception area to talk privately. She mentioned her grand jury subpoena, and Kehir said he would represent her at the grand jury, if she wanted him to. Fine, but there was something she needed to tell him. Her testimony had been a lie concocted by Roy Moody. She'd been paid. Whatever role the Moodys and Ford had played in bringing her to him, Julie Linn-West was now the one Paul Kehir was ethically bound to look after. And knowing nothing of her cooperation with the feds, the first thing he thought was that she was in danger. Roy Moody was in the next room. Kehir's sole concern for the moment became getting her out of there without the Moodys realizing anything was amiss. He could hook up with Julie later for more details about the case, but for now, she was vulnerable, especially since she would be leaving with the Moodys in their truck. The lawyer quickly outlined a plan.

Kehir and Julie joined the Moodys and Ford in the conference room, where Ford asked if she was going to testify the same as she did in Macon, to which Julie obfuscated and said yes. There were a few more questions, then Kehir stepped in and said he'd prefer the quizzing stop until he'd had a chance to read the transcripts. Everyone agreed. When the meeting ended, Kehir thought neither of the

Moodys saw a problem. But Mike Ford thought Kehir looked very strange when he and Julie entered the room, and as things progressed, he looked stranger still.

In the car afterward, Ford put a question to his friend: "Am I in any danger?"

Kehir replied that he didn't think so.

Meanwhile Moody, the whisperer, the note burner, momentarily parted from his painstaking pattern of caution. On the way back from the law office, he whispered he would give Julie that letter— the one Susan had taken from her boot. He asked that Julie and JoAnn make notes from it, after which Julie was to burn the document. She burned Roy instead, giving the pages to the agents, who were elated but incredulous Moody would make such a mistake.

Roy asked about the papers when he returned the next day.

"I burned it like you told me to," Julie said.

The next afternoon, Roy returned to Julie's apartment. He had another letter this time and would not leave it with Linn-West, but when he momentarily left the room, she whispered some of its content into her body recorder. Roy brought an envelope also, the end of which he sort of squeezed open and angled toward Julie. "Here, take this out," he said.

She slid out a $100 bill.

Moody came back on April Fool's Day, this time looking for details on Julie's dealings with investigators, apparently so a complaint could be filed concerning the way she had been treated. He suggested that would work to Linn-West's advantage when the prosecutor questioned her before the grand jury.

"I want him to be afraid to harass you," Roy said. "I want him to treat you with respect, and that's the only way that we can make them treat you with respect, because they're the kind of people, if you let 'em run over you, they'll just keep on doing it."

Moody railed on and on about the government agents, making clear they weren't about to run over him. Finally, Julie's phone rang and she answered.

"Hello. . . . Yeah . . . yeah. . . . Exactly . . . okay. . . . Yeah . . . okay . . . bye-bye. . . . Yeah, I'll be there." Julie laughed. "Okay. Bye-bye."

The caller had been Brian Hoback, who with other investigators was monitoring the meeting from the apartment across the way. "Make the truth known on this tape," he instructed.

She addressed Moody: "I know what the truth is and you know

what's going on and . . . I'm sure about myself . . . and I'm sure about my mom too, but you know how things were in Macon before. What if she got on the stand and said, froze and said, 'Yeah, I lied. Julie lied.' . . . So now what?"

Moody placed his hand to his mouth, as if gesturing to Julie Linn-West to be quiet.

Eventually, he wrote her a note to the effect he would pay Julie and her mother $500 apiece if they did well before the grand jury. Moments before Moody left, Linn-West made a telling vow.

"After this, Roy, I ain't never lyin' to nobody again."

Moody put his finger to his lips. "Sh-h-h. Sh-h-h," he admonished.

———

Julie Linn-West, who had performed splendidly, courageously, in her undercover role, fit a pattern. She was the impoverished single mother coping with her disability. JoAnn, in the 1980s, had yielded not only to Roy Moody's temptations but also, for a time, to cocaine's. Susan . . . Julie . . . JoAnn . . . Roy Moody had a knack for finding vulnerable women. And there was at least one more.

Investigators approached Julie Ivey initially about the same time they found Julie Linn-West. She too agreed to cooperate. Ivey went back even further with Moody, to 1983, and confessed to signing an affidavit containing false statements in connection with the would-be victims in Moody's attempted-murder case in Florida. Ivey also revealed she was paid $100 to become the nominal president of the Associated Writers Guild of America, though she never did any work for the company, other than signing documents. Moody told her it had something to do with his lawsuit against a bank. Julie Ivey had performed at least one more service for Roy. She'd been the one to introduce him to another single mother in dire financial straits, Julie Linn-West.

On March 28, 1990, after both had begun cooperating with the government, the two Julies spoke on the phone.

"Have you told them that he's threatened you?" Ivey asked.

"Yeah."

"Have they given you any protection or anything?"

"Yeah."

"Okay . . . well . . . the boys are tellin' me that they don't think Roy would do anything crazy, 'cause, of course, that would make him, you know, that right there would be pretty much—"

"He wouldn't," said Linn-West. "He himself wouldn't."

"That's exactly what I told 'em. Maybe he wouldn't, but he hired me to do somethin'. Why in the hell can't he hire somebody—"

"Why couldn't he hire someone else to do his dirty work for him?"

"That's right."

"Well, baby," said Julie Linn-West, "that's what he's all about, isn't it?"

The question had only recently taken on chilling new relevance. On a Friday night only a few days before the two Julies spoke, investigators saw Susan leave the Rex house. Her driving stirred suspicions she was trying to ditch the ubiquitous stakeout team. But she was still under observation when she walked in the darkness toward the runway of a small airport south of Atlanta. Minutes later, a car arrived and parked behind her vehicle. Susan and the occupant of the car appeared to be together. It was routine for surveillance agents to take down tag numbers of cars encountered by the Moodys, and somebody wrote down a number this night. The number was traced to a Jonesboro, Georgia, man previously convicted in Tennessee of assault with intent to commit murder, in a case with the earmarks of a professional hit.

12

Bugged

The U.S. government was about to add new depth of meaning to the customized license plate on the 1972 Volkswagen Beetle Susan Moody drove. BUGGED, the tag read. And if investigators had their way, it soon would be. So would the Moodys' house, phone and truck. As with a search warrant, getting a judge to okay this kind of electronic surveillance required a sworn statement laying out probable cause. The affidavit FBI Agent John Behnke signed on April 1 was masterful in two respects: for what it said authorities had on Moody, and for what it said they didn't have.

"The employment of conventional techniques has reached a stage where further use cannot reasonably be required, so that turning to this requested electronic surveillance has become reasonable and necessary," the affidavit read. "It is my judgment and the judgment of other Special Agents of the FBI, BATF, and Postal Inspectors of the U.S. Postal Service familiar with the facts of this case that there are no other investigative techniques reasonably available that will complete this investigation. Potentially successful investigative procedures have been tried and failed. Remaining investigative procedures appear to be unlikely to succeed if tried, or are considered too dangerous."

Roughly one hundred days after the bombings, searches of the Moodys' house, cars, boat, storage areas and an airplane hangar in Griffin had yielded no physical evidence that matched the bombs,

156

other than similar glues and the odd piece of pipe found in the Chamblee basement. The major-case prints made of Roy and Susan had yielded no significant matches. Moody, the Behnke document said, appeared intelligent, highly motivated, secretive and savvy.

"He has been the subject of a prior bombing investigation and prosecution, as well as an attempted murder investigation and prosecution, and has made note of his prior mistakes in leaving incriminating evidence behind. He has complete command over and the total loyalty of Susan McBride Moody. The Moodys are alert for law enforcement activity."

But in addition to laying out what made Moody such a formidable foe, Behnke's sworn statement detailed why Moody was worthy of pursuit. Behnke included a confluence of events involving Moody and the Eleventh Circuit Court of Appeals in the months leading up to the bombings. In June 1989, the court denied Moody's appeal based on Julie Linn-West's now-discredited testimony. But records revealed also that on August 21, 1989—the day the "Declaration of War" letters were postmarked—the court denied Moody's request for a rehearing. It was true, as Moody's February press release said, Judge Vance did not sit on the panel of judges that had ruled on that case. But Vance *had* heard two matters involving Moody. Both grew out of the civil suit over his arrest in Florida. Vance was part of a panel that dismissed one of Roy's appeals and was also one of the judges to hear arguments on a second issue Moody brought. The latter had not been ruled upon when Vance was murdered. On March 16, 1990, three months to the day after the explosion in Mountain Brook, the court ruled in Moody's favor.

The affidavit also covered Susan's participation in Roy's adventures, the Julie Linn-West affair and the mysterious late-night meeting by the runway. Behnke looked at court papers and newspaper stories about the suspected hit man's previous conviction. He'd been one of two men ostensibly hired by a country singer to assault a songwriter, the result of business discord. The man authorities feared may have met with Susan at the airport and the songwriter were both shot in a scuffle. The former got twenty years and was out on parole and now under surveillance by the mail-bomb task force, a chore requiring considerable manpower and causing controversy within the investigation when measured against the option of simply confronting him face-to-face.

Judge Freeman okayed the bugs and gave federal agents permission to secretly enter the house, the Volkswagen and the pickup truck to install equipment. Roy, of course, probably believed his house was *already* bugged, meaning investigators couldn't afford to put all their chips on the chance he'd leave his brass and brilliance and cool calculation at the doorstep and make their case for them with careless pillow talk. So the plodding, grinding checking of routine leads continued. ATF Agent William "Spanky" McFarland was given a lead to follow that Hoback had generated back in early February, when he'd purchased most of the generic mail-bomb components in the Griffin Servistar Hardware, one of the stores to which Moody had been followed. McFarland, a thickset, good-natured agent from the Jacksonville office, was assigned to interview people working in the store and show them photo spreads that included the Moodys. He took a young agent, Beth Hoggatt, with him.

Shown the spread of six, Walter Phillips picked out photo number five as a customer at the store. He remembered him because, before Phillips came to work at the Servistar in 1982, he had a business in Riverdale that number five patronized. Riverdale is in metropolitan Atlanta, so it was strange to see him again in Griffin, which is not. Phillips said number five came in the store twice in December 1989 and once asked if the store had ammunition components. The store didn't have what he wanted, so Phillips recommended he go to The Shootin' Iron, a gun shop elsewhere in Griffin.

Photo number five was Roy Moody.

James Paul Sartain was a tall, heavyset man who looked as if it hurt just to walk. After twenty-seven years with Ford Motor Company he retired on medical disability. He started working at The Shootin' Iron occasionally to keep himself occupied. He didn't get paid for it, but he helped Allen Williams, the owner, keep up the records and he filled in at the counter when Williams wasn't in the store. Sartain was a likable guy, and the agents had to like that he vividly recalled the sale of a large canister of Red Dot smokeless powder—the kind of powder in all four mail bombs—and some handgun primers in December 1989. He remembered it because it was the only time he sold so much Red Dot and so many primers at once. The customer asked for the powder, then followed him to the storeroom and stood at the door. Instead of the large canister, which weighed four pounds, Sartain asked if the man would prefer four one-pound cans. Once a can was opened, the powder absorbs mois-

ture from the air, which might affect the quality. But the man indicated he wasn't worried about such things because he was going to
use it all at once.

The buyer was in his forties or fifties and worn looking, by Sartain's description. His reddish brown hair looked unnatural, as if
dyed. The man wore tinted glasses, the kind you might buy in a
drugstore for reading. But piercing through all this were the eyes.
Though sunken, with deep circles or bags under them as if he had
not slept in a few days, they were magnetic. On April 4, Sartain
looked at the spread of black-and-white photos, including one of
Roy. But he didn't pick him out. He said he couldn't identify any of
them as the customer, but he thought he could identify the man if
he saw him again in person.

Sartain said he'd search the store records for a copy of the receipt,
and the next day he reported finding a carbon. A few days later, he
perused a second photo lineup, this one in color. There was one picture he said that looked the most like the powder purchaser. The
eyes stood out. But the problem with the picture was the hair. The
picture was of Roy Moody, but once again Sartain had failed to give
a positive identification.

When Julie Linn-West made her grand jury appearance on April
6, she, her son and her mother had already been put up in a hotel,
with twenty-four-hour protection. Later there would be an apartment, at government expense. Investigators figured Moody probably knew by now something was up, and he was already suspected of
killing two men who had posed far less danger to him than Julie
Linn-West. Ray Rukstele asked Hoback to put together a presentation of the events surrounding Linn-West for federal prosecutors
from around the South and Washington. On a Saturday the agent
took his four-and-a-half-year-old son into the task force offices,
along with cookies and toys, to work on it. The next day—Palm Sunday—he worked until almost midnight running through the hidden-camera videotapes for the same project. Soon afterward, he was
also asked to write a formal report for a potential obstruction-of-
justice case against Moody, in time for a meeting in Washington
scheduled near the end of the month. The government didn't have
nearly enough evidence to charge Moody with the bombings, but an
obstruction case might at least get him off the street. And just as important, such a case might offer an opening investigators had long

awaited, a chance to sledgehammer a wedge into an especially
gnarly stump, to split, physically at least, a nearly inseparable couple and see if Susan remained reticent.

For now, the only key figures out of circulation were the two
women transformed from Moody's star witnesses to the government's. And both seemed cool to being kept in cold storage, even if
it was to be hidden from harm. Julie and JoAnn wanted to go back
to their jobs, and Ekstrom, in particular, made clear she wanted out
of the hotel, and not into a government-sponsored apartment either. She wanted to go home. A representative of the U.S. Marshals
Service Witness Security Program delivered a spiel to both women.
It wasn't a sales job, but an even-handed explanation. They could be
relocated, set up with new identities, probably new careers. But family contact would be limited and some friendships would flat-out
have to go. Both women cried, but they turned it down on the spot.
Eventually, Ekstrom moved home, but not Julie, setting up a memorable holiday for two families.

The Hobacks had just returned from Easter services when a
young FBI agent called. Julie was upset. She wanted to attend a
family gathering at her mother's house, a clear breach of the security
protocol. Hoback had given up too much already to leave his own
family on Easter, but the star witness couldn't be allowed to wander
around unprotected; nor, Hoback believed, should she have to
spend Easter sobbing in some hotel room. So he loaded up his wife,
daughter and son—in his personal car, not the government's ride,
since he was too much the straight arrow to dent the rules even in
view of the sacrifice he was making—and they headed to Julie's hotel.

Julie was tearful and grouchy and Hoback didn't blame her. They
compromised; agents would watch over her from somewhere on her
mother's property but wouldn't intrude on the party itself. But Julie
was not the only young mother for whom the meeting held meaning. To Kathy Hoback the case that had taken away husband and father was finally palpable, the people real. She felt for Julie, the
young woman near her own age whose family life had been jarred
and marred just as her own had—by Roy Moody.

———

The task force soon called Julie Linn-West into action again, but
this time only over the telephone. When Julie called the Moody
house, Susan answered and told her Roy wasn't there. But the inves-

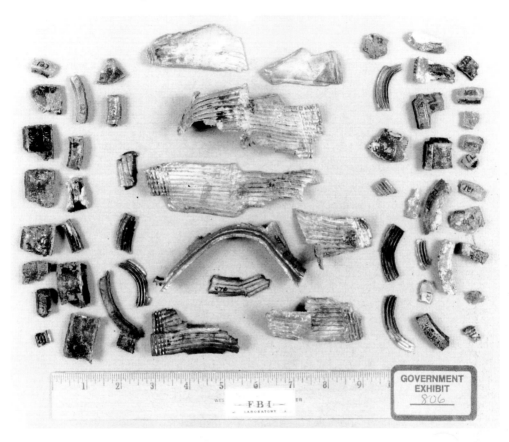

GOVERNMENT
EXHIBIT
806

Fragments of the Birmingham bomb. Note the corduroy pattern where the force of
the explosion seared the imprint of the nails into the metal.

Opposite page, top: The X-ray image of the Eleventh Circuit bomb package as Court Security Officer Steve Grant saw it on the morning of December 18, 1989.

Opposite page, bottom: Bill Briley examining the Eleventh Circuit bomb package next to the portable X-ray machine.

Above: The Eleventh Circuit bomb package before it had been rendered safe.

Robbie Robinson's law office in Savannah.

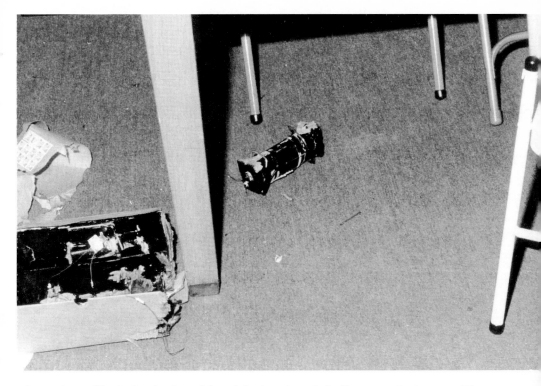

The Jacksonville device in the midst of the bomb techs' efforts to take it apart. The black object under the table is the pipe bomb.

The Jacksonville pipe bomb.

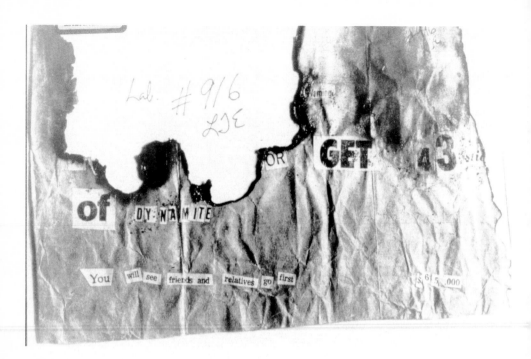

Pieced-together remnants of the threat note from the 1972 case.

The Chamblee device in the suburban basement where it was discovered.

The inside of the Titusville storage locker, with the three footlockers.

Susan and Roy Moody.

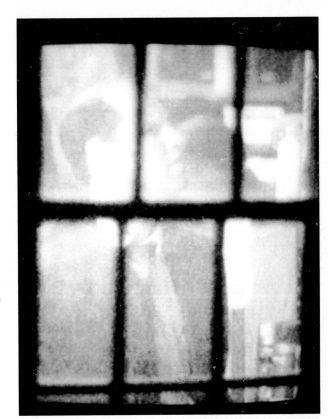

Right: February 8, 1990: Brian Hoback looks around the Rex residence for the first time. (Trace Reeves, WSB-TV)

Below: February 8, 1990: Leaving the Rex house after the first search. Right to left: Terry Byer, Terry Pelfrey, Lloyd Erwin, David Hyche. (Trace Reeves, WSB-TV)

Opposite page, top: Roy Moody during the investigation. (Trace Reeves, WSB-TV)

Opposite page, bottom: Mike Ford in his law library. (Trace Reeves, WSB-TV)

Right: Frank Lee, outside Roy Moody's house. (Courtesy WSB-TV)

Below: Judge Alaimo in his Brunswick chambers. (Andrew Artis, WSB-TV)

Above: Judge Devitt leaves the courthouse in St. Paul. (Andrew Artis, WSB-TV)

Opposite page, top: Don Samuel, on the left, and Ed Tolley in St. Paul. (Andrew Artis, WSB-TV)

Opposite page, bottom: Brian Hoback, Louis Freeh, Attorney General Richard Thornburgh, Howard Shapiro, and John Malcolm.

The prosecution team in St. Paul with Judge Devitt and, to his right,
his courtroom deputy, Deb Siebrecht.

Brian Hoback with President Bush at the White House.
(Susan Biddle, The White House)

tigators, of course, had other ways of knowing when Roy wasn't home. Julie told Susan she wanted to talk to her.

"I've already told them the truth," Julie announced, suggesting she did so to save herself. Susan said to let her off the phone and she would pass on the information. Julie urged Susan to reconsider her position. That was the idea of the phone call, to try to draw Susan out. But the idea didn't work, couldn't work on a young woman inured by nine years with a man in total control, unceasing in his demands. Roy abused her—there'd been instances here and there where she might hold the keys to keep him from leaving when they were having trouble, and Roy would twist her arm until she let loose. But, while the violence made her aware of his power, Susan's was largely a story of emotional abuse, of the silent treatments, days on end during which Roy would refuse to carry on conversations with her, when he wouldn't respond even to her attempts simply to learn what her offense had been, when he wouldn't even look at her. He seemed unmoved by her crying. She tried to discern a pattern by marking a calendar with teardrops, but no pattern emerged. Mainly, Susan tried to do whatever would please Roy, to turn all her attention toward him, to redeem herself. Always, she assumed herself the offender.

But Susan Moody wasn't numb to every nuance of the mail-bomb investigation. Nothing—not the constant surveillance, not the traffic stops, not Julie Linn-West's tears—bothered Susan Moody as much as when the probe affected her family. Her mother, Ann McBride, worked as a public-health nurse, coordinator of the tuberculosis program for the DeKalb County Health Department. Her father was a retired Air Force officer. They lived in a ranch-style home with a daylight basement in a desirable DeKalb County section not far from downtown Atlanta. The family was close-knit, with five children reared to work hard and tell the truth. Ann McBride had this feeling hers wasn't the kind of family to which this sort of thing was supposed to happen, and yet she had believed for years Roy would cause Susan big trouble. Now that he had, Ann simply tried to get through day by day.

Mrs. McBride was more scared than shocked one Friday afternoon when Susan brought over the warranty deed for the house in Rex, along with financial records and the phone numbers of Ford, Harvey and a bail-bond company. She gave the material to her mother and explained she would need it—to arrange bail if Susan and Roy were arrested.

"You're not going to be arrested," Mrs. McBride said.

"Just in case," said her daughter. "We need to be prepared."

"You are not involved in this, are you?"

"Neither of us are involved. They have been following me as intensely as they do Roy. There's no telling what they'll do."

"Then leave," the trim, blond mother said flatly.

"Leave what?"

"Roy."

"Why?"

"So they'll stop harassing you."

"I'm not going to leave Roy."

It was Mrs. McBride's turn to ask why.

"Why should I?" Susan responded.

Susan's mother told her she was never mentioned in connection with the case on television or radio, or in the newspaper. It was true Susan rarely appeared in the news coverage, other than in the background or as an appendage to Roy, who actively courted the attention.

"The media isn't informed by the FBI. You never know what they're going to do. . . ."

Mrs. McBride intimated she'd been warned by agents that Susan should get away from Roy because the situation would intensify in a couple of weeks.

"No matter what, I'm not leaving Roy."

"I don't know how you live day to day with this happening."

Susan did not respond. This wasn't the first time Susan's mother wanted her to leave Roy. She had begged her to. Ann McBride had hated Roy Moody from day one. For Susan's sake she tolerated him. If only her mother realized, thought Susan, that she had already considered every conceivable scenario wherein she could leave Roy. But the young woman couldn't figure out a plan that would work, not both physically and emotionally. If she came home, Susan decided, she wouldn't be leaving a nightmare but bringing it with her and visiting it upon her parents. She couldn't bear the thought of one day getting arrested in front of them. The daughter could articulate none of this to her mother. They rarely spoke so frankly. And anyway, Roy's hold was so strong she couldn't stand to tell anyone of such thoughts. It would be like an act of unfaithfulness—or disobedience. If she told someone she wanted to leave, she believed he would find out somehow. Her body language, her guilt would give her away.

———

Only because Susan wanted her to—otherwise she had no desire to participate—Ann McBride found herself a few days later sitting in her living room next to her husband John, facing Mike Ford and a video camera. Her lips pursed, the tips of the outstretched fingers on one hand tapped tensely against the fingertips of the other hand; she seemed ill at ease. John, a big man with a Hemingway beard, at fifty-seven close to the same age as his son-in-law, seemed more comfortable. Ford, whom they had not previously met, was at their home to take an unusual "video deposition."

Ford swore in the suburbanite couple, then asked John McBride what had happened when the FBI came to see him.

"I drive a bus part-time for the retardation service," McBride said. "I arrived home and two FBI men were waiting here . . . and they said that they would like to see my workshop."

"Did they tell you why?"

"No. . . . I asked them if they had a warrant. They said, 'No, do we need one?' And I said, 'Yes, I think so.' And the agent said, 'Why, do you have something to hide?' And I said, 'No, I have nothing to hide . . . but I don't want to read in the paper about I had the makings of a bomb in my workshop.' I said, 'I'll tell you right now I can probably make one out of what's in there. But it's all common stuff . . . and you seem to have a pipeline directly to the newspaper and television, anything that happens seems to go directly to them. And I don't want to read about myself in the newspaper.' "

McBride recounted other questions the agents put to him and recalled they took down the names and addresses of family members including their children and Mrs. McBride's parents.

"What comments did they make to you about Mr. Moody?" Ford asked.

"Well, I started by making a comment: 'Why on earth would you think that Roy Moody would have anything to do with the bombing?' And the FBI agent in charge said . . . 'We know we've got the right man.' "

McBride said the FBI asked to take a sample from an electric typewriter at the house, and he complied.

Ford shifted his focus: "Mrs. McBride, I appreciate you working with us on this. I know you're very uncomfortable about giving a statement."

The lawyer quizzed her about a visit two federal agents made to her office.

"What kind of questions did they ask?"

"They said they could not find any evidence that Susan and Roy were married, that they had looked and searched everywhere. . . ."

"They were asking you about—"

"They asked me about the ceremony here and what the judge looked like and if I knew his name." Just a few months earlier at the McBrides' house, Roy had finally married Susan after years of co-habitation.

Ford: "Could you think of anything that could conceivably have to do with this bombing case everybody's talking about?"

If he was looking for Roy's mother-in-law to answer in righteous indignation at the government's prying, he may have been disappointed. "I think his point he made was he felt like this was a scam that Roy was pulling on Susan. . . . This marriage was a big—he used the word 'bamboozle'—on Susan . . . to make her think that they were married because they knew that she had been trying to get him to marry her for a long time. And that this might be a big sham that he had pulled so she would think they were married."*

She reported one of the agents said they felt Susan's life was in danger, "and if I loved her, that I would try to get her to come forward. And that they had evidence . . . they were getting ready to leave the area and they were fearful for Susan's life." Her voice, formerly terse, now trembled. She too believed Susan was in a great deal of danger.

"At the time that they told you that, what did you think they meant?" Ford queried.

"Well, the implication was that they were afraid Roy was going to hurt Susan, and then it kinda seemed to shift to he may have pulled her into this bombing and that she would be implicated with him."

"What did you think about that from your knowledge of Susan and Roy?" the lawyer asked.

But Ann did not respond about Roy, only about Susan, and her voice was breaking, perhaps with anger at the suggestion Susan might be involved, or perhaps with anger at Roy.

"I told him my daughter wouldn't do something like that."

Mrs. McBride said that, when the interview seemed over, she told the agents she had something she would like to say.

"I told them that I didn't appreciate some of the tactics that had

---

*Ultimately, no evidence surfaced that the marriage was not real.

been used on our friends and family . . . I understood that they had a job to do, but I thought some of it was unnecessary and solely meant to harass and embarrass our family." She kneaded her fingers, her gaze sweeping uneasily around the room. The interview of Mrs. McBride's parents, who barely knew Roy, had stung Ann, as did the episode with the wedding present Susan noted in the journal. The groom's family, old friends, called the McBrides and asked them not to come to the wedding.

Mrs. McBride continued: "Kirkland said, well, it's going to get a lot worse in the next couple of weeks."

Ford indicated he was considering giving the video or parts of it to Judge Freeman "to show him what's going on." He said it might be used if "we end up filing a civil action against certain agents."

But the agents, of course, didn't retreat. Four days later, Susan went to a birthday party for her brother, the kind of occasion, of course, where making photos is commonplace. Only Susan was taking pictures of surveillance vehicles. She spotted feds parked alongside a road with a view of the house, as well as driving by and pausing in front. All this was the subject of another journal entry, with an added detail:

"While there took Grandma for a ride because she wanted to see my 'tail.'"

13

The Lineup

All things work together . . .

Harry A's sat on a sandy St. George's Island street, two quaint and quasi-nautical stories shaped like an oversize houseboat done in driftwood gray, swimming-pool blue and the brown hue of creosote pilings, with a long screened window running from one end to the other, interrupted by a door on each side of which hung a white life-preserver ring. The tavern seemed a suitable setting for a Jimmy Buffett video, but an unlikely backdrop for what some would see as one of the most glaring blunders of the Moody investigation.

Roy and Susan had headed to Florida on their motorcycles, surveillance in tow, including, by Roy's reckoning, automobiles, motorcycles and aircraft. The Moodys somehow found room on their bikes to take their video camera along, and at St. George's Island, Susan wound up inside Harry A's videotaping a table of five men she believed to be part of the surveillance, touching off a chain of events that culminated with somebody's grabbing the camera and an FBI agent tearing the tape to pieces. Susan went to the trash can and reclaimed the remnants in Roy's helmet. A deputy sheriff arrived, and Roy told him he wanted the five men prosecuted for assault and criminal destruction of property. The agents told the man from the sheriff's department they were conducting an investigation and had asked not to have their pictures taken. The agent who tore up the tape admitted it to the local officer and offered to pay for the cassette. Susan declined.

But the most important damage wasn't to the tape. The agents involved in the incident were brought in strictly for the surveillance, and in Atlanta, some of the investigators trying to build a case, grappling with Moody day in, day out for the psychological edge, were angry. The agents in the bar had played into Moody's hands. When Roy and Susan returned from Florida, a television photographer waited on the corner of Skyline Drive for shots of them on their motorcycles. Roy, in Ford's library, went on camera with WSB, dumping from a clear plastic bag onto the teak table pieces of the victimized videotape.

"I think they made the move because they feel like they are above the law," Roy declared. His seemed a self-satisfied indignation, as if this authenticated his claims about the egregious conduct of federal agents, the same sort of unbridled behavior he might have you believe resulted in his unjust arrest in 1972.

"I think somebody has to come forward and say look what these people are doing. Not only it's unethical, it's illegal. They're violating the law. Now what I want to know is, can citizens depend upon the justice system to protect them against these type of federal agents. If we cannot, then the American people need to know that."

It was interesting talk, indeed, from the man investigators suspected of writing the letters from Americans for a Competent Federal Judicial System.

"You have to be victimized by these people to understand how they operate. It's surprising and alarming to a lot of people. It's alarming to me but it isn't surprising. They've done numerous things that implies to me that they either don't have the capacity or the desire to differentiate between right and wrong, between truthfulness and falsehoods, between ethics and the lack of ethics."

Mike Ford fired off letters to Ray Rukstele, prosecutors in Florida, FBI Director William Sessions and Larry Potts, an FBI inspector recently arrived in Atlanta to take command of the mail-bomb investigation. The letters all read similarly.

"If you dispute any allegations, you should make your position known . . . within the next seven days," Ford wrote. "If you do not so advise, civil action will be instituted based upon the allegations and criminal prosecution will be requested at the State and Federal level."

But Roy Moody wasn't the only one who took a Florida vacation. So did Paul Sartain, the volunteer counter clerk at The Shootin' Iron in Griffin. A neighbor collected his mail and newspapers in his absence, and when Sartain got back, he went through the papers for the week he was on vacation. He saw a story about the St. George's Island episode. "Moody Wanted FBI Agents Arrested," read the headline. And there was a picture with it, a picture, Sartain decided, of the man who had purchased the powder and primers in December 1989. He called ATF.

Between Julie Linn-West and Paul Sartain, the momentum of the investigation was finally shifting against Roy Moody, but not without fits and false starts, like an addict poised on the brink between sobriety and self-destruction, redemption and relapse.

Ray Rukstele had assigned to the case a second prosecutor, Tom Bever, whom he considered talented and hardworking and who, in Rukstele's opinion, had unselfishly delayed leaving for a job with the Iran-Contra special prosecutor to see the Moody case move forward. In late April, Bever accompanied Rukstele to Washington for a meeting at the Justice Department with Department officials and prosecutors from other federal court districts involved in the bomb investigation—from Georgia, Florida and Alabama. Rukstele and Bever had prepared their theory of the case, flown up the night before and discussed how they would make their presentation. The plan Rukstele outlined to the gathering was this: bring a conspiracy case against the Moodys for obstruction of justice, perjury, subornation of perjury and mail fraud, all based upon the events surrounding Julie Linn-West. He urged the use of the Racketeer Influenced and Corrupt Organizations—RICO—law, which, originally designed for mobster prosecutions, had been used against a wide range of non–Cosa Nostra conspiracies. The Atlanta prosecutors believed the elements were in place for a strong case against Roy and Susan. An indictment on these charges would not only get Moody off the street but leave an opening to pursue Susan's cooperation.

But Rukstele and Bever left the meeting angry and disappointed. Not a single other lawyer at the conference seemed to Rukstele enthusiastic about the plan. Rukstele was struck by how provincial the prosecutors proved to be, as attorneys from different districts brought reasons why the mail-bomb case should ultimately be prosecuted on their respective turfs. Lawyers from two U.S. attorneys' offices came across as openly hostile. The bottom line: no approval for arresting the Moodys, not yet.

———

April 30 was a doubly dark day for Roy Moody. His vanity-press operation had been the subject of consumer complaints and scrutiny by postal authorities for years, and the mail-bomb case reinvigorated interest. On the thirtieth, an administrative law judge ordered all mail for the Associated Writers Guild of America, Inc. detained for the breach of an earlier consent agreement, a devastating blow for a business that depended on its mail to survive. The same day, attired in suits and ties, Hoback and FBI Agent Gary Morgan showed up outside Mike Ford's office and waved down Roy, who was about to leave in the black pickup.

"Can you give us just a few minutes here, back over here at Mr. Ford's office?" Hoback asked Moody. Roy, this time, was cooperative enough. This time, it was the agents' turn to deliver a letter.

> *Dear Mr. and Mrs. Moody:*
>
> *This letter is to advise you that you are targets of a federal Grand Jury investigation in this District into violations of federal law relating to the murder of Judge Robert S. Vance, United States Court of Appeals for the Eleventh Circuit, and attorney Robert E. Robinson of Savannah, as well as the mailing of package bombs to the United States Court of Appeals for the Eleventh Circuit in Atlanta, and the Jacksonville, Florida, offices of the NAACP, and other matters in violations of federal criminal laws.*
>
> *On February 22, 1990, a letter was sent to The President of the United States. The letter was signed by "Roy Moody." The letter states in part that "In preparing to respond to the government's action, information was unexpectly [sic] uncovered which my attorneys and I feel could lead to the arrest and conviction of the perpetrator of these crimes."*
>
> *The Grand Jury has asked me to extend to both of you an invitation to appear before the Grand Jury at 9:30 A.M., on Thursday, May 3, 1990, to testify about these matters that are now under investigation.*

> *Both of you must understand that a decision by you to*
> *testify is a completely voluntary decision by you and that*
> *your testimony could be used against you if any criminal*
> *charges should be returned against you.*
>
> *I would appreciate it if you or your attorney would no-*
> *tify me in writing by close of business Wednesday, May 2,*
> *1990, as to whether or not you will accept the Grand*
> *Jury's invitation to testify. If you or your attorney has not*
> *contacted me by that date, I will assume that you do not*
> *wish to testify.*
>
> > *Sincerely,*
> > *Ray Rukstele*

A third prong poked Moody that day, but he wouldn't feel it until the next; the Justice Department approved a second search warrant for Roy's Rex residence and miniwarehouse. On May 1, from the back of a station wagon parked in Moody's driveway, Hoback and Pelfrey, both in blue jeans, toted tools, including a vacuum cleaner. Frank Lee, Dave Kirkland, Harold Jones, Spanky McFarland and others prowled the premises as well. Two key missions this day: vacuum the place to look for powder traces in the dust, and search for evidence in the Julie Linn-West case.

A long line of television cameras faced the house. And soon after the search was over, while one of the stations broadcast live from the scene, Roy Moody emerged. He was not his usual charming, dapper public self. Dressed in faded blue overalls and a long-sleeved, white T-shirt, he seemed no longer insouciant but enervated.

"I'll make a statement," he said to the hurriedly huddling press of cameras and microphones. "I'm not going to answer questions but I will make a statement.

"About three weeks ago Susan and I went on vacation to Florida. When we returned, we . . . saw the shoeprint of a male in our shower, and we could also tell that somebody had been in our laundry room, moving stuff around. . . . It's my belief that the people that were in my house during that period of time were federal agents. I think they planted evidence. I think they came back today to get that evidence."

Roy turned from the crowd of reporters and photographers in his driveway and walked back toward his house, but he wasn't walking away yet from his public pokes at his antagonists. Mike Ford addressed letters to both ATF's and the GBI's internal affairs units alleging Hoback and Pelfrey "have attempted to persuade Ms. Julie Linn-West to testify in a particular manner.

"Obviously, that effort, in and of itself, may be a violation of the law," Ford charged. "Mr. Pelfrey apparently threatened her with ten years in jail if she did not recant her previous testimony."

Ford referred to enclosed statements from the Moodys concerning Linn-West. "I request that this incident be promptly investigated and that both agents be required to take polygraph examinations conducted by outside sources to the investigation and agencies involved."

But Ford's client took things a step further. A mailing bearing Roy's signature went out to Georgia news organizations.

May 14, 1990

To: NEWS MANAGER

Dear Sir,

> *On several occasions, members of the "media" have requested that I provide information relative to the so-called "mail bomb" investigation.*
>
> *In response I am providing information which reflects our conern [sic] regarding what appears to be an illegal attempt by government agents to influence the testimony of a grand jury witness.*
>
> *It is interesting to note that after said witness testified, she called my wife and said, "I had to do what was necessary to save my neck." To me her statement is an admission her testimony before the grand jury was influenced by the threat of ten years imprisonment.*
>
> *The above phone call was intercepted by government agents who have my phone tapped. Shortly thereafter, I learned the witness had been taken into "protective custody."*
>
> *When you examine the effects of "protective custody," it becomes apparent three benefits issues [sic] to the government;*
>
> > *1. It is difficult if not impossible for the media to question the witness about the threats made by government agents to influence her testimony.*

2. *It is difficult if not impossible for the media to determine that "protective custody" substantially improved the witnesse's* [sic] *lifestyle and may be in fact a disguised "pay-off" for yielding to said threats.*
3. *The false impression is created that the witness could have reason to fear me thereby painting me as a dangerous person, an image that would help the government in any forthcoming attempt to prosecute.*

If you are interested in receiving additional information concerning other similar concerns, send me a copy of the transcript or tearsheet relative to your presentation of this news item.

Sincerely,
Roy Moody

Moody didn't run this one by his lawyers either. For all the time Moody spent in law school, in law libraries and in lawsuits, it was clear to Bruce Harvey and Mike Ford that Moody knew enough about the law to be dangerous—at least to himself. In this instance, he had just provided to the feds one long piece of text for linguistic comparison to the bomber's letters, and for whatever other tests they wanted to conduct. Harvey and Ford had already decided Moody was his own worst enemy. Nonetheless, the day after the postmark on Moody's latest attempt to throw the light of public scrutiny into the eyes of the mail-bomb investigators, Harvey, Hauptman and Ford found themselves in Judge Freeman's chambers. The government meant to pull Roy Moody under some lights of its own—in the lineup room at Atlanta's city jail.

———

Moody wore a pale blue shirt with a dark tie. The other five men, carefully selected by investigators for resemblance to Roy, likewise dressed in light-colored shirts with ties, and each, like Roy, had thick, dark hair. Amy Levin Weil, a tough, smart Assistant U.S. Attorney, questioned Ford to make sure he had no problem with the logistics. He did not. The lighting was such that Moody couldn't see the witness through the glass separating them. Neither Moody nor his attorneys would be told the identity of the witness or whether he could finger Moody.

The witness was Paul Sartain. Spanky McFarland, one of the ATF agents who had found The Shootin' Iron in the first place, told the lumbering retiree to look at each man in the lineup and, if he could identify the buyer of the gunpowder and primers, to indicate his number. Black numbers were painted on the back wall of the lineup room.

Sartain picked number four. There was no doubt, the man from the gun store said, number four bought the powder and primers in December 1989.

He picked Roy Moody.

"Were you involved in a lineup?" Moody was asked outside where a TV crew had arrived.

"No comment," he said at the time. Later he dubbed the procedure "an inconvenience."

Just two days later the legal system slipped Roy another bitter pill. A prosecutor in Florida elected not to bring charges against the FBI agent who ravaged Susan's videotape, although an assistant state's attorney acknowledged on television that the agent technically committed the crime of criminal mischief.

But, the lawyer added, "It is my firm belief, and I've tried a lot of cases . . . if this case was presented to a jury, a jury would probably, you know, sympathize with the agent's actions.

"He had asked her in a somewhat reasonable manner to stop [videotaping] and she didn't."

The prosecutor confessed confidence in an FBI internal investigation of the matter and said he was satisfied appropriate action would be taken, a conclusion one could hardly expect Roy Moody to share.

"I think it sends a signal to all citizens that we are dealing with a police force that's above the law," Moody told a reporter. "And I think it's a force to fear. I think it's a force to be bridled."

But this time Roy was bridled, by Bruce Harvey, who monitored Moody's remarks. The interview took place in Harvey's brick-walled office in the converted Union Mission building in downtown Atlanta.

"I don't want to talk about your criticizing the judicial system," Harvey admonished, and he halted Roy's attempt to answer a question about whether he thought he would be arrested.

"I believe they intend to charge him with something," Harvey said. "Whether it's anything related to the mail-bomb investigation, I doubt very seriously because there have been a lot of recent developments but nothing specific. If they had any hard facts, if they had any connections, he'd be indicted already. I don't think there is anything there."

Harvey was in his favorite place—onstage—and he was building to a crescendo.

"They have had now at least sixty days to do any kind of independent testing or analysis of the items taken from Mr. Moody's home in February. They've had a considerable amount of time to do any kind of testing they wanted to the evidence they took out of Mr. Moody's house the second time. If they have anything, let's see it . . . and if they don't have anything there, let 'em tell the grand jury, let 'em tell the public that what they've seized shows no connection between the mail bombings and Roy Moody."

Harvey was correct in his assumption the government had no single piece of physical evidence to prove Roy Moody the mail bomber. But Harvey sensed something the government *did* have deeply bothered his client. Roy seemed obsessed with learning the identity of the lineup witness. His legal team added a private investigator, and one of the PI's first missions was to follow the powder trail, to track down the witness and find out whether he had indeed identified Roy and what else he had told the government. When a reporter found out about the detective, Harvey said the Moody camp was conducting its own "shadow investigation."

Within two days of the lineup, Spanky McFarland got a call from Walter Phillips, the manager at the Griffin hardware store who had steered him to The Shootin' Iron in the first place. Phillips reported he'd just been interviewed by somebody identifying himself as a private investigator, who showed photos of Roy and Susan and asked whether he had talked to federal agents. Phillips indicated he had answered the way McFarland had told him to in such situations, telling the visitor he knew nothing about the investigation beyond what he had seen on the news.

The pressure preyed and weighed on Moody now, and he showed it. The Moodys returned from an overnight trip, and after a seemingly trivial discussion about the family dog, the coldness toward Susan settled over Roy. The young wife tried to find out why, and he turned from silent to violent, showering her in vile names. *Bitch!* he called her. *Slut! Whore!* She followed him from room to room, trying, as usual, to find out what she had done. He had a toothbrush in his hand, the handle of which he jabbed into the soft flesh under her chin. Suddenly she suspected what had angered Roy. She was too friendly with a neighbor, another man. *How could you think such things?* Susan asked. *You are crazy,* she said more than once. Roy was seated in his big orange easy chair. Susan positioned herself so she straddled his knees, sitting facing him, trying to force him to look her in the eyes while she spoke. He reached up, put his hands to the base of her neck and squeezed hard enough that later bruises would emerge. But she made no move to stop him, just waited until he let go on his own. And when he did and got up to walk to his office, she continued to follow him, still trying to get him to talk face-to-face. Somehow, he got her to the floor and pinned her under his legs, then picked up her head between his palms and pounded it on the floor, which was made of particleboard, uncovered as part of the Moodys' ongoing home renovation.*

He stopped suddenly, got up and told Susan to pack a bag and leave. She threw some things in the Volkswagen and hit the road, her usual retinue of surveillance agents behind her. She had a vague idea of heading to her sister Nancy's house in the Florida panhandle and, with that in mind, got on I-285, a perimeter highway encircling the core of metropolitan Atlanta. But she started thinking about the consequences. She thought so long and hard that she never got off on Interstate 85 to head south toward the Gulf coast, but instead she drove the entire circular perimeter route, which took Susan—and her faithful escort—about an hour, maybe more. She realized the feds wouldn't stop following her. *How can I bring this to Nancy's?* she thought. *Where am I going to get money? How am I going to survive?* She feared the round-the-clock scrutiny was making Roy stranger than he was already; she figured the pressure was to blame for the beating she had just taken. But at least if she stayed with Roy she wouldn't envelop an innocent sister in the circus her life had become. Susan believed if she were patient she would eventually be free of Roy; one or both of them would sooner or later go to jail. When she got back to the interchange where she had gotten on I-285, she turned and headed back to the house in Rex.

*This is based on Susan's account of events. Later, in court testimony, Roy would contend Susan hit him in the chest area when he was in the chair, "just as an expression of anger, not in an attempt to hurt me." He said she was "still being physical" when she followed him to the office area. While this account of Roy's omitted the choking and the toothbrush jabbing, he admitted to slapping his young wife and beating her head on the floor.

Near the same time, Mike Ford suddenly resigned as Roy's attorney. And he wasn't the only lawyer leaving the case.

Ray Rukstele learned of his replacement from a reporter. A woman from the *Atlanta Journal-Constitution* called him at the office, where, since the start of the mail-bomb investigation, he was apt to be at nine-thirty or ten at night. She told him Louis Freeh had just been appointed to take over the investigation. Freeh was with a U.S. Attorney's office in New York and renowned as the lead prosecutor in the "Pizza Connection" case, which involved drug trafficking by Sicilian mobsters who used pizza joints as fronts. The reporter wanted Rukstele's comment, but he declined. He told her he didn't know anything about it. He didn't believe it. Later that night, one of the attorney general's top assistants called and talked about the problems in the case. The main problem, as Rukstele understood, was the fractious relationship between prosecutors in the various locales involved. The Justice Department official mentioned he was thinking of bringing somebody in. The next morning he called and said he was appointing Freeh.

Rimantas "Ray" Rukstele knew about surviving hardship. He was born to it in Lithuania in the closing days of the Second World War, fled the communists with his family and millions of others, and wound up in Germany shuttled from one displaced persons camp to the next until 1949, when the Ruksteles joined Ray's uncle in Detroit, Michigan. Rukstele told himself he had never viewed the mail-bomb case as a career builder, as he believed others had. But he dearly wanted to see it through at least to indictment. And now that it was taken from him, he was crushed.

Rukstele told the man from Justice his office would be at Freeh's disposal, and anything Freeh needed he would get. Soon the New Yorker and a second newly appointed special prosecutor, Howard Shapiro, came to Atlanta. Rukstele was impressed.

Freeh was young, bright and extraordinarily tough. Shapiro, who as a law clerk watched Freeh in action in the Pizza Connection case, was bright, tough and extraordinarily young—a day past his thirtieth birthday, a month shy of his third anniversary with a federal prosecutor's office in New York when Freeh invited him into the case. Shapiro was flattered and surprised at Freeh's invitation; it was his first substantive conversation with Freeh in close to a year.

Brian Hoback was apprehensive when he heard about the special prosecutors. While the mail-bomb task force had become in some ways a model of cooperation, the scars had barely formed over the wounds to interagency relations from the early days of the investigation, and Hoback heard that Freeh, before his prosecutorial career, had been an FBI agent. But the ATF agent's first dealings with the New Yorkers allayed his anxieties.

"I know who you are," Freeh replied when Hoback introduced himself. Hoback quickly discerned both special prosecutors had done their homework.

In Titusville, Florida, three agents visited Ted Banks, a salty sexagenarian who acknowledged serving six years for counterfeiting. Predictably, he said he was innocent. He met Moody in the pen and they stayed in touch afterward. Banks said he trusted Moody like a brother and would be surprised if he was involved in the mail bombings. Banks had questions of his own for the agents, particularly about the O'Ferrell end of the investigation.

Postal Inspector Dave Kirkland, one of the agents who visited Banks in Florida, made clear to Hoback afterward he didn't buy the Floridian's story. And in his report about the Banks interview, Kirkland noted "there were several items of interest in the carport. These included tanks that were associated with welding equipment."

Banks continued to meet with both agents and prosecutors, questioned not only about the bombings—not very fruitfully—but also about suspicious business dealings in which he'd been involved with Moody.

Finally, Terry Pelfrey and FBI Agent Gary Morgan interviewed Banks in Titusville on June 7. He refused a polygraph test and said he didn't want to talk to any more agents unless he was on the witness stand.

Other investigators converged on Titusville, from the FBI, ATF, Postal Inspectors and the Mountain Brook Police. A swatch of the Florida map from Titusville to Melbourne and toward Orlando was divided into grids. Each agent was assigned a grid. They went to grocery stores, hardware stores, motels, restaurants. They were looking for origins of the common household items that had been used to build the bombs, and such wide-ranging canvasses—a similar operation was undertaken in Georgia—symbolized the dearth of incriminating physical evidence uncovered so far. Andrew Bringuel, who didn't even go to work for the FBI until February 1990, about two months after the bombings, was among those sent to Titusville for the searches. But that wasn't where his singular contribution to the mail-bomb case came. And it wasn't in Birmingham, his home office, either.

When he got back from Florida, he was asked to continue looking for the nails. Somebody showed him pictures of the nails from the bomb that killed Judge Vance, shiny, eightpenny nails with an offset punch on the head and tool marks just below on the shank. He would later guess he spent 90 percent of June looking for those nails. He contacted wholesalers. He reached retailers. He had nails sent to his office. But none were the ones that could nail Moody; none of them matched those from the bombs.

The rookie agent still commuted on weekends to and from Peachtree City, Georgia, a pleasant planned community about a half hour south of Atlanta and maybe fifteen miles from Rex. The Bringuels still had their house there up for sale. On Sunday, July 1, Bringuel and his wife went to a Kroger supermarket. Mrs. Bringuel mentioned she'd broken a piece of furniture and needed some wood glue, and they headed to the hardware section. As he looked for the glue, he caught sight of something else on the rack. Those look like the nails I've been looking for, Bringuel told his wife. He bought them and took them back to the office in Birmingham, where an agent who had been collecting evidence agreed.

Interviews and polygraph tests concerning the supposed hit man from Susan's late-night airport encounter helped push Hoback to the conclusion the tag number may simply have been miswritten. Susan, he now believed, had never met with the man. But Hoback had a new witness worry. Paul Sartain, now potentially the most valuable witness in the bomb case, seemed to think somebody was following him. Then came hang-ups. Days later those evolved into threatening calls, and the caller not only knew Sartain's stepchildren were out of town, but where. Although one call was traced to a phone not two miles from Moody's house, there was nothing to implicate Roy in the harassment.

14

The Deep

> I was looking at him when he was prying my
> fingers loose from the boat. He had a de-
> ranged, mad look on his face. I've never seen
> anything like that before.

Brian Hoback had a fresh look if not a fresh outlook when he got to the office on July 10, a Tuesday. That morning, Hoback happened to wear a blue blazer, gray slacks and a white shirt with a tie, rather than his routine blue jeans and sports shirt.

Sartorially fortuitous, as it turned out.

"Whaddya got going?" asked Howard Shapiro.

"Just the usual stuff," Hoback replied.

Louis Freeh was there. "Can you help me this morning? I need you to go with me."

"Sure. Where are you going?"

"I'll get back with you on all that."

Freeh told Hoback to make sure he had with him the tapes and transcripts of Moody's meetings with Julie Linn-West. The young agent thought he caught strange looks from a couple of supervisors—a sort of studied ignorance—as he and Freeh headed for the side door of the building. In a small, fenced-in lot in the shadow of a downtown viaduct, they started to get in Freeh's dark blue

179

Chrysler New Yorker, rented for him by the FBI. The typically contained Freeh seemed unusually irritated when he realized he had
forgotten something and had to go back upstairs. Hoback wondered
what was up.

On his return, Freeh slid into the driver's seat, unusual since,
when they traveled together, Hoback usually drove while Freeh used
the time to read documents pertaining to the case. As Freeh steered
the car up a ramp toward Forsyth Street and neared the sliding, au-
tomated chain-link security gate, he tossed a stapled stack of papers
in the agent's lap.

"This is what we're gonna do today," Freeh announced.

Hoback started reading and started sweating. It was an indictment, against Roy and Susan, for obstruction of justice and related
crimes, centered on the events surrounding Julie Linn-West.

"I want you to read it," Freeh said. "Make sure we haven't made
any mistakes. Make corrections, and when we get to Macon, we'll
make the corrections down there."

Macon—that meant the case would be brought in the Middle District of Georgia, where Moody was originally convicted, in 1972.
The trip usually took about an hour and a half. The New Yorker
pulled onto the interstate highway.

"Who all knows about this?" Hoback asked.

Only about ten people, Freeh replied, adding that some were getting briefed on it while they drove. Freeh rattled off those in the
loop: a handful of supervisors, Shapiro, FBI Director Sessions, Assistant U.S. Attorney Sam Wilson in Macon and a few others.

"And now you," Freeh said.

"Well, what about Stokes and Hinshaw, do they know?"

"Nope." And, Freeh informed the increasingly anxious agent,
they weren't going to know, and neither would the other investigators assigned to the case, until after the indictment.

This is bad, Hoback thought; Stokes will go ballistic, through the
ceiling. And the other agents would figure he knew about this all
along and didn't trust them. Hoback was sweating. What should
have been a triumphal procession after months of battle against a
brilliant enemy had become one of the most agonized car rides of
Hoback's life. It ranked with the drive from Memphis to Atlanta to
take the ATF job, leaving home for the first time, leaving his young
wife behind with small children and hitting the highway in a 1975
Cutlass he doubted would finish the trip. That was barely three years

past, and now he was rolling down the road on the biggest case ATF had going, anywhere.

All this secrecy, Hoback knew, was to prevent a press leak. Freeh was cool to the media anyway, and this case was already haunted by the publicity fiasco in Enterprise and Judge Freeman's resounding rebuke in February. If word of this got out early, Freeh informed Hoback, "we ain't doin' it."

The lawyer agreed to Hoback's request to at least notify ATF's director and apologized for not telling Hoback sooner.

"I'm glad you didn't tell me," Hoback said. ". . . I'd have been a nervous wreck," which, at the moment, he was anyway.

As he spoke, the lawyer was, as usual, purposeful, but calm, as if he might have been just as easily driving to the supermarket, giving Hoback a grocery list instead of the game plan to put Walter Leroy Moody Jr. in jail—except Freeh drove with the exigency of the moment, fast in the southbound lane. Hoback looked up to see, northbound, a chocolate-brown sheriff's car.

"He's got you, Louie," Hoback said.

"He's going the other way."

"He's pulling into the median strip now. . . . Louie, he's coming after us. You'd better pull over."

Blue lights flashed behind them, and Freeh pulled to the side and stopped. Hoback looked toward the patrol car and thought he discerned deep irritation in the deputy's face. The local lawman, tall, trim, clean-cut, in aviator glasses and a campaign hat, beckoned with one finger, as if to say, "Come here." Freeh and Hoback got out of the Chrysler and the deputy pointed at Brian. "Not you," the deputy said, then he pointed at Freeh. "Him."

Hoback, in plainclothes and packing a gun, put his hands on the car for safety's sake, then said, "Hey, we're federal agents."

"You're what? Fed-er-al agents!"

The cop turned, took off his hat, and flung it in his squad car, then cut loose with a tirade that exaggerated their transportational transgressions.

"Well, I'm sorry, officer . . . ," offered Freeh. The two federal men explained they were running late and trying to make up time.

"Y'all get in your car and get out of my county," came the terse reply. Hoback's irrepressible boyish smirk sneaked onto his face at some odd times, and this was one of them.

"You think this is funny?" snapped the deputy.

"No, sir."

"Y'all just go on. And be careful."

Back in the car, the agent flashed the prosecutor his what-did-I-tell-you look. Freeh, in mock lawyer talk, said, "The guy stated some material facts incorrectly." Both men broke out laughing. The tension broke too. Hoback still knew Stokes might tear him to pieces, but he no longer obsessed over it. Having stayed out of jail, they moved on to Macon to make sure Moody could not do the same. That afternoon, the grand jury indicted Roy and Susan Moody for obstruction of justice, bribery, subornation of perjury, witness tampering and obstructing a criminal investigation.

Freeh offered to let Hoback drive back to Atlanta to help out in the arrest, but it was uncertain whether he would get there in time. Hoback badly wanted to see the cuffs clicked on Roy Moody, but he opted to wait in Macon.

———

Shortly before six P.M., a crowd of agents showed up at the Moodys' door on Skyline Drive. Susan answered. Bill Grom, the deputy marshal, along with FBI Agents Tracey North and Glen Hunter, had been designated ahead of time to arrest Susan, who seemed to Grom just as she had every other time he'd seen her—emotionless, an automaton. But that belied what Susan Moody felt inside. She was suddenly living one of the happiest days of her life, just being free from Roy. She was ready to sit in jail for fifty years, so long as her reward was getting away from her husband.

John Behnke from the FBI, Postal Inspector John Farrell and David Hyche, the rookie ATF agent who had spotted the odd pipe in the Chamblee basement, comprised Roy's arrest team. They moved past Susan and split up. Hyche headed straight for Roy's study, a cluttered lair looking like a law library crossed with the back room at a pawnshop. Moody was there, on the phone, calmly telling somebody agents were coming in his house. Hyche stood in the doorway and called out to Behnke and Farrell. Somebody told Moody he was under arrest. I'm on the phone to my lawyer, came the reply.

FBI supervisor Harold Jones took the phone away and hung it up. Moody said little else, other than asking about Susan. Hyche patted him down and inventoried his wallet, which contained $241. Hyche, trained as an emergency medical technician, was also assigned to look after Moody's physical well-being and checked the handcuffs to make sure they weren't cutting off his circulation. Five minutes after their arrival, investigators had Moody in custody and on the road. Hyche again checked the circulation in Moody's hands. The suspect said he was uncomfortable but his hands were okay. John Farrell read him his rights, which Moody said—of course—he understood. The prisoner asked to see the arrest warrant. He not only got to see it, but Farrell read it to him. Moody asked where he was going. Macon, came the response. The suspect said little else on the ride, other than making short, calm responses to inquiries about his comfort. Hyche would later recall that while most people under arrest either look at you for sympathy, as if they want to make a deal, or with smoldering enmity, neither inclination was manifest in Roy's visage. Barely more than an hour after leaving Rex, the entourage reached the federal courthouse in Macon.

Once it had been confirmed Moody was in custody, Freeh had cleared Hoback to call the Atlanta ATF office, where he reached ASAC Rich Rawlins, who was stunned.

"You're kidding me?" said the man who six months before had written Moody's name on the back of Bob Holland's retirement notice, based on Lloyd Erwin's luncheon recollection.

"No. I'm not kidding you. We arrested him today." Hoback explained about the secrecy and recapped the day's events.

"I gotta find Stokes."

But Frank Lee got to him first, calling from the Moodys' house. Lee didn't like the way it went down either. He was summoned to the task force office on a pretense, and an FBI official stopped him when he tried to leave to make a phone call to alert his bosses about what was happening. There would be no leak, the FBI man warned. Lee felt as if he were under house arrest. He too expected Stokes to be furious, and he was right. The ATF SAC had just driven eight to ten hours on his way back from vacation and was not in a good mood anyway, a condition probably exacerbated when, during the call from Lee, the call-waiting on Stokes's home phone clicked in and Stokes's boss at ATF headquarters let him know about the indictment and arrest. "I know. I'm watching it on television," was his sarcastic response. The way Stokes saw it, he was supposed to tell headquarters what was going on, not the other way around. Stokes told Lee, whom he had known close to twenty years, he'd never been so disappointed in him.

Moody wore safari shorts, rumpled, like his hair, a white T-shirt with some kind of aviation crest on the breast, and the handcuffs binding his wrists behind his back as Behnke and Farrell, one holding each arm, walked him across a loading dock and into a door by which Hoback stood like a sentry until the others were inside. Moody was uncuffed and placed in a holding cell. David Hyche sat in an adjoining area, out of sight but within earshot, not ten feet from the star prisoner. Hyche heard the suspect talking and thought, at first, Roy was talking to him. The young investigator got up and walked toward the cell, but the prisoner just looked at the floor, mumbling, not even acknowledging Hyche's presence. Roy Moody, the agent realized, was talking to himself.

About an hour after Moody's arrival, Bruce Harvey and Michael Hauptman made it to the Macon courthouse. They met with Roy in a small, spartan room with a chain-link partition between attorneys and client. Early in the conversation, one of the lawyers made a dramatic revelation concerning the strength of the government's case—one witness didn't find the exact words nearly so memorable as the reaction they got. Instantly, Roy's eyes rolled back in his head and he fell flat backward, his skull bouncing off the cement floor with an audible whack. Hauptman ran for help, but by the time the deputy marshals got there, Moody was coming around.

His initial appearance before a judge that night lasted less than ten minutes, a formality. The critical proceeding, the one that might set the course for the rest of the mail-bomb investigation, would be the detention hearing, in which the government would attempt to convince a federal judge the Moodys should be held without bail pending trial. That hearing commenced the afternoon of July 12.

———

"These two defendants involve a serious risk that they will obstruct, attempt to obstruct, threaten, injure, intimidate, and attempt to do so with respect to these witnesses," said Sam Wilson, a lanky, likable lawyer with a country twang.

"Mr. Moody is a dangerous person. He has been since 1972. . . . Mrs. Susan Moody, we expect to show that she assisted Mr. Walter Leroy Moody in his endeavors in recent years and that she serves primarily as his contact with the outside . . . his messenger and legman, so to speak."

Bruce Harvey predictably proclaimed the presumption of innocence, suggested Moody was not a threat to witnesses the government was watching after anyway, and argued Roy was entitled to bail and had the wherewithal to make bail in a reasonable amount. Susan's lawyer, a federal public defender from Atlanta named Stephanie Kearns, offered no opening statement.

The government's first witness was Warren Glover, a well-spoken, forty-three-year-old Georgia native with a master's degree in psychology. In 1982, he went to work at a Moody company called Superior Sail Drives. Roy had developed an engine to power sailboats when they had no wind to propel them back to the dock. Glover testified Roy took out $750,000 "key man" life-insurance policies on him and two other employees, Daniel Fiederer and Timothy Williams. Eventually there was a trip to the Florida Keys to test the engine, and one last outing, ostensibly to get some underwater photos. But before Glover got to the heart of the narrative, Harvey asked if he could approach the bench.

"You may."

"I understand where the government is going with this," Harvey told Judge Wilbur Owens Jr. in hushed tones. "This evidence goes to a 1983 prosecution in Florida for attempted murder against Mr. Moody of this gentleman right here. The end result of that prosecution was a hung jury after a trial and a nol-pros of the charges after that. . . . What I'm doing is moving . . . to prohibit them from continuing on and presenting evidence of that kind of material because it just doesn't go to the issues that are before Your Honor. The fact that he went to trial in 1983 for attempted murder, I mean, we'll stipulate that he did, there was a hung jury, and then the charges were dismissed."

"Will you stipulate that he attempted murder . . . ?" asked Howard Shapiro. Tall, with dark, thick, unruly hair and a gangling comportment, he looked even younger than he was.

Harvey: "No. We'll stipulate that he went on trial, this man testified before a jury, the jury was hung, and then—that the state dismissed the charges, nol-prossed the charges against him."

Relations between lawyers for the two sides lacked the collegiality one often finds in Georgia courtrooms.

Shapiro: "We think it's highly relevant, that it will be one piece in a pattern of behavior of Mr. Moody, about his willingness to strike out violently for personal advantage."

The judge ruled for the government, and Glover plunged into a Benchleyesque tale of terror at sea:

A storm hit the night before, so the seas were rough. The three employees suggested not going out at all, but Moody insisted. Furthermore, he said sharks had been spotted in the harbor, and they were out close to four miles when they finally anchored the boat. Moody tied Williams, Fiederer and Glover together with what was supposed to be a safety line, run through the loops of their cutoff jeans, to keep the trio from drifting apart. All three went in the water together, none trained as underwater photographers. Their technique consisted of one person holding the camera and the other two holding him under while he took the pictures. They'd done it two or three times when suddenly the boat lurched forward at full speed. They tried to get hold of the craft, but Moody threw the ladder off. All three jumped up and held on to the side about thirty or forty-five seconds, but Roy grabbed their fingers, pried them loose from the side and pushed them off. He was saying, "I can't hold it, I can't hold it, I can't hold it."

Glover looked at Moody when he was peeling his fingers loose. Roy had a deranged, mad look on his face, like nothing Glover had ever seen before. He didn't know whether the lifeline to the boat broke or was cut, but it was loose and all three men were in the water. Tied together as they were, they couldn't float. They unclothed and separated in the rough sea. Glover guessed they were apart about two hours until he and Williams drifted back together.

"Have you seen Dan?" Glover asked.

He's on top of the channel marker, Williams said. Fiederer had climbed onto a marker standing perhaps thirty or forty feet high in the harbor.

Williams's head bled. Glover asked him what happened.

I was at the channel marker and Roy told me to come get on the boat, and as I swam to the boat and reached to get on, he hit me in the head with an anchor and pushed me underwater, came the response.

About the time they talked, they heard the boat coming back, Moody aboard. He passed them, screaming, "Get on the boat," but never slowed down. He made four or five passes at full throttle. The first time, Glover thought Roy was trying to get close, but after that, he should have known Glover's position. Glover believed Moody was trying to run him over.

He kicked off the boat with his hands and feet, one time diving under the hull. Then the boat went away and Glover was alone again for maybe an hour. Then Moody and the boat returned.

I found the ladder. Get on the boat, Roy said.

Glover was tired. It was either get back on the boat or drown. He chose the boat.

The first thing Glover did was hit his soon-to-be-former boss two or three times, getting him in a sitting position. Then he told him to bring a flare gun out of the cabin. Roy handed him the flare gun and Glover fired two rounds to summon the Coast Guard, which he spotted in the harbor.

You have a third round to fire, Moody told him.

"If I fire it, if you come toward me, the third round's yours."

When the Coast Guard arrived, Glover said, "The man's tried to kill us. Can I get on your boat?"

But Glover was told to go ahead and take the boat in, and that another sailboat had picked up one of the other men and that the third would be picked up too. Glover took the boat into Bonefish Harbor, then hired a man to take him back out to fetch Fiederer and Williams off the other sailboat.

———

Hauptman cross-examined Glover, reemphasizing that Moody was not convicted in the case, and eliciting that Moody was suing Glover. Stephanie Kearns established Glover did not believe Susan was involved in any plot to kill him.

The next witness was a licensed polygrapher who testified Moody solicited him to falsify a polygraph test for $1,000. He declined the money and reported the incident to the Board of Polygraph Examiners. Cross-examination by Harvey couldn't change the facts. Again, the cross by Susan's lawyer was brief.

"Mr. Williams, back in 1983 during your dealings with Mr. Moody, you did not have any dealings, did you, with a Susan McBride?"

"No."

"And you don't know of her, do you?"

"No."

After hearing from a lawyer involved in Moody's tangled litigation against an Atlanta bank, the prosecution played videotape excerpts and other highlights of Julie Linn-West's undercover work, mostly introduced during ATF Agent Bill Bass's testimony, which was often interrupted by objections from Harvey when Freeh was asking the questions, and objections from Freeh during Harvey's interrogation. Postal Inspector John Paul followed Bass on the witness stand with revelations suggesting Moody's audacity had not suffocated under the surveillance he'd suffered since early in the probe. Paul talked about a consent agreement with the Postal Service Roy had signed in 1982 in behalf of the Associated Writers Guild of America and a related company, the North American Data Verification and Testing Service. Then Paul recounted the administrative law judge's order on April 30, 1990, to detain the mail for the two organizations, after an alleged breach of the agreement. The shocker came when he described Moody's formal response to the action, made through Mike Ford and including a copy of the consent decree—or what purported to be the consent decree. It turned out to be a phony, altered in key areas. Ford told a postal lawyer he got the document from Moody himself. Scamming a little old lady with a bogus document is one thing. But daring to defraud an outfit that investigates fraud for a living, especially when you are probably under more intense scrutiny by federal law enforcement than any other man in America, rises to breathtaking heights of chutzpah.

Paul was still on the stand when court recessed at nine P.M., to resume the next morning. Prosecutor Sam Wilson called the judge's attention to Moody's demeanor.

"He's been sitting behind me and I have observed he's been writing notes and reading documents and conferring with his lawyers, watching the proceedings. He appears to be fully alert and aware of everything that's going on."

Moody's ability to help with his defense would be relevant to any future attempts Moody might make to claim insanity or diminished capacity.

"The court has carefully observed the defendant," Judge Owens said, "and observed that he has been awake and attentive and participating in the proceeding."

Hoback considered it unprofessional to stare at the defendants, but he stole glances here and there and thought he detected that smug self-assurance in Moody again, as if he didn't expect detention. The agent was impressed with the courtroom work of Freeh and Shapiro, but thought they too were brimming with bravado.

The next day would say whose self-confidence was self-delusion. The next day was also when Howard Shapiro mentioned the bombings.

———

The government contended the Moodys should be held without bond so they could not continue to obstruct witnesses, and since bombing the judiciary is certainly obstructionist, the bombings were relevant to the hearing. But the young prosecutor had barely uttered the word *bomb* before Harvey asked for another bench conference. The judge quickly moved the proceeding into his chambers—out of the hearing of the press and public.

Shapiro referred to "substantial evidence" linking Roy to the bombs, and as for Susan, "the evidence overwhelmingly establishes that she functions at his requests, at his behest, carrying out all of his schemes, and that they are together virtually all the time. . . . The production of four mail bombs meticulously produced is something that takes quite a bit of time and would be difficult to hide from one's spouse and close companion, so that at a minimum, it is reasonable to infer knowledge on Mrs. Moody's part of Mr. Moody's mail-bombing activities."

While Moody himself had long ago described himself on TV as a suspect in the bombings, there had been scant official confirmation. Now the defense, naturally, didn't want the bombing allegations aired in public.

"This is no ordinary situation," Harvey argued. "We're talking about evidence of what has been described as the number one priority crime in the United States right now by George Bush . . . and we're talking about using that in public before there's been any charges preferred."

The judge had sided with the prosecution on a number of objections to this point, but went with the defense on this one, suggesting the bomb information could prejudice Moody's right to a fair trial.

"If the government wants to charge him with that crime, they have a right to do so," Owens said.

The government had the right. But they didn't have the evidence. The outcome of the detention hearing, however, kept them in the hunt. The judge locked up Moody with no bond.

"He utilizes the court system in a way that it is not intended to be utilized," Owens observed. "He takes the offense, using tactics designed to deter others from using the system in the way that it is intended to be used.

"He, in the court's best judgment, as a human being, is a danger to other persons, a danger to the community; if not controlled, [he] could be expected to attempt to retaliate against those who are witnesses against him."

The government failed to get the same for Susan, although one of the conditions of her release on bail might have been just as good: no contact with Roy.

15

And the Devil Leaned Back and
Did Us a Mail Bomb

Even after the hearing, Brian Hoback, for one, felt no particular
high from Moody's arrest. Roy had yet to be indicted in the case that
could keep him off the street forever. The government put it suc-
cinctly in secretly filed court papers: "Normal investigative procedures have been tried and have failed or reasonably appear to be
unlikely to fully succeed if tried." It echoed what John Behnke's earlier affidavit said, with two key differences. First, months had passed
since that initial assessment by Behnke; that the same could still be
said testified either to Moody's cunning or innocence. Second, this
time the electronic surveillance for which authorities sought court
permission was unusual. They wanted to bug the High Security Unit
of the Atlanta Federal Penitentiary, where the suspect sat in solitary
confinement pending trial.

Behnke acted as affiant once again, noting in his statement
Moody "regularly talks and whispers to himself." Once again, a
judge approved.

That authorities made a public plea for help finding the typewriters similarly signaled the search for physical evidence in the bomb
case remained frustrating. These days, Moody's letters were handwritten, not typed. He wrote to Stephanie Kearns in Atlanta, one of

Susan's lawyers, with "information Susan must have to defend her case," prefaced, however, with something else.

"Sometimes Susan and I would go out to eat and I would be preoccupied about first one thing or the other," he began. "She would become annoyed by my lack of attention and grab my hand and shake me, saying, 'Will you look at me!' I sure would love to look at her and touch her now."

Soon he dispatched another message to Sandra Popson, Susan's lawyer in Macon, a letter suggesting that, while Roy Moody's person was locked up, the layman litigator in him remained unfettered, even in his element.

"As you will note my theory of defense involves prosecutorial misconduct," he postulated. "In my view, intrinsic to that defense is the need to show how the intense psychological war directed against Susan and myself affected us.

"I consider it essential that I meet with a psychologist or psychiatrist familar with psychological war and behavior modification tactics. I want him or her to explain to the jury the effects of such torment.

"I strongly suggest that Susan do the same, using a different expert. I feel it would be much more effective if two 'different' authorities corroborated each others [sic] testimony that mitigated our culpability while increasing that of the government. I think Susan knows the government can gain access to the doctor's records without difficulty."

Roy outlined other key elements of his theory: he would maintain he was convinced agents were conspiring to entrap him and Susan and "ultimately cause our wrongful execution"; Roy determined the only way he could expose the conspiracy—and save Susan's life, along with his own—was in the public forum a trial would provide; thus he intentionally misled agents into thinking he was attempting to influence Julie's testimony so he could get himself arrested.

Regardless of how far-fetched the story read, Roy miscalculated. He was in for a surprise—probably many surprises—where his young wife was concerned. Susan and her lawyers were developing a drastically different defense from what Moody outlined. In August, Susan started seeing Dr. Marti Loring, a clinical social worker who had testified in cases involving allegations of spousal abuse and was executive director of the Atlanta-based Center for Mental Health and Human Development, which specialized in family-violence issues. Dr. Loring had a soft voice, big, engaging brown eyes and auburn hair short but for long wisps sinuating pixie-style down from her temples and about her brow. She came across as immensely bright and capable, but with a delightfully offbeat way about her. She found Susan at first terrified, anxious and depressed. The young woman hardly spoke above a whisper, but in any case had difficulty trusting enough to talk about her situation. The doctor found her patient, at times, shocked, numb or depressed. Susan had contemplated suicide. Such characteristics added up to posttraumatic shock disorder, but that wasn't the diagnosis that explained most fully why Susan felt so free even as she headed to jail, and it wasn't the diagnosis that would have the most impact on Susan's future.

"Ms. Moody has had symptoms characteristic of the Battered Woman Syndrome," Dr. Loring wrote in one report, "including isolation, depression, terror, learned helplessness, financial dependence and low self-esteem." She loved her husband and she feared him. She depended on him. She was easily manipulated. He controlled every physical and emotional aspect of her life. Susan was coerced; her spirit, as Loring saw it, imprisoned. The social worker knew about the choking incident and the arm-twisting, but to her, the case of Susan McBride showed the power of *emotional* abuse, which could be every bit as potent as its physical counterpart. Loring found that Susan unquestioningly performed whatever tasks Roy set before her. For Susan, obedience was how she survived.

Unable to reach satisfactory financial arrangements with Roy, Harvey and Hauptman left the obstruction case. Moody had ten days to get a lawyer. Near the end of it, he asked the court to appoint Harvey back into the case. The judge said no. Moody asked whether, if he represented himself, he could have an investigator, law clerk, legal secretary and an "associate" attorney to assist him. Prosecutors opposed the taxpayer's picking up Moody's legal bills, citing the nearly $75,000 worth of property he attempted to put up for bail, a $43,000 inheritance check he cashed less than a year earlier and the $155,644 in assets listed for one of the Moodys' companies. He owned two planes, two sailboats, a motorcycle, a Datsun 280Z sports car and his '85 Ford pickup. Finally, U.S. Magistrate Judge Claude W. Hicks Jr. fashioned an arrangement whereby Moody's property would be held by the government as collateral for his legal fees.

Edward Tolley was trying a murder case when Hicks left a message for him. Tolley returned the call.

"Can you guess why I called?" the judge asked the defense lawyer.

From the way he put the question, Tolley *could* guess. He immediately agreed to represent Roy Moody in the obstruction case. He prided himself on never refusing a court appointment—and this one posed an irresistible challenge. Tolley's hadn't simply been the next name to come up in the regular rotation of court appointments. The stakes were too high for anything other than conscientious, competent counsel. Ed Tolley practiced in a college town, Athens, Georgia, and his client list ran the gamut from the University of Georgia athletic department to a fifteen-year-old serial killer, in whose defense Tolley succeeded in gaining from the Georgia Supreme Court a precedent-setting bar to the execution of juveniles. He had lots of experience with murder, having tried sixteen death-penalty cases without a single client sentenced to die.

A dapper but not ostentatious dresser, Tolley was clean-cut and black-haired, with a neat mustache on a smooth, mildly swarthy face. He parlayed studied Southern charm, legal ability and confidence into a courtly courtroom manner that seemed to win him at least the affections of judges, if not always their rulings. Two things Tolley knew he didn't handle especially well: liquor and losing. Now the test was how he would handle Roy Moody, who went through lawyers like a hypochondriac goes through doctors. Judge Hicks had Tolley fax some biographical information. The magistrate personally delivered it to Moody to let him know the caliber of counsel he'd arranged.

The first face-to-face took place in the austere kitchen of the high-security unit at the federal pen. Tolley brought with him Mark Wiggins, a young attorney from his firm. Tolley assured his new client that, guilty or innocent, he would do everything he could for him. Innocent, Roy told Tolley. Otherwise, Roy said little in the three-and-a-half-hour conference. He wanted to talk about the bomb case, but Tolley didn't. Harvey still represented Roy in connection with the mail-bomb investigation.

Before the call from Judge Hicks, the defense lawyer had known little about the bomb case beyond what a casual consumer of the news knew. So he was surprised on his arrival to meet what seemed the stereotypical Southern gentleman, obviously intelligent, friendly and courteous to the point of deference, appending "sir" to his yeses and nos. Tolley couldn't help but notice Moody's electric eyes. Roy, in khakis and a T-shirt, sat across from the lawyer by a window. In later visits, Roy always seemed to prefer that perch by the window, sometimes in a thermal T-shirt, even when the weather was warm and muggy. Even when it was hot, Tolley noticed, Moody was cold. Tolley eventually had a doctor see Roy because he thought something might be physically wrong. He never found out what, other than Moody was just cold-natured.

But Roy didn't limit what he had to say to conversations with his lawyers. Ominous, if inconclusive, Moody mutterings picked up by the electronic monitoring:[*]

> *I'll assassinate you, I'll blow you . . . up.*
>
> *You screwed me one time, in secret. You put the screws, you should* [unintelligible] *a judicial rape at one time, in secret, it will never happen again!* [pause] *It will never happen again! You put the judicial raping to me one time and see? I'll guarantee you, it will never happen again. Now you, you don't believe me, you're in for a rude awakening.*
>
> *And the devil leaned back and did us a mail bomb. Man, if you hadn't delivered the mail bomb, what in the heck would the government expect, fella? Someone to . . . take one out without a gun!*
>
> *That's why if you find out that the person who was shot in the face has a pistol and is punishing the man who shot him in the face, it is a different story. It's natural under the circumstances. The circumstances in this case is, I was subjected to a judicial raping by a court and a bomb jury.*

On October 4, Roy scored a legal victory. District Judge Wilbur Owens, who was to have heard the obstruction trial, recused himself. He said little in his order beyond "my impartiality might reasonably have been questioned." Owens had been involved in pretrial proceedings in Moody's 1972 case in Macon. The issue of his removal had been raised in a handwritten motion by Roy himself, then cemented in a motion by Ed Tolley. Owens was eventually replaced by District Judge Anthony A. Alaimo, whose office was in the coastal-Georgia town of Brunswick.

But that small success, however redolent it was of headier times in

---

[*]Controversy later developed about the audibility of government intercepts. With that qualification, I am using the government's version of what was said.

February and March, was dwarfed by the legal action Moody found out about soon after. Roy got word Susan was filing for divorce. He felt faint and was taken to the hospital for a check, followed by his return to the high-security unit and a twenty-four-hour suicide watch lasting several days. Moody was interviewed by a psychiatrist and the watch stopped. But a few days later—because the divorce filing hit the news, Moody surmised—the watch was instituted once more.

Moody complained, claiming it was "detrimental to my defense." He needed his concentration to assist his lawyer in preparing his case, or so he explained in a memo to the warden.

"I should call to your attention," the memo said, "I have no history of attempted suicide and have not been diagnosed as being suicidal. And, for the record, I would like to state emphatically that it is the furtherest thing from my mind."

Susan filed the divorce complaint herself—*pro se*—having learned from a master of the art. "The marriage between the parties is irretrievably broken," it said.

"There is no property to be divided. The marital home, aircraft, boats, vehicles and personal property belong to the husband."

Though they'd been together for years, the divorce papers noted the Moodys' marriage only took place around October 13, 1989. Close to the same time the divorce papers were served, FBI agents talked with another woman about dealings with Moody in the fall of 1989. She had taken an overnight trip with Roy to Chattanooga, Tennessee, less than a half-day's drive from Atlanta, in what could hardly, from Moody's point of view, be described as a spontaneous failing of the flesh; Moody contacted her through a personal ad, then wooed her in letters dated before and after his marriage to Susan. "I don't smoke or use drugs," Moody wrote. "I do drink socially but never get bombed."

Roy, however, maintained Susan was the only woman he ever loved in his unusual "Response to Complaint for Divorce."

> *In my wildest nightmare, I never thought my last communication with you might be this response to your complaint for divorce.*
>
> *The general perception is that our marriage of one year has come to an end.*
>
> *However, in my mind and in my heart, my marriage to*

you began as I watched you pick out the various items you needed to spend the few days we shared on Jekyll Island nearly ten years ago.

Each day that has followed, my love for you has grown. Today it is more profound and complete than ever. Tomorrow it will be stronger. I do not have the capacity to control it, nor do I want to.

I have the uncanny ability to recall in vivid detail the countless tender moments we have shared. I have so many wonderful memories of you. They are my strength and my weakness.

I have been told that everyone you have come in contact with since our arrest has tried to get you to divorce me. I can understand how such a relentless force could become irresistible.

However, when I recall how you have expressed your love for me in so many beautiful and convincing ways, I can not belive [sic] *you no longer love me.*

You are the only woman I have ever loved, and my faith in our relationship has provided more meaning and stability to my life than anything.

You are the only person I can trust, and for me to believe your love for me has died, would require you to sit me down, look into my eyes and tell me it was over.

I hope that when the phoney investigations are over you will sit me down and explain how you feel. If you still love me, I want us to continue to share our lives together. If you don't I will force myself to accept it. But I need to hear it from your lips, and I need for you to be gentle with me because I have no defenses when it comes to you.

It would be so sad for us to win the legal battles then not be able to locate each other. If you move, please keep my attorney advised of your address when you are free to do so. His name is Ed Tolley. . . .

I have made two payments on the house so you should still have access to it. You and your Dad are welcome to anything there, tools, machinery etc. I'm sure you know that.

Give Max [the name of their Great Dane] *a big hug for me and tell him I still love him too.*

Susan never laid eyes on it.

Marti Loring dated her psychosocial evaluation of Susan October 17. "Susan Moody suffers from the Battered Woman Syndrome," it began. "She developed this disorder in 1981 after becoming involved in a relationship with Roy Moody. During this relationship, she experienced emotional and physical abuse."

The report detailed the abuse and its ramifications and ended with an update: "There has been considerable improvement in her depression and self-esteem since her separation from Mr. Moody in July of 1990. She has obtained a job and is attending college."

The diagnosis would be pivotal in a court motion by Sandra Popson in Susan's behalf. Perhaps surprising no one unless it was Roy himself, Popson's idea of how to pursue the case veered sharply from the entrapment-based theory Roy espoused in his earlier letter. Instead Susan's lawyer outlined a defense underpinned by the contention Susan *believed* Roy when he told her Julie Linn-West and JoAnn Ekstrom corroborated his story about Gene Wallace planting the bomb. She believed Roy, the theory went, when he claimed government agents were intimidating Julie, trying to get her to lie to the grand jury about her 1988 testimony. Roy, according to Popson's papers, convinced Susan his 1972 sentence was unjust.

The motion referred to the battered-woman syndrome as the reason Susan accepted Roy's version as the truth. "She obeyed his requests and directions, and they seemed reasonable to her because of his dominant hold over her," the motion read. "Susan Moody was a compliant tool in Roy Moody's hands. She was easily manipulated and lied to."

In pursuing such a defense in a trial, Susan's side would want to call witnesses who could describe the surveillance on the Moodys, the media attention on the bomb case and the effect of the probe on their family and friends.

"The bombing investigation and its effects are crucial to an understanding of what Susan Moody knew and, thus, why she believed Roy Moody's version of events," the Popson motion said, adding her defense "will give the bombing investigation prime billing."

And the bombing investigation was one thing Roy Moody's lawyers likely did *not* want mentioned in front of any jury hearing the obstruction case. So Susan's motion asked the judge to sever her case from Roy's, to try them separately.

So far she had moved to split from Moody in a marriage and a court case. Such moves might have proved grievous personal injuries to Roy, but the question was, what implications would they have for the mail-bombing investigation? One man on each side of the equation picked up clues at a hearing at which both Moodys had to be present.

Both Ed Tolley and Brian Hoback took note as Susan walked past Roy and sat down without so much as a glance at him. Hoback hoped it a harbinger of something; Tolley viewed it as the beginning of the end.

The defense lawyer, however, had in mind a strategy that might diminish Susan's importance to the case. He had already filed preliminary notice of an insanity defense.

————

If Moody was the mail bomber, why he targeted Vance, Robinson and the NAACP in particular remained mysterious. Howard Shapiro walked the few blocks from task force headquarters to the Eleventh Circuit courthouse and looked through opinions Moody was suspected of seeing at the Eleventh Circuit courthouse. He took particular interest in an opinion by Judge Vance favorable to the Jacksonville NAACP.

"The remoteness in time of the school authorities' intentionally discriminatory actions is irrelevant," the decision said.

By contrast, when the Eleventh Circuit turned down Moody's efforts to use Julie Linn-West's supposed new evidence to overturn his 1972 conviction, the court ruled the legal vehicle Moody used, called a writ of error coram nobis, "cannot be available for new evidence only potentially relevant to a factual issue decided long ago by a jury. . . .

"Such a remedy would prolong litigation once concluded, thus thwarting society's compelling interest in the finality of criminal convictions."

In other words, loosely interpreted, in the Jacksonville NAACP case, violations of civil rights were never too old to fix. But in Roy Moody's case, his claims were too old to reconsider.

16

Susan's Song

By November 1990, investigators closest to the case were convinced Moody was the mail bomber, though there was still no direct, physical evidence to pin Moody to the bombs even after one of the most technologically advanced forensic searches ever made. The case in hand was perilously circumstantial, but nearly eleven months had passed in this high-profile, high-pressure probe. So prosecutors made a bold move, getting a federal grand jury to return a lengthy indictment against Roy Moody for the mail bombings and related crimes.

Attorney General Dick Thornburgh and FBI Director William Sessions stood side by side at the news conference.

"It is absolutely essential," Sessions said, eyes sweeping the room, "where a country determines that it will rule itself by law that we give the strong support to our courts and the protection that our courts need and should be afforded. So today is a particularly important day to us."

Said Thornburgh, "Much as I'd like to discuss the evidence in detail, I think you recognize it would be inappropriate to go beyond what is stated on the face of the indictment at this time. The evidence will be presented in open court at the time of the trial.

"The indictment charges that he acted alone. No investigation is really ever closed, however."

Bruce Harvey went on TV too. "You know what they do is they try to exhaust every avenue available to them, and they apparently have exhausted those avenues and what we have now is what we got. There ain't no more. The fat lady has sung."

A reporter asked Harvey if he had reason to believe Susan would testify against his client.

"Other than the fact that she is not in the indictment, not named as a codefendant in the indictment, which could give us a good guess, I have no specific knowledge of that."

Susan had not cut a deal, not yet anyway.

The next day Moody was arraigned on the mail-bomb charges. Several agents attended, including Hoback and FBI Agent Todd Letcher. After the hearing, Letcher went in a room to take another set of prints from Roy. The other investigators waited outside, except for Hoback. Hoback wanted to be in there. Much as in the confrontation when the first prints were taken, in the mobile home, Hoback wanted Moody to remember him, to know Brian Hoback had a part in putting him here. This time, Moody said nothing in response.

But something else was happening the day after the mail-bomb indictment, a meeting in Macon. Louis Freeh was there, with David Hyche from ATF, FBI Agent Glen Hunter and Sandra Popson.

And Susan.

It took place in a conference room in Popson's office in a historic building in downtown Macon. As Susan understood it, the government had approached Popson after a court hearing. What even her lawyer may not have known is that Susan had wanted to talk to investigators from the very beginning, had even hoped she would be arrested. Then, her life would at least—at last—change. But she had been afraid they wouldn't believe her, which might have seemed strange to those who haven't, in spheres from lovemaking to law-breaking, served a master manipulator like a slave.

Louis Freeh made apologies for what Susan's family had been through. In court, he came across as a particularly prosecutorial prosecutor. But now he looked Susan straight in the eye and she felt him warm, unthreatening, not at all accusatory. The two agents on the trip said little, but Hunter didn't fit the starchy stereotype she attached to FBI agents. He spoke slowly and came across as fatherly. Hyche was about her age. She appreciated the respect they seemed to show.

Susan still trained her eyes downward. She covered her mouth with her hand. Popson did most of the talking for that side, and Su-

san didn't say much, but she said enough. When she revealed she
had bought some typewriters, she could feel the excitement in the
room. Even Popson's face changed. The lawyers got together and
hammered out an agreement.

Susan would plead guilty to one count of the obstruction indictment, a conspiracy charge carrying a five-year maximum. If she
complied with everything else in the pact, she would not be prosecuted in Georgia or Alabama—state or federal—for any crimes relating to the mail-bomb murders of Vance and Robinson, to her
activities concerning Superior Sail Drives, the Associated Writers
Guild of America, Inc., or North American Data Verification and
Testing Service, Inc., among other things. Her end of the deal included full cooperation with the FBI or other law enforcement officials and a willingness to testify truthfully to a grand jury or in court.
The rest of the charges she faced in the obstruction case would be
dropped at her sentencing. Also, charges she had picked up in Atlanta for perjury and contempt would be dismissed. Prosecutors
would tell the judge and the probation department about Susan's
cooperation, but the sentence would be up to the judge.

If the young woman were to lie to investigators or break the law
again, her immunity, in essence, would be null and void and her
own statements could be used against her. She signed it "Susan
McBride-Moody."

Freeh told her she'd be working with Hunter, Hyche and a third
agent, a woman. And about the last thing he said before leaving was
that they would be doing a lot of work together and he suggested
she consider moving into a government-supplied apartment. Meanwhile Hoback and other agents waited much of the day and into the
night for word on what had happened. Finally, Freeh returned and
investigators crowded his office to hear Susan had agreed to a plea
bargain.

The third agent in Susan's entourage would be Tracey North, a
young, reserved law-school-trained FBI agent, who with Hyche,
Hunter and Susan, set out in a car headed for Brunswick, the
coastal-Georgia city five hours from Atlanta where Judge Alaimo
presided. Hyche and Hunter did most of the talking that first trip,
trying to draw Susan out. But she found it weird to be alone with the
agents for the first time in a car and slept much of the way. They
stopped at a restaurant where Susan ordered only fries, at which she

merely picked. Her weight had dropped to 112 pounds. Before the bombings she had weighed as much as 145.

Hoback noticed how skinny and pale she looked when she arrived at the back of the federal courthouse in Brunswick early the morning of November 10, a Saturday. He guided her entourage into the mail-dock entrance. He asked Susan how she was doing, but she said little. Once again, her gaze trailed downward. The hearing before Judge Anthony Alaimo would be quick and quiet, by design—no press present. Pleas are normally taken in open court; a secretive Saturday session for such a thing was extraordinary. Susan was there to plead guilty to the single count from the indictment, as her agreement mandated. The young woman had already committed to the course she would take, so, to her, the plea itself was not an occasion of great moment but a technicality, just something to get past.

The foursome—three federal agents and one shy girl—immediately got to work, heading from Brunswick to Jacksonville, about an hour down Interstate 95. It was the first of many jaunts across the Southeast where she would play tour guide, retracing the steps she had marched when Roy Moody was her drum major. Moody had always given Susan lists of things to do. And she said that, beginning in the summer of 1989—half a year or less before the bombs were mailed—he began giving her lists of things to purchase along with bizarre instructions on how to do it. She was to go to stores far from home, refrain from parking close to the entrances of stores she visited, keep her name a secret and avoid the sort of contact that would leave fingerprints. Sometimes she was supposed to wear a disguise, which was nothing new. She'd done it at least once in connection with the Julie Linn-West scam. And in 1985, when Moody ran newspaper ads in a thinly veiled search for helpers in one of his schemes, responses came to a mail drop in Smyrna, Georgia. To check the mail, Susan donned a black wig and fastened a mixing bowl under her clothes to look pregnant.

It was fitting that Susan's first foray with her handlers would be to Jacksonville; that was the destination on the first out-of-town trip she could remember involving Roy's lists. He went with her on that first expedition but waited nearby in a restaurant while Susan went into an Office Depot and bought scissors, boxes, tan package tape and brown wrapping paper. On another trip she dropped Roy at a Jacksonville library before setting out with her list of errands. Now back in Jacksonville more than a year later with the investigators, Susan, understandably, couldn't remember at first every place she'd been in the city and only vaguely recalled others. So they drove around a lot to catalyze her memory.

Once back in Atlanta, Susan was installed in a government-supplied apartment. She was provided with a rented car as well. The agents met with her nearly daily—Hyche, for instance, logged thirteen straight seven-day workweeks—usually at a designated time at her new place, which she kept meticulously neat and where she nearly always had refreshments for her visitors. Usually there was a predetermined, specific topic to work through. Susan never seemed impatient about it, though some topics took days to sort out. Glen Hunter took the lead in one of the early subject areas, concerning Titusville, Florida.

———

Roy hooked up with his old prison associate Ted Banks, in Titusville sometime in the early '80s. Thereafter Moody made several trips to the central-Florida town. Susan told the agents Roy had obtained a variety of items from Ted, including chemicals, a drill press and guns—interesting, since both Banks and Moody were convicted felons, legally forbidden from possessing firearms. She said Moody also got a grenade from Banks—an olive drab cylinder, flat-bottomed, with a pull-ring or some similar apparatus attached. Somebody showed her a photo of a tear-gas canister. Similar, she said.[*] The item had stayed in a sock at the Moody house, but after he got back from a trip in August 1989, he asked for it, and of course, she fetched it, never to see it again. August 1989 was when the tear-gas device detonated at the regional NAACP office in Atlanta.

Investigators had been to see Ted Banks several times before Susan's cooperation began. The visit where Postal Inspector Dave Kirkland noted Banks's welding tanks had been in early April. He was interviewed again that same month in Titusville and at the Russell Building in Atlanta. Banks said he had never heard Moody make derogatory statements about the civil rights movement, and he held fast to his position he did not believe Roy was involved in the mail bombings. In June, Terry Pelfrey, from the GBI, and Gary Morgan, from the Atlanta FBI office, interviewed him yet again in

---

[*]Banks says the item was actually a smoke bomb.

Titusville; that's when the old ex-con said he didn't want to talk to agents anymore, except from the witness stand, and he refused a polygraph test. Even when Roy's lawyer, Ed Tolley, and a private investigator, ex-FBI agent Tim Huhn, visited Banks on November 14, Banks essentially said Moody wasn't guilty of anything, though he did say the government had asked him about a letter to a lawyer he'd written at Roy's request. Banks indicated he had admitted the document was "a crock of shit." The next day, Banks had several more visitors, but they weren't from the Moody camp.

"Ms. Moody's information has already been corroborated in several respects; none of her information has proven to be unreliable," said Gary Morgan in the affidavit for the search warrants. Susan had reported Roy packed a number of guns into one footlocker, packed a second footlocker with chemistry books, among other things, and brought the trunks to Banks in Titusville.

When agents raided Banks's house, Frank Lee was among them. He asked Banks if he had any guns in the house, a standard question when executing a search warrant. "Yes," was the reply. A nine-millimeter pistol, new and still in the box, was under a sofa. Banks claimed he had bought it for a friend. Lee also asked Banks whether Moody had brought him any guns or footlockers on his trips to Titusville. No, Banks told him.

That didn't jibe with what investigators found when they searched a unit at All Purpose Storage in Titusville. There they discovered three footlockers, containing guns, ammunition, chemistry books, along with a copy of *The Anarchist's Cookbook*, a sort of do-it-yourselfer's guide to wreaking havoc through, among other means, homemade explosives. And there was pornography, including film from overseas, four home videos, one commercially obtained video, and magazines. In sum, the footlockers contained precisely the kinds of things Roy would presumably not have wanted federal investigators to find if they searched his house. A number of items had Roy Moody's name on them.

Informed about the discovery of the footlockers, Banks admitted he had lied, but claimed Moody had told him the trunks held only books. Banks also denied having a key for the footlockers. Told that a key on his key ring opened their padlocks, Banks said it was for a padlock in his workshop. At least three locks from the shop were checked; it opened none of them.

Other discoveries at Banks's home included a diagram for a remote-controlled bomb. "As God is my witness," he said, "I have never seen that paper before."

Banks again denied knowing about Moody's making bombs, or providing Moody with a tear-gas canister. He said he thought Moody was innocent of the bombings.

The next day, FBI agents Clifford Botyos and Morgan, ATF Agent Spanky McFarland and Postal Inspector John Paul showed up at the place where Banks worked and arrested him. The charge: felon in possession of a firearm.

"Cheap shot," the sixty-three-year-old boatbuilder said. "The gun is my mother's."

———

Susan felt no pressure from the agents to produce; she put pressure on herself to help as much as she could. Perhaps nothing in the months she worked with the trio of feds distressed her more than the failure to find the right typewriters. In June 1989, Roy had asked her to buy four of them in a manner, as she understood it, that would not draw attention to her. She found three of them at yard or garage sales. With the agents, she drove around neighborhoods where there had been such sales and identified thirty-two addresses whence a typewriter might have come. Roy told her he picked up the fourth on a trip back from Florida. She remembered him remarking about one of the machines, that one of the letters appeared raised above the others when typed. She suspected that in January 1990—which was after Moody's name first surfaced in the mail-bomb investigation—Moody threw one typewriter in Lake Lanier, the huge man-made lake about forty-five minutes north of Atlanta.

She was emphatic that she did *not* buy a typewriter in Enterprise, Alabama, though it seemed as if investigators asked her about it a hundred times. They even took her to Enterprise just in case she had visited and hadn't known it. They drove her by the boll-weevil statue and by Wayne O'Ferrell's store. But Susan was resolute that she had not been there.

Soon after her release, Susan had been hired at a building-supply store, but she was fired when details about her background were revealed. She simply left blank the space on the application where it asked whether she had ever been arrested. Susan considered herself a good employee and felt good to be working at something legitimate; even digging ditches twelve hours a day, she felt, would rank

ahead of running Roy's businesses. Eventually she took a job helping a woman named Eva Roswall at a hole-in-the-wall restaurant
that served hearty home-style vegetables and meats in plentiful portions. The place was in an old movie theater, and behind the restaurant Eva's husband had a recording studio and live-music showcase.
Her job never interfered with her cooperation with the government,
which was her top priority. Susan offered to let Eva replace her during the months when her travels with her retinue of agents kept her
away from work for long periods, but Eva had become not only boss
but friend and confidante and would not hear of her quitting. When
she did work, agents escorted her to and from the restaurant.

Ironically, for Susan, an emotionally battered woman, there was
no question about the investigators' earning her trust. The way she
saw it, she had nothing to lose by trusting them from the start. It
wasn't quite the same on the other side of the equation. Hyche
found himself, at first, trying to keep in mind that she might have
been in on the bombings. But she steadfastly denied knowing what
Roy had been up to, and in time he came to believe strongly she was
telling the truth, that her participation had been unwitting. Hyche
never noticed her hesitate when there was something useful she
could tell them about Roy Moody.

Besides Jacksonville, there had been a number of other list-driven
shopping trips in and out of Georgia. Among the items she'd
shopped for: pipe, acrylic tubing, a kitchen scale, stove exhaust
pipe, charcoal water filters, muriatic acid, balloons, metal end caps,
distilled water, X-Acto knives, dry ice, rat pesticide, a propane torch,
rain suits, shower caps, black paint, metal washtubs, rubber gloves,
string, big bolts, boxes in a variety of sizes, and nails. She said Roy also
asked her to shoplift some nails. Susan said no, fearing getting
caught even more than Roy's wrath for refusing. Roy, she related,
lifted them himself from a Kroger supermarket.

Many of the items matched, generically at least, the components
comprising the mail bombs, or equipment an extraordinarily meticulous bomb builder—which the man who killed Vance and Robinson
certainly was—might use to prevent detection. However, many of
the items—the muriatic acid, the dry ice—seemed to fall in neither
group. It became apparent Moody had been working on two endeavors in 1989. Investigators dubbed the first the Chemical Project.

It lasted most of July. Susan guessed Roy was trying to make some kind of liquid or gas and had come up with a distilling process. He worked mostly under the house in Rex, and he was cautious, making sure neighbors were not in their yards before he slipped into the crawl space. He told Susan to keep Max the dog away from the space, which she took to mean something dangerous was under way. At least once, she smelled burning charcoal throughout the house. Roy also worked in the front bedroom, designating it off-limits to Susan. She didn't know Hazel had reported a similar mandate concerning the room where she was injured by the explosion in 1972. Eventually, investigators came to a startling conclusion, which related to that first communiqué from the bomber in August 1989, the "Declaration of War."

> THE COURT'S FAILURE TO RENDER IMPARTIAL
> AND EQUITABLE JUDGMENTS IS DUE TO RANK BIAS
> AND THE MISTAKEN BELIEF ITS VICTIMS CAN NOT
> EFFECTIVELY RETALIATE.
> THEREFORE, CITIZENS OF DENSELY POPULATED
> CITIES SHALL BE SUBJECTED TO HIGH
> CONCENTRATION LEVELS OF CARBONYL CHLORIDE
> AND CYANODIMETHYLAMINOETHOXYPHOSPINE
> OXIDE. THE ATTACKS SHALL CONTINUE UNTIL
> WIDESPREAD TERROR FORCES THE COURT TO
> ADDOPT [sic] THE IMPARTIAL AND EQUITABLE
> TREATMENT OF ALL AS ITS HIGHEST PRIORITY.

However whacko the letter sounded in August of 1989, now it suddenly seemed something else. Moody, investigators decided, meant to manufacture the deadly war gas the letter threatened. Only after the Chemical Project failed, the government theorized, did Moody move on to the Other Project.

The NAACP tear-gas package would have been the dry run. He sent Susan for more boxes, for wrapping paper, mailing labels, postage and other items matching components of the package bombs. This time everything went into the front left bedroom, where the door was never locked but always closed; it was understood Susan would not enter it. She had no desire to, anyway. From the room once she heard a loud bang, an explosion. She was in the yard and thought the neighbors must have heard it too. About a month later, near Halloween, Roy had Susan take him down a nearby highway, late at night when other cars were scarce, and he stuck his arm out of the truck. He told Susan not to look. Another bang. Several weeks later, at midafternoon on a Sunday, Moody wanted to go for a ride, and he brought with him a metal pail holding something covered with a towel. He had Susan drop him off in woods. She was to return in about fifteen minutes, and when she did, she spotted in the bucket some sort of disfigured metal object. Roy said something about how he thought somebody driving by had "heard it."

She described Roy dumping items in a variety of places and, after the February search, burning some papers. She remembered twice taking Roy to hotels and signing him in under pseudonyms. Once in Chamblee, just north of Atlanta, Moody climbed out of the truck with two dark-colored garbage bags in hand, and in one of them she could make out the clear outline of a typewriter. The second hotel was in the same area, and she checked him in after first, at his request, picking up disposable shower caps. Investigators would theorize the shower caps were to prevent hair from falling into a package or a letter, where it might yield DNA.

Perhaps Susan's most important trip with Roy—and consequently, close to a year later, her most important trip with Hyche, Hunter and North—was to Florence, Kentucky. As she tells it, Roy didn't tell her exactly where to go to find the items on this latest list, so long as it was within a day's round trip. She departed about three A.M., November 21, 1989, headed toward Cincinnati, Ohio. By midmorning she decided Florence, Kentucky, would do. At the post office there she bought about $20 worth of cellophane packages containing stamps and Priority Mail labels. She picked up aluminum cake pans and canned peaches, both on her list. She got mailing labels. And she visited Ric Lohr's Quickprint, a copy shop in a strip mall, and made copies of several documents. She wore gloves, along with a coat, sunglasses, and a scarf on her head, and she placed open manila folders over the originals and over the tray where the copies slid out, so neither she nor anyone else in the store could see the copies. After doing all this, she went outside and placed the copies in plastic garbage bags, which she put in her Volkswagen Beetle before visiting another store in the shopping center to buy the shipping boxes described by Roy on his list.

It might seem incredible to some people that a young woman could drive hundreds of miles to copy a few sheets of paper and not succumb to the urge to read them, just as some doubtless would look askance at a wife's claim that her husband labored mysteriously in a bedroom in her house and she chose not to even sneak a peak. But David Hyche, for one, believed Susan. He thought she knew Roy was doing something illegal, but she didn't know what. He believed she did not look not because Roy didn't want her to, but because Susan did not want to know what he was doing.

When she headed back toward Florence with the agents, Susan didn't at first remember the name of the town. But once she came upon it, there was no doubt it was the right place. The foursome returned from Kentucky on Susan's birthday. It would be a while before the feds knew what kind of present Susan had given *them*.

17

Trial Run

Brunswick, Georgia, is about halfway between Jacksonville and Savannah and is home to the Federal Law Enforcement Training Center, where many of the mail-bomb investigators matriculated. Slightly south is Jekyll Island, turn-of-the-century vacation enclave for names like Rockefeller, Vanderbilt, Morgan and Pulitzer, owned now by the state of Georgia. Sea Island, still a bastion of big money and site of The Cloister, not a convent but a posh, old-school resort, is just the other side of a toll bridge from Brunswick, as is St. Simons Island, the lush and lovely location of hotels, beaches, golf courses, dream homes and Bloody Marsh, the scene, in 1742, of a successful ambush by Britain's Scottish Highlanders of Spain's crack Cuban Grenadiers. Some believe the battle helped stanch the Spanish expansion in North America. Now Brunswick was scene of the latest skirmish in Roy Moody's ongoing hostilities with the United States government.

Sam Wilson handled the opening statement for the prosecution table, where Freeh and Hoback also sat. Mostly he delivered a straightforward account of Moody's dealings with Julie Linn-West, JoAnn Ekstrom and Julie Ivey and an explanation of the specific charges in the indictment. Near the end, Wilson briefly addressed Moody's motive.

"One observation that you might make, that Mr. Moody wanted to get this '72 conviction out of the way for any of a number of rea-

sons. The first one that comes to mind is that he was so involved
with legal proceedings that he had aspirations of becoming a lawyer.
In 1986 when this was all going on, you could not be a lawyer in the
state of Georgia if you had a felony conviction. That's the reason for
all these activities surrounding this 1972 conviction."

Tolley's turn came. He introduced one of his law partners from
Athens, Jay Cook, who sat at the defense table with him. As was Tolley's custom, he delivered a preamble of perfunctory pleasantries,
referring to the jury as "ladies and gentlemen" almost every other
sentence and tossing in a homespun saying: "Each pot sits on its
own bottom." (Consider each charge separately, was his point.) Tolley even complimented the prosecutor for the great detail with
which he outlined the case. Then he got down to business.

"He has very gingerly stepped around the fact," Tolley said of
Sam Wilson, "that the three principal witnesses in the case against
Mr. Moody—that is Julie Linn-West, Julie Ivey and JoAnn Ekstrom,
the mother of Julie Linn-West—are, very frankly, an array of liars
and cheats. And there's no question about that."

According to Ed Tolley's defense, Roy Moody was the victim.

"We submit to you, ladies and gentlemen, that there were plenty
of people in this case, including various lawyers that Mr. Moody
hired, that, regardless of the fact that this was all harebrained, were
glad and willing to take his money. Not to take his money to counsel
and advise him, not to take his money to be their friend, not to take
his money to help him, not to help him because he was obviously
somewhat disturbed, but to simply take his money, ladies and gentlemen. And not a one of them will you see stand trial for the events
that have occurred in this case."

Tolley recounted Moody's 1972 conviction, his prison time and
his steadfast claims of innocence.

"It left Moody a disturbed man, an uncomfortable man, a man
who came out of prison with a lot of problems, a man who was vulnerable to the kind of people that work in strip joints* and take
their clothes off for money." Tolley knew, after all, this was a small-
town, South-Georgia jury.

"These type of folks recognize a victim when they see one. And

---

*An investigative report lists many jobs JoAnn Ekstrom had held over the years,
mostly in the beauty salon business. It also indicates that some years before the trial, and
prior to meeting Moody, she *had* been a dancer in an Atlanta lounge.

it's true enough that on these tapes Walter Leroy Moody sometimes appears rational, sometimes appears to be in control; but at all times, ladies and gentlemen—and you think about this—at all times it was these gals who were really in control because they, for example, were the ones that were running the tape recorders and they were, for example, the ones that had the television cameras, and they, for example, were the ones that knew what they needed to do to get immunity out of the case.

"Because in the final analysis, they were the ones that actually committed the crimes."

To dispute basic facts in the case would be futile, in the shadow of stacks of video and audiotapes. The argument would be over what those facts added up to. Hoback took notes while Tolley spoke. He thought the defense lawyer was effective, and that he seemed to be doing what Freeh had told Hoback he suspected Tolley would do; he was setting up an insanity defense.

"The man did it to simply clear his name," Tolley said. "If he's nuts for doing it, then maybe he's just nuts. But to him, being convicted of something he says he didn't do eighteen years ago and spending five years in the federal prison for it was important. And it left him, ladies and gentlemen, with a lot of scars."

Tolley added: "I submit to you that when the evidence is over and you go out to the jury room on the last day of this case that you'll find it far from intricate. You'll find it idiotic. You'll find it simplistic. You'll find it childlike. You'll find it the product of somebody who must really be confused."

It was late afternoon when Tolley finished. The witnesses would not begin until the next morning. Judge Alaimo sequestered the jury in a hotel with the usual admonitions to ignore news accounts about the case. "I assure you," he added, "that you will know more about this case when we get through with it than any of these news reporters will."

———

Bill Grom, who had recently left the Marshals Service to join ATF, was the first witness. Louis Freeh used him to introduce several of the documents and tapes involved in the case. Julie Linn-West was next.

With Freeh feeding the questions, she recounted the three-car accident in Kentucky in 1970 that left her in a wheelchair. She was diagnosed a quadriplegic, but she said she could move about as a paraplegic. She testified she kept her own household, supported her son and drove a car.

"I direct your attention to 1972," Freeh said. "Would you tell the jury, please, where you were living?"

"In 1972 I was living in Milwaukee, Wisconsin."

"Who were you living with at the time?"

"My mother and stepfather and my brother and sister."

"And when did you first come to Georgia?"

"In 1977."

The story advanced in Moody's recent appeals, of course, had been that she was in Georgia in 1972 and hanging out with Gene Wallace.

Freeh guided her to the 1988 hearing. "Did anyone pay you not to tell the truth?"

"Yes, they did."

"Who was that?"

"Walter Leroy Moody."

The prosecutor elicited that she was under oath when she lied in Macon, and also when she signed false affidavits. He was attacking her negatives head-on, thereby revealing them on his terms and limiting the emotive impact they would have if revealed for the first time during Tolley's cross-examination. She acknowledged she was currently getting $500 a month she understood to be from the FBI "to supplement my rental income." She acknowledged the government had agreed not to prosecute her for perjury in Macon if she agreed to tell the truth. Ms. Linn-West also admitted to the use and sale of drugs in the past. That out of the way, she described her entrée to Roy Moody, which had come through a friend, Julie Ivey.

"What was your financial condition at the time?" Freeh asked.

"I was in dire straits."

She recounted meeting Moody and agreeing to become his Gene Wallace witness. Linn-West recalled seeing Susan Moody regularly to practice the story in sessions lasting up to three hours.

"I was supposed to go to the Macon library, first of all . . . to let my face be seen so that if there were any questions as to if I was actually there, that there would be people that had seen me there.

"Also on the trip there they had showed me copies of newspaper articles concerning his charges brought against him in 1972, and I was supposed to go into the library and—they had given me a list of the microfilms I was supposed to ask for and actually go through the motions of looking at these particular articles that they had shown me concerning the 1972 case in Macon."

Susan went to the library with her, after stopping on a side road and donning a black wig, changing her glasses, adding makeup and a scarf around her neck. The idea, apparently, was for Susan to look older, to look like Julie's mother.

"I asked the librarian if she could instruct me on how to use the microfilm machines," Julie testified. "And then once I was finished reviewing the articles, we went back downstairs.

"There's a lost-and-found right before you go out the door, and I was instructed by Roy to ask the lost-and-found lady if there had been a Cross pen bearing my initials on it that had been found in the library, because last time I had been at the library, I was to have lost that pen and I was asking if it had been found and returned."

Julie Linn-West, of course, had never been to the library before that day, nor lost such a pen. But Roy's idea, she explained, was to let her face be known by the lost-and-found attendant.

Finally, her narrative reached the 1988 hearing.

"Do you remember leaving the witness stand or leaving the place where you were testifying and returning to the other part of the courtroom?" Freeh asked.

"I left the witness stand and went into the audience."

"And did Mr. Moody make any gesture to you at that time?"

"Thumbs-up and smiled and patted me on the back to let me know that I had done good."

Much of the rest of her testimony involved more recent events, especially her dealings with Moody once she began cooperating with the government. The prosecution, of course, made extensive use of the undercover tapes. And the tapes, to Ed Tolley, were devastating. As he readied for cross-examination, he knew he needed to tear into Julie Linn-West's motives and credibility, but also that he had to be careful not to tear so viciously into the young mother that he created sympathy for her among the jurors—or caused them to dislike him.

The defense lawyer eased into the hard stuff, making innocuous inquiry about where she had lived, where she had worked—"Just trying to find out a little bit about you," he said. Eventually he worked his way to the period when Julie Ivey stayed with her. Linn-West acknowledged they had both been involved with drugs.

"What were you doing?" Tolley asked.

"On a daily basis we would smoke marijuana, like five or six joints a day, and—"

"Excuse me for interrupting you."

"Excuse me."

"These folks may not know what a joint is," said Tolley, as if mindful, again, of the rustic jury pool. "Why don't you tell them?"

She complied, and he asked her some more drug questions.

"The reason I'm asking these questions, ma'am, is because I had gotten the impression that you were, quote, *financially destitute* when Mr. Moody met you." He underscored her earlier admission she used to sell drugs. "You had money from public assistance, you had money from child support, and Ms. Ivey had a job cleaning houses, and y'all had a little drug business going. Between all of those sources of income, as you said, you had enough money to keep your heads above water on a month-to-month basis; is that correct?"

"Barely, yes."

"So the truth of the matter is, when Walter Leroy Moody approached you with this scheme that you have described—that is, to help him set aside his 1972 conviction—while you wanted the money and you could certainly always use the money, you certainly didn't have to have the money, did you?"

"Yes."

"You think you had to have the money?"

"Yes."

"And the only way you thought you could get that was to participate in this scheme?"

"I thought it was an easy way out."

Tolley moved on to Susan's involvement. "Did you and Susan ever discuss the fact that Roy felt that morally he had been wronged by that 1972 conviction?"

"He felt that he had been wronged, yes."

"And I picked up somewhere also that even though you were doing this for the money and even though, apparently, you knew it was wrong, you, likewise, felt that perhaps you were serving some high purpose as well. I think you've communicated that. Is that correct?"

"I don't understand what you mean—'higher purpose.' But I know that I believed after I got to know Roy better that—I had sympathy for his situation."

"In some respects, he was kind of a pathetic character in your mind, wasn't he?" suggested the defense lawyer.

"No."

Hoback figured Tolley had scored a few points in the cross, but overall the agent thought Julie had held up well. The next witness, however, was not easily predictable, as Roy Moody had learned the hard way. But the government fared better when JoAnn Ekstrom took the stand the following morning and described posing as a screenwriter, at Moody's instigation, essentially to gain information from somebody involved in his Florida civil suit. She also covered her delivery of the bogus testimony in Moody's 1988 hearing. Next up was Julie Ivey Burbage, thirty and a single mother too. A looker, though not in a soft way, she had long, tousled, reddish brown hair, tawny skin, curves and a sexy way of walking in high heels. Her voice had a sandpapery quality. When she took the stand, Louis Freeh quickly hauled out the baggage—the drug use when she was younger, her immunity grant, the $500 a month the government was giving her for an apartment. But he humanized her when he asked about the first time she met Julie Linn-West.

"She was pregnant and lived in the same apartments that I did, and I noticed that she was in a wheelchair and pregnant. And when she came home with the baby, I made a point to go down and meet the child, see him and meet her," Burbage said.

She confirmed bringing Linn-West and Moody together and described her own first contacts with Roy.

Another man, apparently an acquaintance of Moody's, told her she would be hired to investigate the lifestyles of three people. He later took her to an apartment, handed her a bag of what she believed to be quaaludes, and told her to put them under the bathroom counter. She knocked on the door pretending to look for somebody else. Once inside, she made her way to the bathroom and deposited the suspected drugs as instructed. When she emerged, she was invited to drink a beer, which she did. Among other things, she also talked to the two young men in the apartment about their trip to Florida. The two men were Dan Fiederer and Tim Williams. After she left, the man who had brought her there went to a pay phone, called the police and reported there were drugs in the apartment. It was not clear police ever acted on the call.

Later, the man introduced her to Moody, for whom she eventually testified in Florida. He paid her $1,000. Testifying then, she claimed the boys tried to sell her drugs. Testifying now, she admitted it was a lie.

"What was your financial condition in 1983 when you received that money?" Freeh asked.

"I had no funds, no finances."

"What was your living circumstances?"

"I had nowhere to live."

"How old was your son?"

". . . Two and a half, three. I was living on the streets before I met Mr. Moody."

The next several witnesses were brief: a housewife who confirmed the two Julies knew each other years ago; a former Macon librarian; an FBI agent who participated in the Moody surveillance in March; a former official of the State Bar of Georgia; and the polygrapher who testified at the detention hearing about the attempted bribe.

Witness Douglas R. X. Padgett, a lawyer, was neither brief nor simple. He had represented Roy in the aftermath of the hung jury in the Florida attempted-murder case. He indicated Moody put up a sailboat as security for legal fees. Padgett contended Moody later failed to pay him his cash, so he was to be paid with the boat. But there was a problem.

"I think Mr. Moody told me that it had been repossessed by somebody I think up in Orlando for some expenses that were owed on it," Padgett testified. "Then I got a letter from I believe it was called Kona Corporation in Orlando saying they had repossessed the boat." Sam Wilson read the letter aloud. It was signed by Ted Banks.

Padgett testified he took the fee dispute with Moody to an arbitrator, who ruled the lawyer was entitled to $5,700. That was the first item Tolley attacked on cross-examination.

"Mr. Padgett, in the legal proceeding that went forward in the Superior Court of Clayton County in regard to whether your fee was excessive or not, Judge Ison in fact ruled against you, didn't he?"

Padgett acknowledged the judge had ruled against him, but on a technicality.

"And the dispute," said Tolley, "was about whether or not you had actually done seven thousand dollars worth of work in the case. That's what got it started, isn't it?"

"Well, I assume, yes. I mean, he was saying we did eight hours of work. It was totally ridiculous."

Tolley shifted gears and referred to an interview Padgett did earlier in the year with an FBI agent.

"Did you tell that special agent, quote, Padgett said Moody was crazy and described him as schizophrenic?"

"I can't recall. I may have."

It was another hint about the defense Tolley had in mind, a hint Sam Wilson seemed to have taken when he questioned Padgett again on redirect.

"When you were having a dispute with him, did he represent himself?"

"I think for the most part. I assume he did." Padgett described Moody as very litigious.

"Now, with your experience as a lawyer, did he seem to know what he was doing?"

"Appeared to be."

"Was he pretty proficient at what he was doing?"

"Proficient at nit-picking, yes."

The next witness was Ted Banks. Sam Wilson showed him a letter signed by him to Douglas Padgett. "How did you know what to put in this letter?"

"Well, we sketched it out."

". . . Who is 'we'?"

"Roy Moody and myself just put it together and I sent it for him."

Banks admitted he had not, in fact, repossessed the sailboat. Moody still had the boat when the letter was written. Banks had little more to say from the stand, though there was much more he could have said about his old prison buddy.

A postal inspector testified next and identified a picture of what appeared to be the sailboat in question, sitting in front of Moody's house in Rex not long before the start of the trial. The whole point of the sailboat scenario was to establish that the Julie Linn-West case wasn't the only time Roy had sabotaged the legitimate functioning of the legal system with fraud. The same applied when Dr. Ronald Tolbert, a veterinarian from College Park, Georgia, took the stand. He described a call from Roy, whose eight-month-old Great Dane had died suddenly. Moody was concerned the dog had been poisoned and wanted a necropsy done to determine the cause of death. Tolbert said his initial exam revealed nothing significant about the cause, but he sent some samples to a lab at the University of Georgia. The lab report too showed no evidence of poison.

Dr. Tolbert: "He . . . came to me with, I guess it was an affidavit of some type that contained information that he had summarized as to why the dog had died based on the information I had given him, and he asked that I would sign that so he could use that in the litigation that he was involved in. . . .

"Basically, the letter was indicating that I strongly felt that his dog had been poisoned, and at no time did I ever tell him that I thought the dog had been poisoned. I told him that the information was incorrect and I could not sign it."

The next witness was a pathologist who had worked in the lab, who said the dog's owner—apparently Moody—called him at home. The lab man told the caller he had no evidence as to whether anyone had poisoned the dog. Then Freeh introduced documents suggesting that, concerning the dog's death, Moody had pressed criminal-damage-to-property charges against a man named Thomas C. Allen III. Freeh quoted from a hearing where Roy testified he had spoken to "the vet who made the report to me from the University of Georgia. . . . He thought it was a fast-acting poison." A judge dismissed the charges against Allen anyway.

The several remaining witnesses the government called included Tommy Mann, Roy's lawyer in the 1972 bomb case. On cross-examination, Tolley asked him about the deposition Mann had taken long ago from Dr. Thomas Hall, the psychiatrist, and a recommendation Moody might benefit from additional psychiatric care.

"Now, I know, Mr. Mann, that when a case is over, it's over, and you had no reason in particular to follow this case, but do you have any idea whether or not such care was ever provided to Mr. Moody at that time?"

"I have no idea."

Louis Freeh offered several exhibits into evidence, then read several stipulations—pieces of evidence over which there is no great dispute, so the attorneys for both sides agree on a form in which it can be synopsized for the jury, usually saving time and trouble for all involved. Then the government rested its case.

Tolley's first witness was Susan Miller, an investigator with the Federal Defender Program, Stephanie Kearns's office. She introduced a videotape she'd helped make of the Moody residence, about a month after the arrest. From the stand, she provided a room-by-room narration, making particular note, with Tolley's occasional prodding, of the heaps of paperwork. Even a bathroom had files in it. The lawyer wanted the jury to see it as the house of a madman.

"Ma'am, as you go through it, can you tell me whether or not you formed an opinion as to whether there was any organization to this?" Tolley asked.

"Oh, there was absolutely no organization."

Next Tolley called Delores Cummings, a personable woman with a warm face and dark reddish-brown hair.

"Ms. Cummings, where were you born and raised?"

"Peach County."

"If you don't mind telling us, how old are you please?"

"Fifty-one."

"And what was your maiden name, please, ma'am?"

"Moody."

"And what is your relationship, if any, to the defendant, Walter Leroy Moody, seated over my left shoulder here?"

"He's my brother."

She was the sister Roy had sued, but still she showed up to testify for him, and about family matters—personal matters—that required her to be horrifyingly candid.

Tolley: "I want to direct your attention to 1972, ma'am. In 1972, did you suffer any psychiatric difficulties?"

"Yes. I had a nervous breakdown where I lost touch with reality."

"And were you hospitalized?"

"Yes." She said she had received medication and shock treatments. Under questioning, she said there was another brother, Bobby.

"Along about the same time—that is, 1972—are you aware or familiar with the fact that Bobby Moody suffered any psychiatric difficulties?"

"He had a breakdown also. . . . He was hospitalized in Augusta."

Both siblings, according to Delores's testimony, had breakdowns in 1972—the year of the bomb conviction with which Roy had become obsessed.

"Now ma'am," Tolley continued, "I want to ask you to be the family historian for a minute. Is there anyone else in your family that you're familiar with that had a history of psychiatric difficulty?"

Freeh objected but the judge overruled.

"Let me just ask you very plainly," Tolley said. "Did anybody else in your immediate family have any psychiatric difficulty that required hospitalization that you were aware of?"

"Yes. My grandfather on my daddy's side."

Freeh handled cross-examination.

"Was your brother the defendant ever hospitalized, to your knowledge?"

"I know that he has been under a psychiatrist, but I don't know if he was ever hospitalized."

"And the only other question I have, do you know what the medical problem was with your grandfather?"

"They said that he was just completely insane."

"Do you know if he had any other problems, physical problems?"

"I think that he had a very bad drinking problem."

"I have nothing further." The prosecutor had done his homework. His cross had been brief, but that is often an indication of how effective a witness has been on direct. Tolley's paralegal, Janet Westbrook, escorted Delores away from the courtroom. She liked Delores a lot and admired her for sticking by somebody like Roy just because he was her brother. But she sensed Delores was embarrassed about him, and that she knew Brunswick was just the beginning of a painfully public ordeal.

Tolley next called Dr. Howard Albrecht, a clinical psychologist from Decatur, Georgia.

Customarily, lawyers march such witnesses through a long list of questions to establish their credentials as experts before getting to the heart of their testimony. It is not unusual for opposing lawyers to ask their own questions before conceding that the other side's expert is indeed an expert, and sometimes no such concession is made, in which case the judge must decide. In this instance, however, Judge Alaimo took charge from the start and himself interrogated Albrecht about his education, experiences, publication record and licensure. Alaimo did it with a deftness, thoroughness and precision not every judge would be able to muster. But Alaimo, before becoming a judge, had been a much honored, topflight trial lawyer. Tolley was comfortable that nobody could qualify a witness better than Alaimo. And when he had, the prosecution declined to challenge Albrecht's qualifications.

Albrecht had met with Moody in November, about three weeks before the trial, four times in the space of a week, a total of eleven hours. He then reviewed for the jury various tests he had administered to Roy, and the results. The first he described was the Wechsler Adult Intelligence Scale, Revised.

Albrecht: "He was operating in his thinking at a different level than what is customary in everyday communication. By that I mean that our customary communication is guided by a certain . . . logic and a certain reason. And within Mr. Moody's test results there were indications that his thinking departed from that kind of logic. . . . It didn't make sense, in simple language."

He added: "Mr. Moody sees the world as a threatening place and sees other people as being potentially harmful to him."

Next was a personality test. Moody, Albrecht said, was "extremely distractible, in that he had difficulty focusing." He also suggested the test showed evidence of verbal and physical child abuse.

"The test also indicated that Mr. Moody becomes obsessive and overwhelmingly self-preoccupied . . . that he is unable to distinguish right from wrong and is not in control of his actions or thinking."

Judge Alaimo interrupted. "You cannot testify to that. That is for the jury to determine."

The psychologist said a word-association test suggested Roy had poor relationships with his parents. Albrecht next covered the results of the famous Rorschach inkblot test.

"On this test, it was very clear that Mr. Moody cannot distinguish reality from fantasy."

Furthermore, Albrecht said, the test revealed Roy as paranoid, seeing harm where none exists. His thinking was schizophrenic. "In Mr. Moody's case we're talking of someone whose thinking departs radically from reality, who responds to the givens of reality and essentially takes the ball and runs and elaborates on reality and applies to it his fantasy life."

Tolley asked if people suffering from the illnesses Albrecht described can appear normal in everyday life.

"Yes, they can; particularly someone who is as bright and intelligent as Mr. Moody."

Albrecht noted that Dr. Hall had diagnosed Moody with ambulatory schizophrenia in 1968. Tolley asked if the conditions he'd described tend to get better or worse if untreated.

"In Mr. Moody's case, his condition does appear to have become worse."

Tolley: "And could that have anything to do, for example, with being imprisoned?"

"In Mr. Moody's case it most definitely had an effect. Because I believe that as a result of his imprisonment—he reported that he was raped while in prison. I have data to indicate that he does suffer from posttraumatic stress disorder as a result of that rape—that means he has residual effects of that, as well as I believe that he responded in a very significant way to his father's death in 1970, as did his brother and sister, who were both hospitalized shortly afterward, his sister a year afterward and his brother within the same period."

Wilson cross-examined.

"Now this prison rape that you just talked about, did you check the prison records to confirm that that did in fact occur?"

"No, I didn't."

"You just took Mr. Moody's word for it."

"I took Mr. Moody's word for it, but the results of the—or the consequences, the effects of the rape were also apparent in some of the psychological test data that I obtained from him."

"This prison rape was supposed to have occurred when?"

"He reports that the prison rape occurred shortly prior to his being released from prison."

"So he's having this posttraumatic reaction in 1990 from something that happened in 1975?"

". . . Yes, he has had this reaction since 1975 because the rape, unfortunately, coincided with Mr. Moody's worst fear of being dominated by someone and being harmed by other people. This is a long-standing fear. And in a sense, what happened was the rape actualized or made that worst fear come true for him."

Wilson also elicited from Albrecht he had seen Moody before, in 1985, when he was hired to do a psychological study on Moody in connection with his litigation with the bank.

"You did not record that diagnosis of schizophrenia in '85, did you?"

"No, sir. But I did say borderline, which is—it refers to borderline psychotic."

Wilson weighed in with the elements of normalcy, success even, in Moody's lifestyle.

"Did you know that Mr. Moody had not one but several businesses? . . . Did you know that Mr. Moody owned his own home? . . . Did you know that Mr. Moody acquired—or had two automobiles? . . . Did you know Mr. Moody owned two airplanes?"

Some things Albrecht did know; some he didn't. But it was possible the most important thing to the prosecution was not the answers, but that the jurors heard the questions and could consider for themselves whether an insane man could function well enough to lead the lifestyle profiled in Wilson's inquiries.

"I'm just asking you," the Macon lawyer continued, "is your opinion Mr. Moody could make decisions in his ordinary life?"

"Yes."

"Whether to go home or sleep in the street?"

"Yes."

"Whether to buy an automobile or not to buy an automobile?"

"Yes."

"Whether to buy an airplane or not to buy an airplane?"

"Yes."

"Whether to get married or not to get married?"

"Yes."

"Whether to eat supper or not to eat supper?"

"Yes."

"He could do those things."

"Yes. . . . Could I qualify, Your Honor?"

Go ahead, the judge said.

". . . When confronted with a small part of reality at one time, when not having to deal with all of life, Mr. Moody can function okay. When not having to deal with his emotions, his relationships with people, when only needing to deal with a very small portion of reality, he can do okay.

"It's when he has to deal with the whole thing that his thinking becomes a mush, just a mess. That's the way I understand his ability to make these kinds of decisions while at the same time being quite disturbed—indeed schizophrenic—in his thinking."

Judge Alaimo interjected again: "But that did not affect his decision in these small matters."

"That's correct. . . . Mr. Moody is not the kind of man to say that the judge has two heads. He is the kind of man to say that the judge is out to get him."

Judge Alaimo once again interrogated the next witness, psychiatrist Sheldon Cohen, about his background and qualifications. The prosecution again declined to voir dire the witness further. Jay Cook, Tolley's partner, a reserved but genial man with graying hair and lawyerly, tortoiseshell-type glasses, handled the direct. The witness told him he had seen Moody twice, both times in the past month.

"I asked him to tell me about the situation that led to his being here today," Dr. Cohen said. "He told me that in 1972 he was convicted of possessing an explosive device and that his feeling was that this was incorrect, it was unjust. He was put into the penitentiary, Atlanta penitentiary, where he said that he was—to him, it was a very trying situation.

"He said not long after he got there that a cellmate was stabbed to death. That frightened him, as it would, I suppose, anybody. And he said that at that time that there was a degree of anarchy in the prison, that killings were fairly frequent. And he said that roughly two and a half months before he was discharged from prison, that four men came into his cell, two of them grabbed his arms, a third put a pillow over his head, and the fourth pulled his pants down and anally raped him. He said he passed out, fell off the bed, and that the men ran out thinking that maybe they'd killed him.

"I said, well, gee whiz, why didn't you report this, and he said words to the effect, 'Do you think I'm crazy?' Because, if he had, they would have, he said, put him in the hole for his own protection, or if they had let him out, he would have been—would have been victimized. He said that this continued to haunt him ever since, and that in his mind that that physical rape was symbolic of what he considered to be a judicial rape at the trial."

Judicial rape . . . a phrase that had turned up repeatedly during the electronic surveillance at the prison. If Moody truly equated the two, what might that have justified in his troubled mind? Might it have been more than the hiring of Julie Linn-West? The whole rape issue certainly raised the question of whether he had been haunted, driven into horrific acts of retribution at the system he blamed for both. But there were also questions—already raised by the prosecution—of whether the prison rape had ever happened, or whether Moody had simply planted the idea with his examiners that it had. Hoback, for one, did not believe Roy had been raped. The young agent saw it as a ploy for sympathy, and an ingenious one. He was, Hoback suspected, in effect testifying through his doctors. But this way, he wasn't subject to cross-examination.

Cohen continued: "Essentially, this man's life since he got out of the penitentiary has been directed at trying to undo what he feels was this unjust conviction. And he said, look, what I have done might have been illegal but it wasn't unjust. He attempted to come up with—to fabricate proof that, indeed, somebody had taken this package to his house."

The doctor referred briefly to the two Julies. "I think West was the one that he persuaded and coached to fabricate a story that she had gone with Gene Wallace and left this package." Even Moody's own witness acknowledged the hoax.

"He was so intent on proving his innocence that he didn't really pay much attention . . . to the fact that this would be something that would probably be pretty easy to disprove.

"And in a sense, this man was sort of like Don Quixote, tilting against windmills, except that what he was doing was just, in a sense, creating more and more problems for himself, as he felt justified in taking any kind of action similar to what had been taken against him."

The psychiatrist said Roy's preoccupation with proving his victimization took root early in life. He too diagnosed him as paranoid. "I think this man does have a lot of unacceptable angry impulses, but he sees them in others and sees others as out to get him.

"He put it to me very cogently. What he said was it's a variation of the Golden Rule: Do unto others before they do unto you; or do unto others what they have done to you."

Cohen called Moody "bright," with an IQ roughly 127 to 130. But his mental prowess couldn't make up for his mental impairments.

"If he were able to use his assets, he could be doing practically any of the jobs. He could have gone to medical school, law school or done what anybody's done."

———

When his turn came, Freeh pounded on Cohen's reliance on Moody for much of the information used to form his conclusions. Cohen acknowledged Moody told him he had lied to Dr. Hall, the practitioner who testified in the 1972 proceedings.

"Did it trouble you as a psychiatrist evaluating Mr. Moody," the prosecutor pressed, "that he had previously lied, at least on one occasion, to another psychiatrist?"

"Of course it did."

"And did that make his statements to you less reliable?"

"Not being paranoid, but it certainly made me suspicious of what I might hear from this man."

Freeh inquired as to whether Dr. Cohen asked Moody if he read psychiatric books.

"I didn't. But I'm sure he has."

"Why do you say that?"

"Well, he reads a lot of things. He was a jailhouse lawyer. I know he's read and quoted from books by attorneys, and he talked about John Locke and the Bible. I think the man's read a fair amount."

Freeh also established that Dr. Cohen disagreed with Dr. Albrecht's diagnosis of schizophrenia. And Cohen acknowledged the rape might have happened and it might not have. The defense rested, signaling the start of the government's rebuttal.

Dr. Scott Duncan, just shy of his thirtieth birthday, had recently been promoted to chief psychologist at the Atlanta penitentiary.

"When you interviewed Mr. Moody, did he appear to be hallucinating in any way?"

"No, sir, he did not."

"Did he appear to be out of touch with reality?"

"No, sir. Quite the contrary."

"Did he appear to have good habits of personal hygiene?"

"Yes, sir."

"Did he show any signs of illogical thinking?"

"No, sir. He did not."

"Did he appear to be intelligent?"

"Very intelligent." Dr. Duncan described Moody's performance on an IQ test. "In layperson's terms . . . it would be what you would consider a genius, yes, genius-level IQ."

Duncan found Moody competent to stand trial, able to assist his attorneys in his defense. He did not consider Moody, technically, to have a mental illness.

Jay Cook questioned him for the defense and immediately brought up the suicide watch. The doctor described the defendant's passing out at the news of the divorce action. Duncan, it turned out, had been the one to talk with him at the hospital.

"Although he was denying being suicidal," he said, "I requested he be placed on suicide watch for precautions."

The final witness was the government's big gun. Park Dietz, M.D., was a consultant to the FBI's vaunted Behavioral Science Unit. The psychiatrist had also consulted in the prosecution of would-be presidential assassin John Hinckley Jr. He worked with the FBI in the Tylenol murders, the district attorney in the "Preppie Murder" case, and with the state of New York in connection with the Tawana Brawley case. He had interviewed Moody four times in the space of a week.

"It wasn't for the purpose of helping alleviate suffering; it was for the truth-finding role."

He had also interviewed Susan and the two Julies and had met with several of the federal agents who knew about the case. He had reviewed videotapes of meetings at Julie Linn-West's apartment.

Dietz said there was no doubt Moody had paranoid personality disorder, among other problems, but he drew a distinction between a personality disorder and a delusion:

"People who are always getting into trouble with others usually do so because of a personality disorder. But a delusion is a characteristic of mental illness."

Dietz suggested he'd gone to a lot of trouble to determine if Moody suffered from a delusion. He wasn't able to find one. He led the jury point by point through his methodology, including his face-to-face dealings with Roy.

"He accused me of bias as soon as I met him," Dietz recounted. "And he continued on that theme on subsequent occasions, asking if I could possibly be fair with him, pointing out that I'd done work for the government, wanting to know how much of my time or income comes from the defense versus the government in various cases. He showed me, even as he related to me, his distortions.

"But at the same time he had some insight about this. As we discussed what it was he distrusted about me, why he thought it would be biased and so on, he showed that while he has the suspicions, he also has the ability to recognize what it is he's relying on when he is suspicious, that he recognizes his judgment about other people is often faulty . . . and, most surprising, that he still has some humor about some of this, which is not consistent with his being deluded.

"The most striking example of that probably was this past Sunday morning when I went to see Mr. Moody and he spent some time lecturing me on why he thought that my examination of him was a sham and unfair and couldn't be done fairly. And he said that he thought the entire process amounted to no more than brainwashing because of the amount of time I'd spent with him. And I remarked back to him that I don't think he had succeeded in brainwashing me. And he laughed, showing that he understood that he was the one who had presented his story for eight hours on the day he said I was brainwashing him and that's not what brainwashing is about, even in fiction."

Later, Dietz testified that Moody admitted he'd been "deceptive" most of his life. Moody traced it to his childhood and promises to him his parents allegedly failed to keep.

"He said that he basically spent his life deceiving others and telling lies, and that he found that it got more and more complicated to do this and when in custody on the present charges found himself trying to develop a story consistent with the evidence that would make him innocent and wrote many false stories over and over, trying to find a way to do this. But it was too complicated, whereupon he had an uncharacteristic thought, a thought of a kind he hadn't had in the past, which was the thought why don't you just tell the truth. And he said he decided then to do so.

"However, when I asked him later whether he found that he'd been able to suddenly, after all these years, start telling the truth or whether old habits of lying die hard, he said that they die hard."

Dr. Dietz was the last witness, finishing close to five-fifteen in the afternoon, too late, the judge decided, to commence closing arguments. Those, and his instructions to the jury, would wait until the next day. The jury left the room. Hoback had helped brief Dietz before he examined Moody. Now the agent decided it had been well worth the time. But all things considered, Tolley felt okay after Dietz was done. The defense attorney still believed he had a shot. That would change in the space of moments.

Moody leaned over and spoke to him in hushed tones. Tolley stood to speak and appeared troubled. He knew Roy considered the Brunswick trial little more than a nuisance, a mosquito buzzing around his battle to beat the bomb case. But Tolley saw it differently. He had stayed in contact with Bruce Harvey and considered it part of his job to come out of the obstruction trial leaving Moody in the best position possible for the bomb case. That was partly why the Athens attorney felt extraordinary pressure to do a good job for Moody, along with the belief that the judiciary—concerned that the public perceive Moody was getting the fairest treatment possible, unshaded by the identities of his victims—expected something extra from him, or he would not have been chosen. Tolley believed few things could put the government in a tougher position in the bomb case than an insanity finding in Brunswick. But what Roy had apparently just told him would gut the chances of that happening.

"Your Honor, I wanted to address an issue to you before we argue in the morning," Tolley began. He directed the judge to the typed charge Alaimo was to deliver to the jury before it began deliberations. The charge on insanity could be found on page forty-four.

"Now the defendant"—Tolley looked at Roy, hoping he would

change his mind but knowing he would not—"and, Mr. Moody, if you object to this or don't agree with what I'm getting ready to say, you need to tell me, okay?"

Moody nodded.

"The defendant objects to that portion of the charge at page forty-four which would allow the jury to find him, quote, insane of this crime. The defendant says to me—and I must confess there's a measure of logic in this"—even if Tolley thought it a tiny measure—"that all of the experts have indicated that he was competent to stand trial and that he was competent to assist his legal counsel. . . . And as assisting legal counsel, he doesn't want the charge at page forty-four.

"I'll have to tell you that it's against my legal advice, but he doesn't want it and it's his case. So I'm asking you not to charge it."

The timing could hardly have been worse for the prospects of a not-guilty verdict, and Moody's motivation was tough to fathom, unless he had suddenly realized a finding of not guilty by reason of insanity would still result in confinement, at a federal mental health facility, *indefinitely.*

Here he goes again, thought Brian Hoback. The guy thinks he's smarter than everybody else. He thinks he's a better lawyer than his lawyers. Just like 1972.

Judge Alaimo looked utterly amazed.

"But does he understand," the judge said, "there is a difference between the two, that he could be perfectly competent at this time to assist you and understand what is going on here, and, yet, conceivably could not have been competent at the time the alleged crimes were committed?"

"That's right," Tolley said.

"That was several years ago," added the judge.

"That's right. And he says, 'I don't want the jury to find me insane.' And that is at page forty-four of your charge. 'But I do want the jury to consider whether my illnesses have affected my ability to form the intent to commit the crimes in question.' Therefore, I move you to exclude the charge at page forty-four."

"All right. And you would except to my giving such a charge."

"I would except to your giving it," Tolley confirmed, believing he was sealing his client's conviction. He had no choice.

"All right."

Added the lawyer, "I have always tried to adhere to Mr. Moody's wishes, Your Honor."

With a closing argument to deliver in a matter of hours, Tolley felt himself in a nearly impossible position. The one rope to which the defense had clung had been narrowed to a frayed thread. He considered implausible the stuff about Moody lacking criminal intent. And arguing he didn't do it was utterly out of the question. Not only were there videotapes, but Roy had essentially admitted to the Julie Linn-West hoax in his interviews with Park Dietz. Tolley was a never-say-die type and stayed up through the night to craft a closing argument out of what was left of his case, an argument of which he would later be proud. But while his client might or might not have been delusional, Ed Tolley was not.

The next day, less than four hours after the start of deliberations, the jury returned its verdict: guilty on all counts.

———

If Paul Sartain's account were correct, Moody purchased four pounds of Red Dot smokeless powder. The problem was, laboratory estimates concerning the amount of powder in the four known bombs—Mountain Brook, Atlanta, Savannah and Jacksonville—suggested enough explosive remained unaccounted for to build more bombs. Or enough powder remained unaccounted for that more bombs might already exist.

Near the end of the Brunswick trial, discussions developed between Louis Freeh and Ed Tolley concerning what those government calculations showed. A series of negotiations ensued, directed, practically speaking, by Roy Moody, who seized on the opportunity to try bargaining himself out of the mail-bomb charges altogether. In the process he led the government to believe there might indeed be other explosives, in place and capable of detonation. Roy was incarcerated, but he had, after all, demonstrated considerable capacity for getting things done through others. An anxious search ensued, anxiety heightened perhaps by concerns the mail-bomber's code, 010187, could signal something each January 1. Shortly before the last January 1, there had been four bombs. The frenzy subsided after a few weeks passed without a bombing. Negotiations would stretch on, but by June, when the mail-bomb trial was set to begin, no more of the distinctive devices had shown up.

The ordeal, however, had been a fitting initiation for Tolley into the mail-bomb portion of the Moody investigation. At Roy's request, Tolley was appointed to represent him in the bomb case, replacing

Bruce Harvey, to whom the government had objected, alluding to his nominal representation of Susan in the early, pre-indictment stage of the case.

Owing to the recusals of federal judges in Atlanta, Senior Judge Edward Devitt of St. Paul, Minnesota, was named to the case. Close to eighty years old, the tall, white-haired jurist owned a national reputation. He assumed his first judgeship in 1935, his first federal judgeship in 1954, and won a Purple Heart in World War Two and served a term in Congress in between. He was coauthor of an important set of lawbooks, *Federal Jury Practice and Instructions*.

"His stature is clearly one of the most respected persons in the state," former Minnesota Governor Elmer Anderson told a reporter after Devitt's appointment to the case. "There wasn't great surprise when he was invited to take this very difficult case or sensitive case, because he's been called on before for similar things."

Following defense complaints about pretrial publicity, Devitt granted a change of venue, moving the trial to St. Paul. The prosecution prevailed on a number of other motions, but prosecutors weren't Tolley's chief obstacle when he lost one of the most important pretrial arguments. Said a document dated May 18, 1991, about two weeks before trial was to begin:

> *After consultation with counsel, Defendant Moody acknowledges the withdrawal of his insanity defense as to Counts one through seventy-one of the indictment. . . . This withdrawal is made with the understanding that he is in effect waiving the insanity defense.*

18

The Bomb Trial

Gone was the leonine mane. Roy Moody's hair was now conservatively cropped, and in his dark blue suit with red tie, peering over half-lens reading glasses, to the uninitiated he might have fit in with the rest of the lawyers in front of the rail—the sort of fit some suggested Roy Moody wanted all along.

Prospective jurors had filled out questionnaires ahead of time, so relatively few questions had to be put to them in voir dire, and Judge Devitt handled most of those that were. Even in the upper Midwest, several members of the pool had heard or seen news stories about the case, but many were either about the bombings back when they happened or about the heightened security at the courthouse for the proceedings, not the kind of coverage that would prejudice Roy's right to a fair trial. With a judge of less experience or common sense, jury selection in a trial of this magnitude might have stretched on for days. But under Devitt's direction, sixteen jurors, including four alternates, were picked before lunch. They lived and worked in Minnesota locales like Roseville and Red Wing and had Minnesota names like Hollenbeck and Holmstadt, Kranz and Krasky.

Tolley and Moody were joined at the defense table by Don Samuel, a partner in a high-profile, high-priced Atlanta firm, who hardly seemed affected by the image that conjures. He had a perpetual squint from a ubiquitous smile, a thick black mustache, thick black hair, a thick middle, and was by no means the hand-tailored clothes horse so many big-name criminal defense lawyers have become. His inattention to the nuances of haberdashery—in particular his repeated wearing of one objectionable paisley, coffee-stained necktie—prompted Tolley to buy him three new ties in St. Paul. Tolley wanted Samuel in the case, however, not for sartorial style but for his lawyerly abilities, especially his vaunted legal scholarship. A crew-cut college-student law clerk from Tolley's firm, Lance Strickland, was at the defense table for the heavy work, like toting files and Roy's wardrobe.

Freeh and Shapiro had added to the prosecution a tenacious young, Harvard-trained assistant U.S. attorney from Atlanta, John Malcolm, known for attentiveness to detail. Joining the lawyers and Justice Department paralegal Mary Ellen Luthy at the government table was a group of agents reflecting the diversity of the bomb task force: Hoback from ATF, Behnke and Gary Morgan from the FBI, and Postal Inspector John Farrell. Steve Brannan, Spanky McFarland, Todd Letcher, Bill Grom and several more agents would also be in St. Paul for behind-the-scenes work. Others would shuttle in as needed.

Howard Shapiro's opening was powerful and poetic beyond his years:

"For Moody, the ultimate crime, the most serious crime—murder—was the culmination of months of careful, patient and darkly ingenious efforts climaxing years of escalating crimes.

"You will hear that over those years Moody specialized in subverting, undermining and abusing the legal system. Years which he chose to punctuate in such ferocious fashion with an actual war against the courts. This was no quiet, covert action, not simply a letter-writing campaign, but a full-fledged, publicly announced war, a war against the United States Court of Appeals for the Eleventh Circuit."

The young prosecutor led the jury through the 1972 case, the Julie Linn-West sham and the related Eleventh Circuit appeal.

"Moody sat watching in the courtroom, his last three years of work on the line. It was apparent from the arguments at the Court of Appeals that it wasn't going well for Moody. Even worse, as Moody commented to one of his attorneys, one judge seemed unprepared, totally unconcerned about what for Moody were the most momentous issues of the day. That judge was Judge Lewis Morgan, the judge whose name was later placed as the return addressee on the bomb package Moody sent to Judge Vance."

The lanky lawyer recounted the failed chemical project, the making of the tear-gas bomb and its mailing to the NAACP, "an organization which epitomized for Moody the double standard he felt pervaded the court system.

"For years he had made the racist complaint that while there was no justice for the average white guy, what he saw as black pressure groups like the NAACP received preferential treatment. In his rage, Moody had come to see his failure to overcome his own conviction as a symptom of what he perceived as a deeper societal problem, a problem symbolized for Moody by the NAACP, and most of all, by the Eleventh Circuit Court of Appeals."

And in Judge Vance, Shapiro argued, Moody found a symbol of the court he hated, "who eloquently championed black civil rights in a series of well-publicized decisions in an Atlanta school-desegregation case and also in a judicial opinion Moody was sure to have seen during his frequent forays into law libraries, an opinion in which Vance ruled forcefully in favor of the Jacksonville NAACP, the second target of Moody's bombing. In this opinion, the opinion Judge Vance wrote, in stark contrast to Moody's own appeal, Judge Vance explained that violations of civil rights are never too old to be remedied."

The connection Shapiro offered to Robbie Robinson, that he had been involved in another school-desegregation matter, was still tenuous. And Shapiro confronted another, even more serious hole in the government's case.

"Now, you won't see a photo or a videotape of Walter Moody constructing the bombs. And you won't find his fingerprint or anyone else's for that matter on the inside of the bomb devices. It was part of his scheme, part of his method of operating at each and every step to avoid detection and to deflect attention. But you will see an abundance of evidence, both direct and circumstantial, evidence that when taken together will leave absolutely no doubt in your mind about the defendant's guilt."

Tolley took a different tack across the same water.

"I submit . . . ladies and gentlemen, the government will present evidence to you, in the next few weeks, based closely on undisputed fact, but like a good historical novel . . . it will track closely historical fact, but then when the facts are missing, will rely on raw conclusion.

"For example, Mr. Shapiro has indicated to the jury that Walter

Leroy Moody typed and sent letters threatening the judges; but, ladies and gentlemen, there is no evidence to that effect. There is a lack of evidence to that effect."

Nor, Tolley suggested, was there a witness who could testify that Moody mailed the bombs. Tolley painted a picture of Moody—before his 1972 conviction—as a bright young man who seemed bound for good things, until the Sunday the bomb blew up on Hazel. "When he went to prison, he had a business, he had a wife, he had a son, he had a life. And when he left prison, ladies and gentlemen, he had no business, he had no life left. And he has spent all these years in court trying to get back . . . the life he left behind.

". . . He resorted, ladies and gentlemen, to using the courts for all kinds of purposes. He was what I would call a very litigious person. He's the kind of person, ladies and gentlemen, that I submit to you, you probably wouldn't like."

Tolley conceded Moody used perjured testimony "in his obsessive desire to set aside this 1972 conviction." But, he reminded the earnest Minnesotans, that was not the issue. "You don't have to like the defendant Walter Leroy Moody in order to give him a fair trial."

Tolley said Moody had no reason to harm Judge Vance and had never heard of Robbie Robinson. "Robbie Robinson, who was a fine man just ahead of me in law school, as I recall, had no beef with Roy Moody, and Roy Moody had no beef with Robbie Robinson. And while it's true enough that Robbie Robinson, who was an attorney for the NAACP and is a black man and did occasionally serve as counsel for the NAACP on local matters, that Robbie Robinson was not at the forefront of extensive NAACP litigation. He was not on Atlanta television every night, he was not a figure that was known statewide in these type matters. Certainly there were others that were far more high profile than he."

———

Appropriately, the first witness to testify was the first man who injected Roy's name into the mail-bomb investigation. Lloyd Erwin recalled the evidence Chet Bryant brought him early in the 1972 case, and the makeup of the 1972 bomb: the nuts and bolts, the flashlight bulb, the square end plates, the double-base smokeless powder.

Shapiro: "Mr. Erwin, was there anything that was particularly distinctive to you about that 1972 device in terms of its design and construction?"

Erwin: "Yes . . . the thing that makes it very distinct is the fact that
it has metal end plates that are attached by the use of bolts running
through the pipe. That is a very unique characteristic about this device."

"Prior to encountering this 1972 device, had you ever seen a device that had those characteristics?"

"No, sir."

"Did you see another similar device between that 1972 device and
1989?"

"No, sir."

"Did there come a time when you did learn of a device you considered similar in design and construction?"

"Yes, sir."

"And when was that?"

"It was on December nineteenth, 1989. . . ."

Shapiro referred also to the Chamblee device. "And did you form
an opinion as to the design of this device as well as the four 1989 devices?"

"Yes. I concluded that this appears to be the design of the same
person."

On cross, Tolley quickly set about establishing the differences in
the devices described as being so similar. The 1972 device was about
two and a half inches long; the Chamblee device close to a foot. One
was made of steel, the other aluminum alloy. The battery holders
were different between the '72 bomb and '89 bombs. The powder
was different. The old bomb had one battery and the '89 mail
bombs had two. The 1972 bomb was not spiked with nails. And the
veteran lab man acknowledged the use of flashlight bulbs to ignite
powder was common in pipe bombs.

Tolley: "Now, the battery in the '72 device was turned over to the
fingerprint section to be fingerprinted, wasn't it?"

"Yes, sir, it was."

"And no fingerprint identified as that of Walter Leroy Moody was
ever identified, was it?"

"No, sir. It was not."

The next witness was Jerome Braun, a former director of bar admissions in Georgia. His name, title and office address were in a
notebook seized from Roy's Rex residence the day he was arrested.
Braun posited that, at one time, unpardoned convicted felons were
effectively barred from practicing law in Georgia. Later the policy

was modified, but such a conviction still carried considerable weight in such matters. Braun acknowledged, however, no recollection of Roy Moody contacting him about admission to the bar.

Bill Grom was the final witness for the first day of trial, testifying at length about the events in the obstruction case. He was followed, the next morning, by Julie Linn-West, testifying along the same lines as she had in Brunswick. Louis Freeh questioned her about her testimony for Moody in the 1988 hearing.

"Did Mr. Moody tell you why he was buying you new clothes for the hearing?"

"Because I need to look very prominent."

"Did you and he ever have any discussion about the fact that you were in a wheelchair and whether that would make any difference as a witness?"

"It would—he thought it would make a difference as far as them having sympathy for me being in a wheelchair."

Don Samuel also referred to the '88 hearing when his turn came to ask questions: "You went into the federal district court, same court as this United States district court except for the Middle District of Georgia rather than the District of Minnesota, and you lied?"

"Yes."

"And the next day, February second, 1988, you got your final payment for your efforts of another five hundred dollars, and no regrets, job well done; that was it. Fair enough?"

"That's fair enough."

The following day, the prosecution's witnesses included Dr. Tolbert, the veterinarian who testified in Brunswick about the death of Moody's dog, and Timothy Williams, one of the three young men left in the ocean during the incident in the Florida Keys years earlier. The polygrapher who said Moody tried to pay him to falsify test results followed him. Then came Tracey North.

Escorting Susan Moody had not been North's only role in the case. She was also assigned to review Moody's litigation from the past two decades or so. She looked at the writings, letters, briefs he wrote, and more—totaling more than ten thousand pages, she guessed. Using charts, Freeh and North guided the jury on a tour through Roy's courthouse tangles and wrangles. North also read selected portions of Roy's *pro se* filings with the U.S. Supreme Court concerning his late efforts to overturn the '72 conviction: " 'As this case demonstrates, if finality of a criminal conviction is put into jeopardy by the facts of a case, those facts will be changed or ignored by the court. If finality is jeopardized by reason, then reason will be perverted by the court. If finality is jeopardized by the law, then the will of the court will take precedence over the law.

" 'When confronting the finality of criminal convictions, the truth of the matter is the truth does not seem to matter. In pursuing finality, the courts have become Masters of Deceit. . . .' "

Tolley on cross: "Didn't Mr. Moody also say to the United States Supreme Court, and I will paraphrase this to save the court from having to listen to me read a page, that he had an ineffective counsel when he was convicted in 1972? He thought his lawyer did a lousy job, didn't he?"

"Yeah. That was Mr. Moody's opinion."

"And he wrote to the United States Supreme Court that Leslie Harris, the legislative counsel for the American Civil Liberties Union, recently announced on national television that the court's failure to provide indigent defendants competent counsel was a national disgrace. Do you recall he wrote that?"

North: "Yes. That's correct."

"He was upset and felt in 1972 he got a bad lawyer, is that right?"

"That's what Mr. Moody believed, yes."

"And we hope he's not talking about his lawyer today, don't we?" cracked Tolley.

"For your sake," North replied.

———

James Eckel was a young, affable and athletic-looking Atlanta-based FBI agent assigned to the mail-bomb case since the earliest days. He did better than tell the jury what had been found in the three footlockers in Titusville; he showed them. The three trunks were hauled into court, their contents made ready for the jury not just to see but to hold. The weapons had been made inoperable, the ammunition heat sealed so it could be handled.

In cross, Tolley stayed with the essential theme of the defense: what the government didn't have.

"In these footlockers did you find any double-base Red Dot smokeless gunpowder?"

"No, we did not."

"Did you find any paper clips?"

"No, we did not."

"Did you find any saw blades?"

"No, we did not."

"Did you find any glue?"

"No."

"Did you find any string?"

"No."

"Did you find any metal filings?"

"No, not that I'm aware of."

"Did you find any wire cutters?"

"No, we did not."

"Did you find any what will be described later as 1184 cardboard boxes?"

"No, we did not."

The next morning opened with the biggest news to come out of the trial so far for the crowd of reporters covering the case. Ted Banks was of average height, maybe two hundred pounds, with a face like Mr. Magoo. He was sixty-four years old, a boatbuilder by trade, and possibly a bomb builder, he would soon suggest, by mistake.

Banks was a jail inmate when he testified, having pleaded guilty to being a convicted felon in possession of a firearm and lying to federal officers. He had cut a deal.

"Mr. Banks," Freeh said, "would you tell the court and the jury, please, what your understanding is of this agreement?"

"The agreement that I entered into with the government was to tell what I knowed about the bombing thing, the bombing case."

"Did the government promise anything in return?"

"Yes, the government promised that they would not charge me on the bombing case and they would not charge me on any of the scams that I was involved in Roy Moody with."

Freeh led Banks through the story of his incarceration with Moody and their reunion some years later. The ex-con described schemes and scams they worked together, most relating to lawsuits in which Moody was involved.

"Did he appear to you to be very knowledgeable about legal matters?"

"Yes, he is," said Banks, who also said Roy told him more than once he wanted to be a lawyer.

"Did he ever talk about the lawyers that he hired?" Freeh asked.

"Yes."

"Lots of lawyers?"

"Yes."

"Did he ever complain about them?"

"Yes, sir."

"What did he say about them?"

"Well, they's just too lazy to get out and do their work, do their job."

"Did he ever compare himself to his own lawyers?"

"Well, he was a lot better lawyer than they were."

"That's what he told you?"

"Yes."

"Did Mr. Moody ever complain to you about the courts?"

"Yes, he did."

"Did he ever say some people got treated better?"

"Yes, he did."

"What did he tell you?"

"The blacks got a better shake than white folks."

"Did he say 'blacks'?"

"He said 'niggers.' "

"Did he ever express any other sentiments about black people?"

"Well, they took over Atlanta and they ought to load them up on a boat and send them back to Africa." They were oddly unoriginal phrasings to have come from Roy Moody, and while not lacking in malignancy, they were lacking in the sharpness with which Roy regularly edged rhetoric about his enemies.

"Mr. Banks," Freeh asked a short while later, "have you ever had any legitimate dealings with Mr. Moody?"

"None that I remember."

Freeh worked his way around to the fall of 1989, when Moody came by White House Marine, where Banks was plant manager. Roy, according to Banks, hung around an hour or two, picking up a bolt or a nut here, a screw on the floor there. He picked up some pipe and placed it on a table, as he did some "all-thread."

"What is all-thread?" asked Freeh.

"All-thread is just a rod with thread all the way on it."

"Like a big bolt?"

"Yeah. Like a big bolt." In other words, like a threaded rod.

Moody came back sometime around late afternoon while Banks was locking up.

"Mr. Banks, did Mr. Moody ask you to do something for him that night?"

"Yes, he did."

"What did he ask you to do?"

"He asked me to do—he said he was on a little project and he wanted me to do some welding for him."

". . . Had he ever asked you to do any welding before?"

"No. He had not."

"What did he ask you to weld that night?"

"Well, he told me he was on a project and he wanted me to do a job for him. And I says, 'What do you want me to do?' He said, 'Well, I wanted some pieces of pipe—ends welded onto a piece of pipe.' "

"Did you agree to do that?"

Banks said he pulled out the welder, saw and any other tools he needed for the job. "Then I says, 'What size do you want this pipe?'"

"And I cut him a piece of pipe, and it was too long. So, I says, 'Well, okay, show me on this pipe,' which I had in a vise. And he says, 'I want it this long.' I marked it and I cut three pieces, fell down to the floor. I picked them up."

Freeh elicited that the pieces, about six inches long, were cut from the same piece of galvanized steel pipe, about a quarter-inch thick, two inches in diameter.

"Was Mr. Moody there when you cut it?"

"Yes, he was."

"What did he ask you to do next?"

"Weld end plates on it."

Banks described getting a piece of angle iron—like the pipe, commonly used at the marine shop—and cutting six end plates, four inches by four inches.

"What did you do after you cut them?"

"I laid them up on the table, took the welder which I had all hooked up and everything, and I just welded the plates on."

Freeh suggested Banks demonstrate the configuration with a piece of square cardboard and a paper cup.

"After you did the welding, did you cool the metal, did you use any—"

"Well, I welded them up and kicked them off on the floor . . . and they were hot. And I says, get that bucket over there. There is a five-gallon bucket. I said, you run down to the river there. And the water was right close. And dip some water up in that bucket and bring it up here. So he did that, Roy did that, brought it up. And I just reached down and picked them up and throwed them in the bucket."

Moody, according to his erstwhile buddy, had one final chore to ask; he wanted some all-thread cut.

"And so I cut him a piece and it was a little too short. . . . I put another piece up there. I said, 'Show me what you want.' And I cut him about seven pieces. And they were about seven inches long."

Banks said the whole process took about a half hour.

"You said earlier in the day when he was there, you saw him picking things up?" said Freeh.

"Yes. I did."

"Did you see him pick up any nuts?"

"And bolts and screws and washers, yes."

"Any hex nuts?"

"Yes."

Moody asked for the sawblade used to cut the threaded rod and the pipe. Banks complied.

"Mr. Banks," Freeh finally asked, "when you were with Mr. Moody that evening at the White House Marina and you did the things that you told us about . . . did you ask him any questions?"

"Yes, I did. I says, 'What kind of project are you on?' And he says, 'Well, this is—I'm into this project here,' and he would not tell me."

"Did you ask him that question a second time that night?"

"Yes, I asked him a second time. And I had asked him a couple of times. He didn't tell me what he was doing."

"What did you ask him the second time?"

"I says, 'We are not making a bomb, are we?' And he says, 'Absolutely not.' "

"Mr. Banks, did you think you were making a bomb that night?"

"Well, I—yes, I thought I was making a bomb."

"What did Mr. Moody say when you asked him that?"

"He says, 'I am not making a bomb.' "

"Now, before you left that night, did he ask you to do anything else for him?"

"Yes. I asked him several times, you know, just joking more or less. But are we making a bomb here? No. We are not making a bomb. And he asked me as we went out to the car if I could get him some loading powder."

Banks testified he didn't ask Roy why he wanted the powder, and the pair of them went to a restaurant and had dinner. "I says, 'Roy, you're not making a bomb, are you?' He says, 'No. I am not.' He says, 'This is a project I'm on.' "

A week or two later Banks, by his account, called a friend named Tom Bates and ordered the powder—reluctantly, he maintained in court. "I thought he was making a bomb and I didn't want to be involved in the whole thing," Banks testified. Bates had a flea market booth and dealt in guns.

"If I needed any powder or pistols or anything, he would get them for me," said the convicted felon, adding that in this case he paid for the powder but never picked it up.

"Well, I didn't want to tell Roy a lie," the old salt said, "that I didn't order it. I just wanted to say that—he asked me if I could get it; I said yes, I could. And I was into it. And it was just a psychological thing. And I just wanted to have the powder and say that I wouldn't get it for him."

Banks said he called Roy on the phone but couldn't get hold of him in three tries.

"I wanted him to bring my pipes back."

"Why?"

"Because I had a bad feeling."

Eventually, in early December, Moody was back in Titusville for something having to do with one of their financial schemes.

"Did you talk to him about those things you had made in the marina?" queried Freeh.

"Oh, yes. In the course of sitting there, I asked him if I could get those pipes back that I had welded for him."

"What did he say?"

"He said he was into a project and he was using them. And it was, I said, 'You are not making bombs or anything like that?' He says, 'No, sir. I am not making any bombs.' And I let the subject drop."

That was the last time Banks saw Moody, at least until Moody's trials.

Freeh: "Let me direct your attention to December of 1989. Do you remember watching television news one night?"

"Yes."

"Do you remember seeing something that scared you?"

"Yes, I did. I saw it."

"What did you see?"

"An X ray of a bomb on television." One of the Atlanta stations had indeed gotten such a shot of the Eleventh Circuit device.

"Was there anything about what you saw on the screen that was familiar to you?"

"The pipes looked familiar. And I says . . . what has happened here, you know?"

Banks tried to explain why he lied to federal agents. "I wanted to divorce myself from Moody. I didn't want to be part of him. And the bomb thing, and I was afraid of that and I just didn't want to admit to knowing him."

Later, Freeh and Banks were discussing the guns in the footlocker search.

"Did you know he wasn't allowed to have them?"

"Yes."

"You knew he had been convicted of a crime?"

"Yes."

Banks seemed to stop just short of positively stating that what he welded for Moody became three bombs. Shown one of the rendered-safe devices, for example, he described it as "similar to what I did for Roy Moody," noting the pipe was the same size but the plates were smaller. "This weld on this is all piled up," he said. ". . . That's not my welding." The prosecution would suggest Moody simply cut down the plates—perhaps to fit in the box—and added on some welds to ensure the proper functioning of the bombs.

The ex-con also testified that in the spring or summer of 1989, Roy asked him for a typewriter. Banks complied.

Tolley's first question on cross: "Mr. Banks, have you been over these questions and answers before that you've been going over today?"

"Similar."

"Similar?"

"Close."

Tolley reestablished Banks was awaiting sentencing in just over a month. "And you expect, don't you, that your testimony today will help you when it comes time for the judge to sentence you?"

"I hope it does, but I'm not sure of it."

The defense lawyer touched briefly on the fraud schemes Banks had described, inducing the witness to confirm none of them involved violence. He also confirmed Susan's participation in them. Banks also told Tolley, in effect, he could not identify the tear-gas canister from the Atlanta NAACP package as the one he gave Roy Moody.

"Now you told the ladies and gentlemen of the jury that Roy Moody used the word *nigger*. Have you ever used the word yourself?"

"Absolutely."

Tolley brought up Banks's buddy Bates. "Now, as I heard your testimony, what you said in answer to the U.S. attorney's question was, 'If I needed powder and things like that, he would get them for me.'"

"Anything, yes."

Tolley had him cornered for the moment. "Now, for what purpose would you need gunpowder, sir?"

"I never bought any gunpowder," Banks now claimed. "I never received any gunpowder from him."

"I know you say you didn't receive any gunpowder from Bates in regard to Moody. But why did you say, 'if I needed powder'? It's like you'd done this before. Did you buy powder from him before?"

"No. I did not."

Tolley strolled Banks past the landmarks of his criminal past, including the counterfeiting case.

"You printed it?"

"Yeah."

"Do you know about printing and things like that?"

"Yes."

"Now, the judge that sent you to prison was Gerald Tjoflat, wasn't it?"

"No, it was George C. Young in one case and Tjoflat might have been the other one."

"All right, sir. And both of them sent you to prison, didn't they?"

"I don't remember whether it was Tjoflat or it was Young on both of them. I think it was Young, but I had some hearings in front of Tjoflat though."

Gerald Tjoflat, Tolley pointed out, became chief judge of the Eleventh Circuit and was one of the judges who had been threatened. Banks said he didn't know those things "until we got into this." The lawyer followed with questions about newspaper articles agents found in the search of Banks's house—including some about the assassination of Martin Luther King Jr.

"And in particular, you kept articles about James Earl Ray, the man who killed him?"

"Yes."

Tolley was armed with a sheaf of FBI "302s," federal-court jargon for the forms agents fill out to record interviews done during an investigation.

"In the interview of April the fifth, 1990, do you recall that you told the agents, quote, I would be very much surprised if Roy Moody is involved in the recent bombing cases'?"

"That is true."

"On April twenty-fourth, 1990, again in Titusville, Florida, do you recall telling the agents that Roy Moody has never made any comments regarding judges, and specifically judges in the Eleventh Circuit?"

"I never heard him make a comment."

"Okay. So that is true?"

"Yes."

"All right, sir. You also told the agents on that day . . . 'Moody has never made any statements that he dislikes minorities.'"

"I never heard him make any statements," Banks said, which didn't exactly square with the send-'em-back-to-Africa story.

Banks also testified Roy and Susan got along "very good."

"Did he seem affectionate towards her?"

"Yes, he did."

"Did she seem affectionate towards him?"

"Yes, she did."

Tolley: "Did she fit, if you know what a, quote, *battered woman* looks like? Did she fit the profile of a battered wife?"

"No."

"I don't know quite how to ask this to you, so if it doesn't make sense, I will repeat it. But did she act like she was an automaton or battery-operated or under any spell?"

"No, she did not."

On redirect, Freeh sought to clarify the clippings situation, eliciting from the witness that cutting out newspaper articles was a habit shared by other prisoners, and his collection included other stories about other then-current events, like Watergate. Freeh next called FBI Agent Steven McGinty to corroborate the claim.

Tom Bates took the stand later that day. He was seventy-two years old, retired from Cape Canaveral, which wasn't far from Titusville. He said he met Banks in the late seventies through a friend of his wife's and at one point borrowed money from Ted, which he made good by trading him guns.

"Did you try to pay him back more money?" Louis Freeh asked.

"I wanted to but he wouldn't accept more."

Bates confirmed Banks's story that in 1989 he asked Bates for

some powder and primers—the first time, according to Bates, Banks
had made such a request of him. And Bates identified a sales slip
dated December 9, when he bought the materials. Bates said he was
unaware at the time Banks was a convicted felon.

"The week after it was bought," Bates testified, "he came to the flea
market where I had a table in Oak Hill, Florida, and I asked him—I
told him that I had the powder for him. And he said he wasn't ready
for it yet.

"Then the same thing happened the following week." Bates described a third, similar incident. The powder, he said, remained on
a shelf until it was eventually turned over to the FBI.

One of the final witnesses that day was a big, handsome brunette
from an Atlanta suburb. Karlene Shiver, thirty-five when she testified, said she dated Roy in 1980 and 1981. "Roy was quite a charmer
and was a very nice-looking man and . . . the beginning of the relationship was very nice," she said.

She filled in the jury on how Roy's Associated Writers Guild
worked: "He would put ads in the paper for people that wanted to
be aspiring writers. And for a fee they could belong to the Guild and
they would have an opportunity to be published in a book called *Au-
thors to Watch*."

Shiver also referred to the North American Data Verification and
Testing Service. "He would put ads in the paper . . . 'Proofreader,
earn seven to ten dollars an hour,' something similar to that is what
the ads would read. And the people would write in like they were going to apply for the position. He would send them back a letter stating that they . . . had to take a test from the North American Data
Verification Service to see if they were qualified to be proofreaders.
And that test I believe cost twenty-five dollars."

Shiver said she was not an employee of the companies but did a
fair amount of work for Moody. She wanted to spend time with Roy.
Roy spent time, she suggested, at the airport, having bought an airplane during their relationship, and building models, nice models.

"He was very, very good at that, very mechanical."

Howard Shapiro steered her testimony toward conversations
Shiver had had with Moody concerning social issues.

"Did he ever comment to you about the NAACP?"

"Yes, he did. He told me that the NAACP was backed by the Jews,
the government Jews, that the blacks were just a front for them to
get what they wanted." Shiver also testified Roy called Martin

Luther King a card-toting communist, and that George Wallace was one of his heroes.

"Did he ever tell you what he believed should be done with blacks?"

"He said that all the jungle bunnies should be rounded up and put on a boat and sent back to Africa." Then she related an anecdote.

"A few months before I met Roy I had gone home to Alabama to visit my family. I met first with my sister and we were going over to my mom's. And it was raining. It was dark. My car—I was driving and all of a sudden I knew that I had run over something. So I pulled over to the side of the road and my sister was screaming. And what I had run over was a man.

"And for quite some time, I was very afraid to drive at night, and especially if it was raining. And so I was in Roy's company one night when it was raining, and I was sharing with him this experience of what happened and how upsetting it was. And I told him . . . I really couldn't help it. It was dark. It was raining. The man had on dark clothing and he was black. There was no way I could see him. And at the first of the conversation Roy was very sympathetic until I got to the point where I said he was black, and Roy said, I can't believe that you're upset. They should have gave you a trophy. He said they should let you go out and let you run over a few more. That's what he said to me."

Shapiro and Shiver shifted gears.

"Did he ever have a discussion with you about committing a crime?"

"Yes. One time he told me the perfect crime would be to build a bomb, and when everything exploded, there wouldn't be anything left to investigate."

Soon after, Shapiro asked about Moody's ambitions.

"He told me he wanted to be a lawyer," Shiver answered.

Shapiro led her through the demise of their relationship, which included, by Shiver's account, two incidents when Roy hit her and his dating of another woman—Susan.

"Did there come a time when Mr. Moody had an arrest warrant issued for you?"

"Yes, he did." The accusation was embezzlement. And at the hearing Roy denied having any type of personal relationship with Shiver, describing her instead as an employee.

Shiver had been a multipurpose witness. If the jury found her credible, she had buttressed the government's case in several key areas: Roy's litigiousness, abuse of women, frustrated legal ambition and racial animus—the latter one of the most threadbare elements of the prosecution's motive theory. But the Georgia woman had one more bomb to drop on the mail-bomb suspect. And this one was a late-breaking bonus for the government.

"I had occasion to type on his typewriter," she said, even beginning to talk like a prosecutor. "But I can't say that I really did any typing for him because it was impossible to type on the typewriter."

"What was the matter with the typewriter?" asked Shapiro.

". . . Some of the letters would jump. Mainly A's would jump."

"Let me show you government exhibit three eighty-six in evidence, ask you if you have ever seen this before." Government 386 was the Brenda Wood letter, the message sent to the Atlanta TV anchor back in December. In the first two lines alone, the A jumped above the other characters six times. Shiver had seen the document for the first time just before she came in to testify, as she sat in the witness room.

Shapiro: "Is there anything you recognize about that exhibit?"

Shiver: "The A's."

Tolley objected. Comparing typewriting, he suggested, was a job for experts. But Shapiro prevailed and Shiver continued.

"I recognize the A's on here because—this may sound funny to some people—but when I was typing, when I was learning to type, we used to do, 'Now is the time for all good men to come to the aid of their country.' And I remember typing that several times and the *a* in *aid* was always up. And the only time Roy asked me to type anything for him it . . . was a letter that had to do with the Guild and I remember laughing and telling him that this was a joke, that the typewriter was a joke. There was no way that you could type on it. And I never typed anything else."

Tolley opened cross-examination with an insight that did not push the limits of his discernment. "Ms. Shiver, I take it from your testimony you don't like Mr. Moody very much, do you?"

"Um . . ."

"Well, let's be honest. You don't like him, do you?"

"I don't terribly dislike the man. I mean, I have forgiven him for what he's done to me."

"Then your testimony is that you have forgiven him and you like him?"

"No, I didn't say that I like him. I don't necessarily dislike the man."

Ed Tolley referred to his background information. "Ms. Shiver, I notice that on February the [sixteenth], 1990, the FBI came and interviewed you, do you remember that?"

". . . Yes, sir. I remember that."

"Do you remember telling the FBI agents that interviewed you, quote, Ms. Shiver advised she did not think Roy Moody was a racist? Did you tell them that?"

"No. There's been—there was a misunderstanding. . . ."

"Excuse me," Tolley said. "Could you just answer my question first and then you can explain? Did you tell the agent that you did not think Roy Moody was a racist?"

"No, I did not. I did not tell them that."

"Then the agent was wrong?"

"I think the agent wrote it down wrong."

"Well, that's kind of significant, isn't it? And he missed that in your conversation with him?"

". . . I never said that Roy was not racist."

Tolley suggested it was not until a second interview, on April 30, that she branded Roy racist.

"Now," the defense lawyer continued, "the first time the agents talked to you, ma'am, did you tell the agents that you did not know anything about Roy Moody being involved with bombs?"

"I certainly did."

"And the second time that you talked to them, ma'am, you related to them the scenario about Roy Moody and the perfect bombing crime, didn't you?"

"I made the statement of what he said to me about a perfect bombing crime. What I said that I did not know anything about was that he had been convicted, because I certainly would not have been dating a man that had been convicted of building a bomb that hurt his first wife had I known that."

"But you dated a man for . . . years that made jokes about killing 'niggers' and throwing babies in the river; that was okay but making bombs was not?"

"Well, you have to realize that down South a lot of people are very racist." It was certainly an answer that might have been received differently had the venue not been changed.

Tolley asked the young woman if she remembered agents asking who Roy's friends were and who she told them they were. She said she did not recall.

"You said that Roy Moody had two close friends?" Tolley prodded, and she came up with the first name of a college librarian. Tolley kept going. " 'The only other person she knows that she would call a close friend of Moody's was a black female whose name she could no longer recall but who worked with Roy Moody.' Do you remember telling the agent that?"

"No. I do not remember telling the agent that."

"So this agent was really sloppy; he made two big boo-boos, didn't he?"

"Undoubtedly he did because I did not say that."

Shapiro, on redirect, established that Ms. Shiver had not spent much time in recent years thinking about Moody prior to the February visit from agents. "Since then you have been visited on six or eight or ten occasions by agents and prosecutors?"

"At least."

"And has that given you a chance to think and reflect about Mr. Moody?"

"Yes, sir."

———

Seeing that box in front of her at the witness stand brought back terrible memories for Murlene Murray, a pretty, pleasant, middle-aged woman with cinnamon-toned skin, fastidiously applied makeup, a high-necked, peach-colored print dress and a plain peach blazer. Her testimony, with John Malcolm asking the questions, began the second week of the trial. Ms. Murray was a secretary at the Southeast regional office for the NAACP in Atlanta and had been for thirty-one years. In all that time, nothing like this had ever happened.

Around noon on August 21, 1989, the mailman delivered a package to the office and Ms. Murray placed it on the left-hand corner of her desk. Earl Shinhoster, the Southeast regional director, came through and asked about the box, which was addressed not to any particular person, but to the office. Nonetheless, the decision was to open it.

"Ms. Murray, was the box easy to open?" Malcolm asked.

"No."

"Why not?"

"It had two strong pieces of tape on it and you couldn't just get it up easily."

"So you had to struggle to open the box?"

"Yes. I was trying to open it and the box was moving about on the desk. And Mr. Shinhoster put his hand on the left-hand side of the box."

Finally, she announced to the courtroom, she got the corner of the box up. "Something said *pie, pie*, and I saw a spark. And all of this smoke just, whatever it was, just came directly up into my face."

Malcolm asked her what it felt like.

"My face was on fire. My eyes started tearing, and I jumped. Mr. Shinhoster and I both jumped back."

"What were you thinking at the moment?"

". . . That I had lost my eyesight."

Ms. Murray described running down the hall to a doctor's office. She asked him if her face, which she was holding and which was streamed with tears, was on fire. He told her they should get out of the building, which they did, scrambling down the steps, tripping and falling over each other until finally they were in the parking lot. She painted a horrible picture of the scene there, people pouring out of the building, coughing, eyes running water. "It was just a mess."

"How many people did you see?" asked Malcolm.

"Oh, between, oh, thirty and forty people."

"And what kind of people were these?"

"They were elderly people. There was some children. There were women. There were a number of babies."

She said the burning sensation lasted about a week.

Tolley's cross was short and polite. For the government, the chief jury value of testimony like hers was not so much to point a finger at Roy Moody as to paint a picture of the pain he allegedly wrought. Earl Shinhoster was next up. Never had he experienced the personal sense of peril that had hit him that day in 1989, which was saying something for a man who had been involved in the NAACP since 1963, when as a thirteen-year-old he was a member of the organization's Savannah youth council. Savannah, of course, was also hometown to Robbie Robinson, whom Shinhoster had known personally. Shinhoster, a man of keen, almond-shaped eyes, with flecks of gray in his haircut, mustache and goatee, wore a gray, double-breasted suit. He described heading downstairs to call 911 when the gas hit, but instead of immediately fleeing for his own safety, he headed back upstairs to make sure people were trying to get out of the building. And he tried to get back in the office.

"I did open the office door," he said. "At that point I was hit in the face, almost immediately as I opened the door, with this gas. Whereupon almost immediately my face began to burn, my eyes began to burn."

Outside the courthouse after his testimony, newspeople gathered around the NAACP official.

"Does it ever run through your mind," a reporter asked, "that it might just as easily have been Robbie Robinson who received a teargas bomb and Earl Shinhoster who received a mail bomb, a pipe bomb?"

"Yes. And I thank God every day," Shinhoster replied. "I thank God that day that it occurred that it was no more serious than it was. Those of us who are involved in the civil rights movement and struggle . . . we know when we begin this kind of work that the peril exists and that our lives may be endangered. So all we can do is trust God, every day. And that's what we do."

"When that came to fruition, when it became a box smoking, sitting in your office and not just an abstract thought, did you ever think about giving it up, finding another line of work, in all honesty?" the reporter followed up.

"No," Shinhoster answered quickly. "I never have thought from this experience or from any other that I've encountered that perhaps this is not the line of work for me. I'm doing this as much as a calling as an avocation . . . and I'll just have to take whatever consequences might follow."

A procession of lawmen followed Shinhoster on the stand, Postal Inspector John Farrell, ATF agents Sonny Fields and David Hyche, and Terry Byer, from the ATF Atlanta lab. Byer presented detailed, 3-D mock-ups he had made of the Birmingham, Eleventh Circuit, Savannah and Jacksonville bombs and of the 1972 device, and he explained in detail, but in everyday terms, how bombs function. He should have known. He'd been working with explosives, training to handle them or taking them apart, for almost a quarter century, beginning with the Navy's one-year Explosive Ordnance Disposal School and including a seven-year apprenticeship. And Byer testified it was his opinion that, in all likelihood, the four 1989 bombs, the 1972 device, and the pipe taken from the Chamblee basement were all engineered by the same person.

———

"Do you have any grandchildren?" Louis Freeh asked.

"Yes, I have one," replied the middle-aged witness with her jaw set in Southern perseverance, gray sweeping back through her hair, and eyes nearly as arresting in their piercing darkness as the eyes of the defendant sitting catercorner from the stand, hers warm, his chilling.

"How old is he?"

"He is nearly nine months old."

"Was he born after your husband died?"

"Yes, he was."

Helen Vance, her demeanor unflaggingly gracious, recounted in gut-wrenching detail her life with Bob Vance and the day their life together ended. Again, it had little to do with Roy Moody's guilt or innocence, but drove home the human impact of the crimes.

"I got up and I was bleeding," she said. "I was cut on my arms and legs, but I did not feel like I was very seriously hurt. But I looked at my husband and he was not moving and I was sure he was dead. And I thought, well, I've got to get help. I believe he's dead. If he is not, he's going to be. Maybe if he is dead—if we can get help quick enough, we can do something. So I picked up the phone there in the kitchen and I could not hear the dial tone. My hearing was temporarily damaged by the bomb.

"So I went back to my bedroom and got a towel and brought it out and put it over Bob, over his stomach, and then I went out of the house and got in my van and drove to my neighbor's. The houses on my street are very far apart, and the quickest way to get there was to drive to my neighbor's. . . . I got to my first neighbor's and I remember getting out of the car and going up to the door. I don't know if I blew the horn when I came up the driveway or not. I don't know if I hit the doorbell or knocked. Anyway, I could not make anybody hear me. I don't know if they were there or not. They could have been gone. And I waited just a few seconds and then I . . . drove back down their driveway and went to the neighbor's across the street from there.

"And I remember driving into their driveway blowing my horn. And my neighbor came out and saw it was me and started to say

'Come in.' Then she stopped and saw the blood. And I said, 'Would you call the police? A bomb has gone off and I think Bob is dead.' And I got back in the van and drove back home. And her husband followed me just a minute or so later. And I was still sitting in the van. And he came over and said, 'Helen, do you want to go in the house?' And I said, 'No, I think I'll just sit here. And he went into the house to see about Bob and came back out very shortly, and about that time the paramedics and the police were getting there."

When she was done on direct, it was Tolley's turn.

"If Your Honor please, we will have no questions for Mrs. Vance today," he said prudently. He took a similar approach to the next witness, also a widow. Carolyn Layfield's husband, lawyer Martelle Layfield, was spared victimization by the sender of the bombs and threat letters only because he was already dead more than two months when the letter addressed to him arrived.

Mike Ford was among several witnesses the next day, testifying about his role in Roy's appeal of the 1972 case. He also authenticated a letter he had received from Roy on the Moody Motion Pictures letterhead.

> *May 11, 1990*
>
> *Mr. Michael C. Ford*
> *Attorney at Law*
> *Dunwoody Place, Suite B*
> *1841 Peeler Road*
> *Atlanta, Georgia 30338*
>
> *Dear Mike,*
>
> *Smile, I'm going to make you a star.*
>
> *Sincerely,*
>
> *Roy Moody*
> *President*

Before the trial was over, that message would take on an entirely new meaning.

Sue Lee, a reference librarian at the Eleventh Circuit courthouse, followed Ford on the stand.

"Ms. Lee, did there come a time when you spoke with someone from the FBI about something you had seen in the library?" asked Shapiro.

"Yes, sir. The FBI was doing research in the library, and I happened to mention that I had seen Mr. Moody on TV, that he was a suspect. And I said, hey, when I saw him on TV, I said, I have seen him before. He has been in the library."

"And you told that to the FBI?"

"Yes. I did."

"Was there anything distinctive about Mr. Moody's appearance that you recall?"

"I don't know what made me remember him. I believe that he has very distinctive hair and I may have remembered—that may have been what caught my attention."

Later in the day Robbie Robinson's secretary, Joyce Tolbert, took the stand, followed by Emerson Brown, the optometrist who cradled the bomb-ravaged attorney before emergency crews arrived. Christopher Scalisi, the paramedic who attended him, testified in vivid detail. All were startlingly effective witnesses at telling the toll taken by the Savannah bomb.

Since she had yet to testify, Helen Vance had been excluded from the courtroom during the medical examiner's testimony about Bob's death. Now she decided she did not want to hear details about what a similar bomb had done to Robbie Robinson, either. She saw one of Robinson's sisters get up and leave the courtroom. Helen followed and one of the trial's most moving scenes took place not in front of the jury box but on a bench in the hallway, where Mrs. Vance sat with Robinson's sister, two women bound together by the bloody work of one terrorist.

For all the dignity and strength she projected, Helen found the days in St. Paul difficult to get through. Each evening when she would return from court, she would sit in her hotel room and drink a Coca-Cola to calm her stomach. But she knew it would be much tougher to be in Mountain Brook now, to not know everything about what had happened and why. And when she could divorce herself from the personal connection to the case she found the revelation of how the government tracked Moody fascinating.

Dr. Denitto was next and told how death descended in the operating room. Frank Lee finished the day, detailing for the jury his crime-scene investigation and narrating a videotape about Robinson's gutted office: "As you can see, the destruction is complete." The desk is blown—large hole in the middle of it. Papers, books, personal articles, are blown around the room.

"This is the desk—you can stop there for a second. This is the area where the bomb was, okay?

"A mantel, fireplace. We are now looking north from behind his desk. Attempt to focus in on some of the large debris—if we could hold it right there. These were two articles of fragmentation that went completely into the other adjoining apartments. This is a piece of the cylindrical pipe. . . .

"The material that you see is flesh, bone, blood, nails, wire, materials from the desk from the bomb."

Lee also offered the opinion that the '72 device, the Chamblee device and the 1989 devices were designed by the same person.

The next morning Steve Grant—the court security officer who discovered the Eleventh Circuit bomb—testified. He had since gone to work for Coca-Cola at its corporate headquarters in Atlanta.

"Mr. Grant," Louis Freeh said, "when you saw that package on the scope as it was going through the machine, were you the last person who was going to check that package?"

"Yes. I was."

"If the package got by you, would anyone else have x-rayed it?"

"No."

"Would anyone else have examined it?"

"No."

Pete McFarlane was up next, to talk about rendering safe the Eleventh Circuit bomb. He was followed by the clerk of court for the Eleventh Circuit, Miguel Cortez. Then the inimitable Willye Dennis in her full-blown style.

"About ten minutes to six when I got to the car-rental company," she said. "Young lady was in a hurry and she gave me a hard time, but I finally rented a car."

"Hard time because they were closing up?" Shapiro asked.

"Yes. And I had not made a reservation either for a car."

"You didn't know your car was going to break down?"

"No. She said she only had one car available and I told her I could only drive one car."

"Did you take the one car?"

"I took the one car, then she told me it was a sports car. And I told her to look at me, I'm a sporty woman."

John Sheddan, the Jacksonville Sheriff's Office bomb tech, took the stand next and finished near the end of the day. Outside the courthouse in St. Paul, close to fifteen hundred miles from the city where they both lived, and a year and a half after Sheddan undid the package that might have undone Willye Dennis, the two Floridians met for the first time.

Sheddan remarked he just happened to have come in early that morning.

"No, you didn't," shot back Willye Dennis. "You didn't just happen to be. . . . You were just part of the whole plan for *all things working together*."

The jury had now heard firsthand accounts about all four mail bombs and the tear-gas package as well. The proscenium prepared, the next morning, June 13, 1991, Susan McBride would take the stand.

———

When Susan walked into court to testify, she no longer looked the younger sister of the farmer's wife in *American Gothic*. Once limp hair now lustrous, pallid skin now glowing, she wore a short, navy-blue silk dress, a string of pearls, and no glasses. A crusty, old-style local newspaper reporter in the gallery muttered, *Hell, I wouldn't be ashamed to be seen with her*, or something like it. The transmutation was complete, from dowdy, devoted helpmate for a husband twice her age to stunning star witness for the young prosecutors.

"When did you first meet Moody?" Howard Shapiro asked.

"In July 1981."

"And where did you meet him?"

"I was a waitress at a coffee shop in Atlanta, Georgia."

"And was he a regular customer there?"

"Yes."

"Where were you living at the time?"

"I was living with my parents."

"Did you begin dating him?"

"Yes."

"And did you subsequently move in with him?"

"Yes."

"When was that?"

"In August 1981." She was eighteen at the time.

"How old was he?"

"Forty-seven."

The first area Shapiro took her to concerned the Associated Writers Guild of America and North American Data Verification and Testing Service. She explained what they did.

"Did the companies bring in money?" Shapiro queried.

"Yes, approximately one hundred eighty thousand dollars a year."

"That on an average?"

"An average."

Susan said there were some part-time employees. There were none full-time—unless you included her. "I handled the advertisements, the banking, the mail processing, typing. I ran errands and I handled the printing. I did everything."

"How much time did you devote to the companies?"

"All my time."

". . . Did it involve a lot of driving?"

"Yes."

"Approximately how much did you drive on a yearly basis?"

"About fifty thousand miles."

"And most of that was running errands for the companies?"

"Yes."

"Did you draw a salary?"

"No."

"What did Mr. Moody do in connection with the companies?"

"He told me what to do."

"Did he do any of the work?"

"No."

Shapiro shifted gears to their personal relationship. He asked, "Did you spend much time together on social activities?"

"No."

"Did you ever have a discussion with him about friends back when you first met?"

"After we met, about a month after we met, I mentioned that I had some black friends where I previously lived, and it upset him a great deal and he—he was upset and did not speak with me or deal with me for about a week."

"Did you ever see those friends again?"

"No."

"Were there other times when he would isolate you, refuse to speak with you and deal with you?"

"Yes."

"When were those other times?"

"All throughout the relationship."

"How long would those periods of isolation last?"

"Anywhere from three days to over a week."

"Would he talk to you at all during those time periods?"

"Only when necessary."

Asked how she responded to the silent treatments and isolation, Susan said she would try to do anything Roy wanted, stopping whatever she was doing to give him all her attention.

"I would try to redeem myself."

Roy, she added, did not like her to have much contact with her family. Her only contacts with friends were business-related. She didn't use the phone socially when Roy was around.

"Who made decisions about where the two of you would go?" the young prosecutor asked.

"He did."

"Who made decisions about what you would do on a daily basis?"

"He did."

"Who made decisions about when you would go places?"

"He did."

". . . Who made decisions about the most intimate aspects of your relationship?"

"He did."

"Did you have any control about even such matters as when to have sexual relations?"

"No."

"Was there a routine between the two of you?"

"Yes."

"What was that?"

Tolley objected. "Your Honor, please. While this is maybe good fodder for publication, I'm not sure that their sexual routine has any bearing on the issues in the case."

Judge Devitt: "Is there some reason for that?"

Shapiro: "There is reason for that, Your Honor. It's obviously not fodder for publication but to show the complete depth and extent of Mr. Moody's control over Ms. McBride."

Judge Devitt: "That maybe could be shown in some other way."

"Okay," Shapiro said. "Did Mr. Moody date or see other women during the course of your relationship?"

"Yes," said Susan.

"Were you aware of that?"

"Yes."

"How were you aware of that?"

"He wouldn't conceal it. He placed a personal ad in the paper and I saw the letters."

"When was that?"

"That was in 1989, in the fall." That was, she acknowledged, the same time frame in which they were married. She briefly detailed incidents of physical abuse, and Shapiro asked her why she didn't try to leave.

"I was very dependent on him emotionally, financially. I didn't have anything. I had very low self-esteem and I knew that if I did leave, he could find me and I was afraid."

Eventually, she described Roy's regular news watching. Typically, Moody didn't ask her opinion about it, but once he asked her what she knew about a murder case—the Julie Love case. That was the murder the bomber railed about in the letter to news anchor Brenda Wood.

"Did he ever express any opinions to you about the attorneys he had hired?" Shapiro asked, having switched topics again.

"Yes. His opinion was that they were incompetent." Susan also said Roy, in 1989, had asked her to pick up his transcripts so he could know how much he needed to complete law school.

"Did he express any interest to you in becoming an attorney?"

"Yes."

"Did he indicate to you any obstacle that stood in his path?"

"He told me he could not become an attorney as long as he had a conviction."

Susan listed litigation Roy took part in during their years together, including the case against the bank where she said he used close to a dozen attorneys, phonied-up documents, and had a plan to feign mental illness. She also related the inside story of the Julie Linn-West scam. After the regular brief morning recess, she started the story of the Chemical Project.

"What was the nature of your relationship in 1989?" Shapiro asked.

"It was very unstable, very unhappy. He was very unhappy."

"And what, if anything, were you doing about that?"

"I was constantly trying to make him happy, doing anything to please him."

"In the summer of '89, approximately how many times would he give you lists with items on them?"

"Approximately six to eight."

The prosecutor asked her what kinds of things were on the lists.

"Boxes, tape, string, muriatic acid, distilled water, aluminum clothesline, wire, Clorox, chlorine, propane torch, solder, gloves, trash bags." Almost always, the list included yellow Playtex rubber gloves and trash bags.

"Were you able to use the items you had at home to fill out the lists?"

"No."

"Why not?"

"He told me to go out and buy them. He did not want to use the items at home."

She described her scavenger hunts at Roy's behest in much the same way she had to the agents. One trip, to Chattanooga, Tennessee, with Roy, illustrated particularly well the furtiveness with which he operated.

"He needed a chemical," she told the courtroom. "And in obtaining this chemical he used a company name, a fictitious company name, Classic Auto Painting, and he set up an account, a mail-receiving account and telephone-answering account in Chattanooga, ordered the chemical from a supply house in Atlanta, and had the chemical shipped to Chattanooga. When the chemical arrived, we went to Chattanooga where he made arrangements for the chemical to be delivered by courier to an abandoned building."

Shapiro: "And did you pick up the chemical?"

"Yes. The chemical was picked up."

"What happened after you picked up the chemical?"

"He told me to drive him to a drugstore, and typing paper and envelopes was purchased at that drugstore. In the truck he had a manual typewriter where he typed a couple of letters while wearing yellow rubber gloves. Meanwhile, he had me wiping fingerprints off of money that he later inserted into those letters. . . . When he was finished, he told me to drive across the street to a car wash where he threw something out that I don't recall what it was. And from there to a nearby post office where he mailed the letters."

She never saw the typewriter again.

Later, Shapiro asked, "During the months of June and July of 1989, how often was Mr. Moody working on what you would call the chemical project?"

"All the time."

"Did there come a time when it became apparent to you that he abandoned the project?"

"Yes, toward the end of July."

"How did you know?"

". . . He was kind of gloomy and he made the comment that he couldn't figure out why it wasn't working."

Moody, she testified, left for a trip to Oshkosh, Wisconsin, and when he returned about a week later, he asked the whereabouts of the smoke grenade Ted Banks had given him. Susan fetched it from a closet.

"At that time," Susan said, "he did close up the front bedroom again for a period of one to two weeks."

Also close to that time, Susan provided him with a wax-paper envelope containing both a Priority Mail label and postage. Roy left on another trip around August 20, and while he was gone, Susan heard on the radio about the smoke bomb at the NAACP office in Atlanta.

"And how did you react when you heard it?" Howard Shapiro asked.

"I felt very afraid. And I was—I felt isolated. And I was very numb."

In early September, after the tear-gas incident, Roy took a couple of footlockers filled with books and guns to Titusville, she said. Susan was able to testify about key dates with remarkable precision, largely because she had a copious cache of receipts for everything from lunch to lodging, which she had used to cue her memory. She used a check cashed for traveling expenses to fix the date of her trip to Florence, Kentucky, on November 21, 1989. She left at three A.M. Susan told the jury, much as she had the agents, that Roy wanted her to go out of state to buy items from one of the lists, to go far enough where she could purchase the items and come back without having to spend the night.

"Did he ever tell you what he was doing with all the items you were purchasing?" the prosecutor asked.

"No. He told me not to ask."

"And did you ask?"

"No."

"Did he give you . . . specific instructions in preparation for the trip to Florence, Kentucky?"

"The instructions were to go in disguise, to pay cash, not to get

fingerprints on the items, and to park away from the storefronts, entrances and exits."

". . . Did he provide you with anything else to do?"

"He gave me several originals to make copies of."

". . . Did you ever read them?"

"No."

"Why not?"

"He told me not to."

She arrived in Florence about ten or eleven A.M. and stopped at a
phone booth "to organize my route." She recounted for the jury visiting a post office and buying about $20 worth of Priority-stamp
packages, with the Priority Mail label, a $2 stamp and a forty-cent
stamp. She told about the aluminum cake pans and about shoplift-
ing, as Roy instructed, a pad of self-adhesive mailing labels from a
Florence office-supply store.

At this point Shapiro diverted attention momentarily from the
Florence trip to ask whether Susan had previously pilfered anything
at Moody's request. She recounted an incident at a Kroger in
Riverdale, Georgia, not far from Rex: "He wanted me to take two
packages of nails. When I didn't want to, he took them."

Back to Florence: "How did you do your copying?"

". . . I had on gloves . . . but I still used an open folder at the bottom of the copy-receiving tray and I used an open folder to cover
the copies as they came out of the machine."

"And how many originals were you given?"

". . . It was more than three."

Susan said her gloves were red. She also wore a scarf, sunglasses,
a blue peacoat, blue jeans and tennis shoes. When she was finished
copying, she said she put the copies in plastic garbage bags and
then in the VW Bug. A couple of doors down from the copy shop was
a box store where she bought a number of boxes close to the sizes
called for on Roy's list.

"Did you ever read or look at the copies you had made?" Shapiro
asked again. This was a crucial credibility issue.

"No."

"Why not?"

"He told me not to."

"You didn't think of doing it anyway?"

"No."

When Susan returned to Rex near midnight, Roy wasn't there but came home soon after, explaining he'd been at a Waffle House for a couple of hours and was trying to phone.

"And he became concerned when I wasn't home by ten. As a result, he packed up the items in the front room, left the house, and decided to wait at the Waffle House a couple of hours, and he said that when I answered the phone, that was his last phone call. Had I not been home, he was going to go to Titusville. . . . His concern was I may have been pulled over by the police, and had they read the items I copied, that I would have been detained."

Apparently with the aid of receipts, Susan ascertained the front room was still closed up on December 4, but opened by December 6. About that time, Roy put down a new plywood floor over the old one in the room. On December 12—just four days before Judge Vance was killed—new carpet was installed in the front bedroom. Susan also purchased a shovel and accompanied Roy into the woods down the road from the house. He dug up a Tupperware container in which she could see envelopes. On December 14, Roy gave Susan more instructions.

"He told me to go through the workshop and pull out items from the workshop that were on the list that he had given me throughout the year."

Shapiro: "And did you find any there?"

"No."

"Did he ask you to collect any other items throughout the house or the premises?"

"Yes. He told me to check the house and check the yards for threaded rod. And I did. And I found about five different lengths of threaded rods, and I placed them in the carport and told him that I did find some and where they were."

"And did they stay very long in the carport?"

"No."

Susan described several other bizarre cleanups, other damaging conversations with Roy, and parts of the Julie Linn-West scenario. Then Shapiro recounted the scrutiny to which the Moodys were subjected in early 1990, the surveillance, searches and subpoenas.

"During all of that time, did Mr. Moody ever take you aside and discuss with you whether he was guilty of the crimes he was being accused of?"

"No."

"Did he ever tell you, 'I didn't do it'?"

"No."

Then it was Tolley's turn. First question: "Ma'am, have you gone over the questions and the answers that were raised here today on a question-and-answer—question-by-question, answer-by-answer—basis?"

"Yes."

"And how many times have you done that?"

"Approximately eight to ten."

"And have you practiced in the chair that you're in now or have you used another courtroom to practice in?"

"I have used this courtroom."

"And how many times have you practiced here?"

"Twice."

Tolley referred to Susan's testimony in 1983 in one of the Florida cases. "Did you testify to the truth or did you lie?"

"I would have to review my testimony." Good answer. An effective witness sticks to specifics on cross, doesn't get sucked in and crossed up.

"In preparing for the case today you haven't had an opportunity to do that?"

"No, sir."

"And you can't remember whether you lied in that proceeding or not?"

"That's right."

"All right, ma'am. In another legal proceeding involving the First National Bank of Atlanta, you gave . . . depositions in that case, do you recall that?"

"Yes."

"So that the jury will understand, can you tell the jury what a deposition is please, ma'am?"

". . . A sworn statement."

"And did you lie?"

"Yes."

He moved on to the Julie Linn-West scenario. "Even though Mr. Moody certainly was involved in the scheme, it was you that met with her most of the time and taught her how to testify, wasn't it?"

"When he told me to, yes, it was."

Then Tolley went back to the issue of her believability under oath.

"Do you recall that on July the sixth, 1990, you were subpoenaed to testify in the United States District Court for the Northern District of Georgia, Atlanta division, to the grand jury in the Richard Russell Building . . . ?"

"Yes."

". . . Do you recall being placed under oath by Assistant United States Attorney Gerrilyn Brill?"

"Yes."

"Do you understand what an assistant United States attorney is?"

"Yes."

"Same as Mr. Shapiro, is that correct?"

"Correct," she said.

"And you were again in a federal district court like this district court, weren't you?"

"Yes."

"And you lied to the grand jury, didn't you?"

"Yes." But Roy told her what to say, she added.

Tolley: "When you testified in that federal grand jury proceeding, did you raise your right hand and take an oath to tell the truth?"

"Yes, sir. I did."

"And that was a lie, wasn't it?"

"Yes, it was."

Later Tolley brought up Susan's plea bargain. "Your understanding is they are going to dismiss all of the related charges against you in Macon, Georgia, except one conspiracy count, right?"

"Yes."

"And your understanding is you are not going to be prosecuted for murder or any of the crimes related to murder in exchange for your testimony here today, is that correct?"

"Correct."

"And your further understanding is that you have got a sentencing pending in Brunswick, Georgia, in front of the Honorable Judge Alaimo with a maximum he could give you of five years in exchange for your testimony here today, is that correct, ma'am?"

"Yes."

"And you are hoping, aren't you, that when you get through here and Judge Alaimo sentences you in July, that your sentence is going to be probation—aren't you, ma'am?"

"I hope for the best, yes."

"And the best is certainly probation, isn't it?"

"Yes."

"What does immunity mean to you, ma'am?"

"Not to be charged."

"Freedom, is that correct? It means freedom."

———

Susan was still on the stand when court resumed the next morning, still under cross.

"Did Roy Moody ever discuss Robert Robinson with you?"

"No."

"Did he ever discuss Judge Vance with you?"

"No."

"Did Roy Moody ever talk to you about school-desegregation cases?"

"Not that I recall."

Tolley also asked her if Roy had reddish blond, kinky, permed hair December 2, 1989—which was about the time of the Red Dot powder purchase from Sartain at The Shootin' Iron.

"No."

"Was your answer no?"

"I have never seen him with that hair."

"Okay. Thank you. The final question then is, ma'am, at any time did you ever see Roy Moody with a bomb or a mail bomb?"

"No."

"Thank you."

There would be redirect and recross, then more redirect. But the essential character of her testimony was set. She was good. She had answered for the most part unfalteringly and with precision. Tolley was able to establish she had lied under oath before and she had plenty to gain from cutting her deal, but she had kept her cool.

Roy still wore his ring from Susan.

"Now will you take that ring off?" Tolley asked his client as she exited.

"No."

The lawyer shook his head.

The next string of witnesses would ensure that Susan's word would not have to stand alone. Juanita Spaulding worked as retail manager for Ric Lohr's Quickprint. She remembered the lady who came in the store dressed conspicuously in dark clothes, all the way to her ankles, with either a scarf or a hood. "She had gloves on," the witness said. "It was not cold out."

Rob Lohr, Ric's brother, was next. He too worked at the shop.

"Let me direct your attention to the fall of 1989," said Shapiro. "Is there any copying incident there that stands out in your mind?"

"Yes. There was a . . . strangely dressed lady that did come in that made some copies."

"And how did you first become aware of it?"

"Juanita came back and brought my attention to it."

"What did you see?"

"A lady dressed in dark clothes with sunglasses, a scarf, you know, wrapped around her head, long overcoat, dark gloves, just real peculiar looking."

"Was it very cold out that day, do you recall?"

"No. It was a rather warm day to be dressed that extreme."

Gordon Horton was an engaging teenager, a junior at Boone High School in Florence, Kentucky, who cleaned up and filled the copiers with paper and did odd jobs at Ric Lohr's Quick Print after school. He testified next, about being fingerprinted by the FBI. His time on the stand was brief, but his significance to the case was about to become huge. This was where the FBI's importance to the investigation—its sheer manpower, systematic following of leads like those Susan McBride generated and its technological capabilities—came coruscatingly clear. The next witness was Robert Gallup, a veteran fingerprint specialist from FBI headquarters. Gallup testified, in effect, that using chemicals and laser techniques he had found two fingerprints on a blank piece of paper accompanying the threat letters from the Jacksonville bomb package. For months, he tried to make identifications. He estimated more than one hundred thousand comparisons were made.

"Did there come a time when you did match a print?" Shapiro asked.

"Yes."

"And how did that come about?"

"Well, I received a set of inked fingerprints in November of 1990, elimination prints of an individual who they thought might have handled this sheet of paper, and I was asked to compare it, and sure enough, the two fingerprints found on here were made by one in the same individual—or were the same fingers of the one individual."

Shapiro: "Let me show you government exhibit seven seventy. Is that the set of inked prints you received?"

Gallup: "Yes. Gordon Lee Horton."

Nobody ever found any of Roy Moody's fingerprints on the bombs. But the fingerprint of the earnest cleanup boy represented hard, physical evidence in corroboration of Susan's story. The prosecution segued from one important evidenciary skein into another. Barely a month after the bombings, long before Roy Moody emerged publicly as a suspect, Atlanta-based ATF Agent Joe Kennedy, part of the surveillance team watching Roy, spotted him entering the Griffin Servistar Hardware store. Walter Phillips, the hardware-store manager who had indicated to investigators he steered Moody to The Shootin' Iron, testified next.

Shapiro: "Can you describe the customer who had the conversation with you?"

"Oh, he was approximately medium height. He either had on a wig or his hair was dyed."

"Would you recognize him if you saw him again?"

"Yes, I would."

"Do you see him in the courtroom today?"

"Yes, I do."

"Would you point him out please?"

Phillips complied.

"Describe what he is wearing," Shapiro instructed.

"A blue suit, red tie, light blue shirt."

"The record should reflect the identification of the defendant, Walter Leroy Moody."

During cross-examination, Don Samuel picked away at a seeming disparity between what Phillips remembered now and what he told federal agents the year before.

"Do you remember telling the FBI agents or the ATF agents when they came and talked to you that you recognized him from having come to a . . . store in Riverdale?"

"Yes."

"On several occasions?"

"I believe so, yes."

"And that was a minimum of seven years previously?"

"Yes."

"But now you are not certain about that anymore?"

"Well, yes, it is a possibility I had seen him. But it is just vague in my mind."

For his fiftieth birthday, Paul Sartain, father of five, twenty-seven years with Ford Motor Company, got to lumber to the witness stand in a courthouse about eleven hundred miles from his home in Griffin. At one point, he had risen to the supervision of a thousand people on two shifts at Ford. He cultivated a talent for remembering faces to go with the names of the timesheet. Now, however, he was retired, doing desultory volunteer work for a little gun shop on an out-of-the-way street in central Georgia and the issue was how well he remembered the face of the man who bought that gunpowder in December 1989. Sartain suffered from diabetes, hypertension and nerve deterioration brought on by the taking of insulin. It was not, he said, likely to get better.

"How are your eyes?" Louis Freeh said. "How do you see?"

"My eyes are perfect."

Freeh and Sartain got to the sale of the four-pound "keg" of Red Dot powder on December 2, 1989, a date fixed with the aid of counter receipts and a calendar from the wall of the gun store.

"Mr. Sartain," said the lead prosecutor, "would you please describe to the jury what you recall about the man who bought the powder that day?"

". . . You can hear the door close before you actually see the person that's come into the shop. So when I first glanced up, he was facing the rear of the shop. And I walked over to him and asked him could I help him. And that's when the hair—I really don't know how to explain it. It looked like it just come out of a beauty shop. It was kind of wavy and kinky around the edges, kind of a real dark, dark reddish brown.

"And I noticed the gentleman was wearing glasses. They were dark, plastic frames, slightly tinted, and they were not glasses that I would say would come out of an eye doctor. They looked like something that come from [a] drugstore or something like that. And I did notice . . . dark, heavy circles under his eyes. His eyes were recessed, more or less like magnetic eyes—just stare through you."

Sartain said the man's mouth was "kind of squinched together" like somebody whose dentures hadn't been lined. The witness recalled looking down slightly at the powder buyer, so he put his height at about five feet ten or eleven. "When I have a good day, I'm about six feet one inch," Sartain said.

"Let me show you what is in evidence as seven seventy-six," Freeh said. Exhibit 776 was a blue jacket found in the May 1 search of the residence in Rex.

"How would you compare seven seventy-six to what you recall the man was wearing that day?"

"My opinion it's identical."

Freeh asked the retiree to look around the courtroom for the person who bought the keg of powder.

"He's directly behind you with the blue jacket, light blue shirt and red tie."

Freeh: "May the record reflect that the witness has identified the defendant, Walter Moody."

But still to be dealt with was the circuitous journey Sartain made to finally identifying Roy in the photo lineups. Freeh asked him first about the time he was shown the six black-and-white photos.

"Did you eliminate any of the photographs that appear there?"

"Yes, sir. I did."

"Which numbers did you eliminate?"

"I eliminated all but five and six."

"And you know now that Mr. Moody's picture is in number five?"

"I do now."

The third time he was interviewed by agents, he recounted, he was shown color photos. "They just presented them to me again, told me to take my time, look them over, and see if there was any change from the first one."

Freeh: "By the way, on the first occasion when you did not identify one of those pictures, did you ask the agents for anything in particular?"

"Yes, sir. I told them that before I would make a commitment I would like to see the man in person."

"And that was on April fourth?"

"Right, sir."

"Now on this day, April ninth, when you saw the color photos, did you pick anybody out or identify anyone in any way?"

"Well, in my mind even on the fourth—"

"I'm not asking about the fourth now. Just tell me what you did on the ninth."

"On the ninth, number five."

"What did you tell the agents about number five on April ninth?"

"The hair was different and the puffiness of the face."

"How did you identify, if at all, picture number five?"

"By the eyes."

". . . What did you say to the agents? In other words, you're sitting there with the pictures. They're watching you. What, if anything, did you say about number five?"

". . . To me it looked like him but I couldn't be sure."

Then he recounted his return from his Florida vacation, the newspaper photo, and eventually, the lineup in Atlanta. On paper, the Sartain identification, with the two early misfires, was far from textbook. On the stand, however, Paul Sartain proved a powerful witness. And Tolley knew it.

19

The Verdict

Judge Devitt sat at his desk framed by a window, backlit by the late-afternoon light shimmering like a sunfish belly off the Mississippi River, the old man and the old river, both quietly purposeful at this stage. To his left sat a huge dictionary atop a pedestal. To the right was a cup full of pencils and an unlit, chewed-upon cigar. A porkpie hat hung on a rack nearby. Across from the eighty-year-old jurist sat Roy Moody's defense team, about the best tax dollars could buy. The prosecution knew about and did not object to this ex parte conference; they were smart enough to discern the dilemma facing Tolley and Samuel.

"If Your Honor please," Tolley began, "Mr. Samuel and I are on a collision course with Mr. Moody about the issue of whether he will testify in the trial of this case. Mr. Samuel and I share the firm opinion that he should not testify. We share that opinion for perhaps different reasons. My own personal reason is that Mr. Moody has given us so many, if you will, *versions* of what has occurred in this case, that I would not be comfortable with any version at this point that he would put to the jury."

Tolley measured his words carefully. "I don't want to go so far as to say the client is going to commit perjury. But . . . given the latest discussion that I have had with him, I have some idea what he would

276

tell the jury would—Don, would you agree with this?—be preposterous. Is that the nicest way to put it?"

"Not a bad way," replied Samuel, whose ugly tie was no longer the most important issue of neck wear. Now the question was what kind of ethical noose Roy might slip around his lawyers' throats, and what the judge could do to help them. The prosecution was close to resting, and Moody was thought to be considering a move that might place his attorneys in the perilous posture of putting up perjured testimony. Complicating the picture further, the lawyers didn't know it to be perjury. But perjurious or preposterous, from a practical standpoint, Moody's story was likely to be utterly inconsistent with the defense Tolley and Samuel had advanced in cross-examination of the government's witnesses.

They talked precedents and alternatives, including refusing to call Moody and telling him if he took the stand, he could represent himself for the rest of the trial. But that wasn't going to happen. Roy Moody had made a career—a life maybe—out of haranguing the legal system. Now he stood accused of a murderous assault on that system, the same system that had to try him. The law itself was on trial, and there was no room for halfhearted lawyers on either side, just as there was no room for a judge prone to mistakes. That's why Tolley, Samuel, and Devitt were in chambers together.

"Our feeling is we are going to talk to him one more time and try to talk him out of testifying," Tolley told the judge. "We are going to tell him eventually that we are not going to call him to testify. And then, I think, Your Honor, as I understand the cases, the ball will shift to your court because you can direct us to put him up in narrative form. In other words, I will put him up. I will put him up under oath, ask him his name, ask him to tell the jury his version of the events, and sit down and let him tell it."

The next day, Samuel and Tolley drove about a half hour outside of St. Paul to the suburb of Oak Park, home to a gleaming state-of-the-art state prison, much of it subterranean, where Moody was housed during the trial. In the handsome new prison library with a big window overlooking the prison grounds, Moody sat shackled to a chair, which struck Tolley as unnecessary; the bombings were not the work of a "face killer," an appellation among criminal-defense lawyers to distinguish those who can stab, strangle, or shoot face-to-face as opposed to those who murder from anonymous distance.

Arguing the ethics of perjured testimony might have been a low-percentage play with Roy Moody, an accomplished suborner of same. So the two lawyers addressed their client with as much cool logic as they could muster. Tolley was left with little choice but to tell Moody in hard terms that the testimony he proposed to give would be extraordinarily damaging to the defense.

FBI bomb expert Tom Thurman was on the stand as the third week of trial opened, continuing testimony begun the previous Friday. He went through recovered bomb parts piece by piece, explaining their function for the jury. Shapiro asked him about the Jacksonville bomb: "Let me show you government's exhibit six ninety-one. Is this the powder that was recovered from the device?"

"Yes, sir. This is the smokeless powder."

"And did you determine the quantity of powder that was recovered from that device?"

"Yes, sir. Approximately six point six ounces."

"And when you received the powder and the, at that point, intact pipe, did you attempt to load the powder back into the pipe?"

"Yes, sir. What I did was take another pipe of identical size . . . and poured the powder back into the pipe. And I discovered, actually quite by accident, that all of the powder wouldn't go back in the bomb."

"Would you have been able to pack the powder into the pipe?"

"Yes, sir. If I had pushed the powder down in there and tried to compress it, I could have made it go in."

"Is it fair to say," the young prosecutor asked, "that the more powder, the more destructive power of the bomb?"

"Yes, sir."

Thurman described the devices as ingenious, imbued with "extremely high craftsmanship." Consistent with the other government experts to testify before him, the expert offered an opinion the '72 and '89 bombs were built by the same person, and he listed specific reasons why.

Later that day prosecutor John Malcolm led Andrew Bringuel, the rookie FBI agent, through the story of his eightpenny finishing nails, the ones he found while shopping with his wife at the Kroger in Peachtree City. Through a series of stipulations and testimony, Malcolm established the Atlanta division of Kroger Company was supplied with eightpenny nails by a company called Peyton's; Peyton's got all its finishing nails from Ensar Corporation; Ensar bought all its eightpenny nails from Metalcraft Corporation in Taiwan, and Metalcraft bought all its eightpenny nails from either the Shen-Hua Company or the Chong-Hsing Iron Wire Company.

That set the scene for Malcolm's meticulous questioning of William Tobin, a forensic metallurgist from the FBI lab. Tobin testified the nails from the four 1989 mail bombs were all the same type—eightpenny, two-and-a-half-inch, galvanized nails. All of them, he suggested, had even come from the same batch at the factory. Tobin had also examined nails purchased by federal agents from a half dozen Atlanta-area Kroger stores. They too came from the same batch. The nails from all four bombs and the metro-Atlanta Kroger stores had all come from the same batch, made with the same tools at about the same time.

All of this only became a nail in the case against Roy Moody for one reason: Susan had already testified that when she refused to shoplift two packages of nails from a Kroger store, Roy took them himself.

The prosecution continued with similar series of witnesses concerning boxes and batteries, essential but essentially dry testimony. But if anyone dozed in the gallery, the two women who took the stand the afternoon of June 18 should have awakened them. The first was the woman Roy met through the personals and took to Chattanooga. She was not young but well preserved and well built.

"By the way," Howard Shapiro asked the witness, "on the overnight trip to Chattanooga, did he tell you he had been recently married?"

"No, he did not."

"Did you have any reason to believe he had been recently married?"

"No, no."

But something she said Roy did tell her might have been far more damaging than marital infidelity: "That the Eleventh Circuit court, they were all crooked, they were in cahoots. There was no fairness. There was no justice."

"He made . . . other comments like that to you as well?" the prosecutor asked.

"In that vein, yes."

"How did he appear while he was making those comments?"

". . . He was very upset. I got a little uncomfortable. I thought it was something that was very close to his heart."

"How could you tell that he was upset, that it was something very close to him?"

"Well, I thought of him as a very reserved, charming person. And for a moment, when he started to explain this to me, I remember wondering if he didn't have a—maybe a bad temper that you don't always show when you first get to know someone."

The second woman testified she went out with Moody two or three times in 1980. Roy, by her account, said blacks and whites should be kept separate and that Roy used the word *nigger*.

On cross, Tolley asked, "Are you aware of the fact that he had both a black accountant and a black personal secretary at or around the time you knew him?"

"No, sir."

The government played a few of the Moody musings picked up on the bugs both before and after his arrest. "Now you've killed two . . . now you can't pull another bombing" was one gem mined in April 1990. "Mmm-huh, bullshit, anytime you're dealing with the court, you're dealing with a . . . damn crook" was another.[*] FBI Agent Bill Lewis, who helped put the tapes before the jury, was cleared to step down.

Howard Shapiro: "Your Honor, at this time, the government rests."

Ed Tolley: "Your Honor, there will be matters that I need to address to the court outside the presence of the jury."

Judge Devitt: "Members of the jury. You may be excused for about ten minutes. We will call you back shortly."

Tolley made a perfunctory motion for a judgment of acquittal. He put it forth without argument and the judge denied it without comment. But Tolley and Samuel were not in an utterly untenable position, not so far at least. The government had built a powerful circumstantial case. But there was still room, however tight, to argue the government had made a good case that Ted Banks helped build the bombs, and a good case that Susan bought components later found in the bombs. But there remained not a single piece of direct, physical evidence proving Roy was the mail bomber. That defense, however, could quickly get wrecked if the brilliant, obsessive Roy

---

[*]This is according to the government transcription.

Moody refused to keep his mouth shut. Obsession won over brilliance.

"The defendant has advised me that he wishes to testify in this case," Tolley announced. "I would like to advise the court of the following matter:

"That his testimony will be entirely against my legal advice and that of Mr. Samuel."

Tolley recounted in public what he'd already made clear in private to the judge and to Roy: Moody's anticipated testimony would jeopardize what defense had been advanced so far. He added that Moody could face death-penalty prosecutions in Alabama and Georgia, the states where Vance and Robinson were murdered. An Alabama prosecutor had been present for almost the entire trial.

"I veto his right to testify," Tolley proclaimed. "I have told him I will not let him testify. . . . I'm not going to call him unless the court orders me to."

Judge Devitt summoned Moody and had him sworn in. Roy: "Your Honor, I have made the decision that I would like to testify."

"Good and loud, Mr. Moody, so we can hear you."

"I said, I have made the decision that I would like to testify, Your Honor."

The judge queried the accused judge killer three more times about it, the last like this:

"You're satisfied you want to testify?"

"Yes, sir."

The white-haired jurist directed Tolley to call Moody as a witness, but spared him the indignity of unbridled participation in something to which he had already made clear his fundamental opposition. Devitt would allow Moody to testify in narrative form, meaning Tolley every now and then could simply throw him a broad question to transition into the next frontier Moody wanted to explore.

"You indicated to me your desire to explain the 1972 matter involving the bomb to the jury," Tolley said. "Do you wish to explain that matter to the jury?"

"Yes, I do."

"All right, sir. Would you please advise them whatever it is you wanted them to know?"

"Okay. In 1972, I had a car repossessed by a man in Atlanta by the name of Tom Downing. And when I learned of the repossession, I asked him—I wrote him and asked him the amount of money that would be necessary to reclaim the car. And he advised me of the amount. I subsequently sent him that amount. When he received it, he then advised me that there would be additional cost for various things. . . ."

In exhaustive detail, he served up essentially the same dish, with a few new trimmings, as he had delivered to another federal-court bomb jury, seventeen years before, replete with the mysterious Gene Wallace. In the process, he hardly disabused listeners of an important component of the government's motive argument, that Roy was absolutely obsessed with the '72 case.

As he rambled through the narrative, Moody introduced a pair of letters dated in 1972 that—conveniently, some might say—corroborated his claims about Wallace. Louis Freeh exercised his option to question Moody about the letters before they were allowed into evidence. The prosecutor suggested neither document could be found in the 1972 court file.

Freeh: "And it's your testimony that both of these were written in 1972?"

"Right."

"You didn't just backdate them and attach them to your February 1988 affidavit?"

"No."

"You wouldn't do anything like that, would you?"

"I think it would depend on the circumstances."

Repeatedly, Roy ran the risk of bolstering the government's image of the embittered and vengeful ex-con. "Without a doubt," he pronounced further into his monologue, "the most distressing thing to me regarding this 1972 case has been the propensity for government agents and assistant U.S. attorneys to misrepresent the facts." Tolley cringed. Moody suggested such an inclination carried over into the case at hand. He seemed, at times, more intent on convincing the jury he was not treated *fairly* in 1972 than on positing his actual innocence.

"I am interested in showing that I was never afforded a fair trial in 1972," he said. ". . . The issue of whether or not I was guilty in 1972 has never been fairly decided."

Freeh objected often during Moody's free-form filibuster, including once as Roy transitioned to a new area.

"What I would like to do now," Moody said, "is to try to give you some idea of the reason why no American citizen should be subjected to a prison-type environment unless they have in fact been afforded a fair trial, and unless they have in fact been found guilty beyond a reasonable doubt."

"What I would like to do now," Freeh interposed, "is to object. That is a play for sympathy to this jury, talking about prisons and what it means to be put in prison. I think that is improper." This is what Brian Hoback had expected of Roy's testimony, that the defendant-witness would paint himself as the sympathetic victim in the '72 case.

Tolley weighed in to the discussion and the judge let Moody go on.

"The conditions at the Atlanta Federal Penitentiary was so bad that a congressional subcommittee chaired by Senator Nunn recommended that it be closed. That recommendation was not followed and it was later burned to the ground."* When Roy began to describe an inmate stabbing during his time at the pen, Freeh again objected, unless Moody could produce documentary evidence, and this time the judge sided with Freeh.

When Roy switched gears again, he offered his explanation for the muriatic acid, dry ice and other elements in Susan's account of the period when the Chemical Project was under way. Moody had an alternative to the government's suggestion he was trying to formulate the deadly nerve gases threatened in the "Declaration of War" letter. He described the famous but controversial Pons-Fleischmann "cold fusion" experiment and suggested, in considerable detail, it inspired him to run his own experiment. Roy indicated he worked on it under the house for a time, and inside as well. He said the experiment lasted from about July to November 1989. He even had an explanation for the secrecy shrouding his activities at the time.

"If this experiment had produced heat, I would have determined that it was radioactive," Roy said. "If it had been radioactive, all of the material that I was using would, itself, have been radioactive, and I would have disposed of it. . . .

"Disposing of radioactive material requires compliance with certain regulations. And I did not intend to do that. If the items had been radioactive, I did not want them traced back to me."

Only Roy Moody, Hoback thought, could come up with something this brazen.

*Moody did his time at the Atlanta pen in the early and middle 1970s. The inmate uprising during which much of the prison was burned took place in 1987.

Roy also put forth what apparently was to him a plausible alternative to the possibility Susan had heard him test-firing explosives. It was complex or confusing, depending on your point of view. He set up a scenario where, during his supposed lab work, he needed to determine whether he had produced the right gases in a jar. He described the easiest way: "Remove the vessel, lift it vertically, and then pass a lighted match underneath it. That will cause a characteristic pop, that if you've ever heard it, you'll recognize it. . . . With the type of container I was using, it sounds maybe not quite as loud as a .22 pistol going off."

Early in Roy's pronouncements concerning cold fusion, Freeh exploited another opening to interrogate Moody without having to wait for cross-examination.

"Your Honor," Freeh said, "I have no objection to this if Mr. Moody will qualify himself as a chemical expert."

"Go ahead," said Judge Devitt. "Tell us about your experience."

Moody answered, "Okay. I have had the regular premedical chemistry courses and courses in physics. The curriculum, I think, was referred to as a premedical science concentrate, Your Honor.

"I forgot where I was."

"You were at the fusion reaction," said Freeh, whose momentary assistance was understandable in light of the help Moody had just given him. The government had spent untold hours of investigation to be able to portray Moody as knowing enough about chemistry to make the mail bombs. And in the space of seconds Roy had just in effect declared *himself* an expert.

Next subject: the events surrounding Julie Linn-West's bogus testimony in 1988. "Essentially everything related to newly discovered evidence in that entire proceeding was falsified," Roy confessed. In itself, it was not a startling admission, considering how overwhelming the evidence of perjury was anyway. But in virtually the next breath, Roy went further. "I started to say 'virtually,' but I think I could go beyond that and say everything that Susan did in that connection was under my direction and control." Now he was corroborating the testimony of the most important witness against him, boosting her credibility and buttressing her image as victim rather than coconspirator.

Moody's line was that he had become suicidal, and his alternative was to "right the wrong that I felt had been done me. And I concluded that in my own mind, that the wrong was the result of misrepresentation by numerous people, and that, if the only way I could right that wrong was using the same misrepresentation that they had used in order to inflict the wrong . . . that I would falsify material and use the same unsavory tactics that they had used." Whether or not Roy Moody had truly been suicidal before, his first day on the stand certainly qualified, intentional or not, as an act of self-destruction.

———

The next morning Roy launched immediately into his attack on the prosecution's assertions about the Chamblee device. He left the witness stand and drew on a diagram. "Okay," Roy said, "this is supposed to represent the pipe assembly that was found in the basement of Mr. Wylie's home." He proceeded with another lengthy, purportedly technical explanation.

Freeh spoke up. "Your Honor, at this point I'm going to object to Mr. Moody giving expert advice unless he qualifies himself as an expert in welding and piping and all of the other things he is giving opinions about."

"Yes," said Judge Devitt. "You might qualify yourself, Mr. Moody."

"Okay, Your Honor," said Roy, stumbling toward a snare into which he had already stepped once the day before, as if obsessed to the point of myopia, even blindness. "I have worked with mechanical devices, automobiles, airplanes and things of that nature since I was about ten years old."

Moments later, Moody retook the stand. "What I am doing," he continued, "is giving . . . reasons why the government's contention that this was designed as a hybrid pipe bomb would indicate that that is not what it was designed for. I'm saying that their hypothesis is an invalid hypothesis."

He discoursed on the properties of nuts, bolts and threaded rods and the virtue of one method of construction over another, of fine-threaded bolts versus standard thread versus coarse thread, apparently to bolster his contention the Chamblee device was not meant to be used with a threaded rod.

"The nut on that . . . pipe is a coarse thread," Moody observed. "The threads on a threaded rod is a standard thread. A standard thread is not compatible with a coarse thread. And a rod would not fit in that nut unless it was a specially made rod."

Roy suggested he had not the slightest idea of what the metal assemblage was intended to do.

"Mr. Lee sees it as a pipe bomb. I think he is totally convinced that that is what it is. But I have the capacity to see other things. I'd like to show you one hypothesis that would explain everything that is there, that would also explain that it could have a useful purpose."

He then laid out a fabulously facile description of how the device could be part of a system to apply a type of automobile paint that is sensitive to humidity. "That would be one way that you could use this device. And it would be, so far as a design philosophy is concerned, it would be compatible all the way through."

Hoback had been writing furiously during Moody's testimony about the Chamblee device. And now at the break he huddled with Terry Byer, the ATF bomb expert, who mentioned to Hoback, coincidentally, he used to be in the auto-painting business. No way, he said to Hoback about Roy's theory. He gave a similar report about Moody's contentions concerning the incompatibility of the Chamblee device with a threaded rod. Hoback dispatched an agent to buy a threaded rod. In perhaps ten or fifteen minutes, he was back.

————

If jurors found all this dizzying, they were apparently not alone. Near ten-thirty A.M. on Roy's second day on the stand, he summoned Tolley. Moody said he was faint and couldn't go on. The deputy marshals took him downstairs and let him lie down until the arrival of a doctor, who found no evidence of high blood pressure or heart attack and recommended a mild sedative. That way Moody could sleep for about an hour but still resume his testimony in the afternoon. Roy told Tolley he thought he would continue at two P.M., and at 2:08, another odd episode from this odd witness concluded and he resumed his place on the witness stand. And he confronted the most potent witness against him.

"Susan is a wonderful person and I love her to death," Roy said, probably not intending the double entendre he projected, "but like everybody, she's subject to error."

This professed devotion didn't deter Roy from trotting out a tawdry tale that he implied was a necessary part of his explanation about his whereabouts during August 1989, but that came off as gratuitous. He set the scene at a Florida motel:

"I guess maybe it was probably about one o'clock in the morning. We were in the swimming pool. And Susan was kind of in an amorous and mischievous mood. She wanted to make love in the swimming pool. And I told her that, you know, I had a feeling we would get caught if we did that . . . but anyway, we did." Later, Moody indicated they went back to the same hostelry for a second stay and the manager knocked on their door. "And he said, 'I got some complaints with you guys.' . . . He took me to the back of the lot and pointed up to this condominium about ten stories high. And he says, 'There's an elderly man and his wife who come out every night with their field glasses and check my swimming pool.' And, of course, they had seen Susan and myself and had reported this to the manager."

But what Roy had to say about his ex-wife was tame compared to what he would say about his ex-lawyer. Moody depicted Susan as merely kinky. Early in his third day on the stand, he painted Mike Ford as part of a murderous mail-bomb conspiracy.

———

Moody said Ford called and asked to meet him at a Chinese restaurant. When they met, Roy said, the lawyer looked distraught and asked Roy if he remembered a friend Ford had previously mentioned with whom he went shooting on weekends.

"And I said yes. He said he sent the tear gas to the NAACP. I asked him how he knew."

Freeh interrupted. "Your Honor, may the record reflect the defendant is reading from something?"

Moody: "I'm not reading. These are dates. Would you like to check them?"

"Oh, I'm going to be checking them," Freeh replied.

Moody continued, "I asked him how he knew and he didn't respond to that question.

"He said he [the mystery friend] also sent the mail bombs. My response was . . . damn, who is the son of a bitch? He told me—his response was, you don't want to know. He's affiliated with the Klan.

". . . When he indicated to me that this person was a Klan sympathizer, I asked him what he was going to do. He says, 'I can't do anything.' He said, 'I'm involved in it to some extent.' And he said, 'You may be too. . . . Some of the items that you have provided to me may have been used in the bomb.' "

Moody laid out this story: On June 19, 1989, the Klan files an appeal in a civil case in the Eleventh Circuit. Possibly late in that same month, Moody and Ford talk. The lawyer evinces an interest in get-

ting a place where he can get away from his wife, who is also his law
partner. The suggestion is it would be a place where Ford could take
other women. He wants his client to help him pick up various
items—small furniture and so on—and will knock off some of
Moody's fees in return. Ford doesn't want Susan involved; women always stick together, he explains. The lawyer has a list, which he asks
Roy to copy. The items on the list include a typewriter and possibly
unfolded boxes. Heedless of Ford's directive not to involve Susan,
Roy tells her to get the items. If his attorney is fooling around on his
wife, Roy is concerned about what could happen if he gets caught.
So he tells Susan to handle it so the items can't be traced back to
Ford. When Moody is ready to deliver some of the material, Ford
wants him to get a motel room and meet him there. Susan gets the
room, and Roy meets Ford there, leaving with him the typewriter
and other things he'd wanted. Next Ford wants some copies made
and Roy assumes it involves the lawyer's "lady friends." Ford asks
Moody not to read the material, so Roy relays the same instructions
to Susan. Before he leaves for an air show in Oshkosh, Wisconsin, in
late July 1989, Roy discusses his smoke canister with Ford. Ford asks
if he can have it, and Moody gives it to him around the first part of
August. Eventually, Ford asks Roy to do some welding for him. Roy
goes to see Ted Banks. Ford also wants some threaded rod. Banks
never tells Moody he thinks he has welded a bomb and never asks
Moody to return anything to him. On December 6, 1989—less than
two weeks from the mail bombings—the Eleventh Circuit denied an
important motion in the KKK case.

Ingenious or inane, incredible or not, the story melded actual,
verifiable events with claims the truthfulness of which, by their nature, could only be known to Ford and Moody. However much Roy
had forsworn himself in the past three days, he hadn't lied in that
letter to Ford the year before on Moody Motion Pictures letterhead:

Smile, I'm going to make you a star.

———

"I asked Ford how he had gotten involved in it," Roy testified.
"Ford told me he was interested in embarrassing a couple of people.
He was interested in paying somebody back. The people that he was
interested in embarrassing were listed as return addressees on this—
on some of the packages. And he didn't name any names. He told

me that he had on a prior occasion worked with Mr. Robinson. He referred to him as Robbie Robinson. He said on one occasion that he had asked Mr. Robinson to fix him up with a black lady in Savannah. . . . Robinson got very upset about it and made the remark that he was not a nigger pimp."

Moody maintained Ford later discovered Robinson was telling others about his request and continued to do so after Ford apologized and asked him not to. The defendant also said Ford told him Judge Vance was never supposed to be harmed, and the package sent to the Eleventh Circuit was never intended for opening.

"He said that there had been a major fuckup in the way that the packages had been mailed," Roy related. "The first package was to have been mailed to Mr. Robinson. He said that they were mailed on the fourteenth, on the fifteenth and on the sixteenth. The second package he said was to be sent to the NAACP in Jacksonville.

"The other two packages—the one to Judge Vance and the one to the Eleventh Circuit—were to be mailed on the sixteenth. He doesn't know how it happened, I don't think, but somehow there was a screwup and they were mailed out of order. He expected the first package to be opened. He thought there was a possibility that the second package would be opened. He said letters had been sent that would cause all of the other packages to be intercepted."

Moody's line was that Ford, after the bombings but before the first raid on Moody's house, warned him the FBI would contact him in light of his previous bomb conviction and his pending Eleventh Circuit appeal.

"He said, 'You can bet your ass they're going to contact you.' He said, 'When they come, do not talk to them. Send them to me.' "

Later, Moody alleged, Ford warned him about something else: "Before you run your mouth to anybody, you had better remember who you are and who I am.

"He said, you are an ex-convict that has been convicted of possession of a bomb. And you are the chief—or the suspect in this case. He said, I am an officer of the court and a family man. He said that he had a brother that worked with . . . I think he said Department of Justice. And he indicated that I was the perfect scapegoat.

". . . He told me that if I jeopardized his interests, it would jeopardize people in the Klan. And he repeatedly said, 'These people have killed a federal judge. They will kill you. Do you understand what I am telling you? They will kill you.' "

Roy's direct testimony, and the third week of the mail-bomb trial, ended that afternoon. Before taking him back to Oak Park for the weekend, the Marshals Service took him by a county-hospital emergency room for another checkup.

Monday, Freeh, predictably, handled the cross. And predictably, he was a relentless, voracious shark of a prosecutor. He opened with a staccato series of questions that drummed out of Roy admissions about the Julie Linn-West scenario.

"And you believe that under the circumstances you were justified in lying?" Freeh asked.

"Yes."

"And what is your philosophy about when a person is justified to lie in court when they are under oath?"

"I think in a situation where there has been a deliberate attempt to deny an individual constitutional rights, where this is not an error, but where it is a contrived act by a group of people who are sworn to uphold the law, who are sworn to uphold the duties of their office, when those individuals failed to comply with their duties, when they failed to uphold the law, when what they do is in fact a crime against that person, a crime against the Constitution, a crime against the people of the United States, when those crimes result in a person being convicted of a crime that they did not commit, when that crime results in them being sent to prison, where they are subjected to inhumane treatment over a long period of time, where their treatment results in permanent damage to them mentally, when that damage results in them getting to a situation where they are so desperate that they are contemplating taking their lives, then in that circumstance where they have exhausted all legal remedies and it becomes a matter of life or death, then I think they are justified in using the same tactics to remove the insult as was used to initiate the insult against them."

If the government wanted to prove Roy was angry and embittered at the legal system, they could hardly have scripted a better speech or directed a better performance. Roy finished at the end of the day, the only witness for the defense, perhaps one of the most effective for the prosecution. Tolley and Samuel had at least a half dozen others subpoenaed. None of them, Tolley decided, would fit with the defense Roy had just posited. At nine-thirty the next morning, the defense rested. Moments later Howard Shapiro called the prosecution's first rebuttal witness, Mike Ford.

Even before the trial had started, the Moody investigation had intruded into Ford's personal life unlike any other case in his career. Agents interviewed his brothers, his father, his mother-in-law and his wife. He'd been hauled in front of a federal grand jury. He'd been duped into believing Roy Moody was his friend as well as his client. Now that Moody's St. Paul soliloquy was done, the whole business amounted to the most distressing experience Ford had ever known.

"Prior to last week," the prosecutor asked, "had Mr. Moody ever taken you aside and personally accused you of the bombings?"

"He's never done that."

"He's never done that?"

"No, sir. Not personally."

"Makes his accusations publicly?"

"That's correct."

"Did you have anything to do with any of the crimes charged in the indictment, Mr. Ford?"

"No, sir."

"Did you make any bombs?"

"No, sir."

"Did you provide any components?"

"No, sir."

Through questioning, Shapiro established Ford had opened his law practice in a predominantly black section of Atlanta. Two of the lawyers who helped him the most starting out were black, and Ford had subsequently joined a predominantly black law firm in which one of the named partners was a civil-rights attorney well-known in Georgia.

"Do you have anything to do with the Klan, Mr. Ford?"

"Absolutely nothing."

Ford produced boarding passes and airport parking receipts suggesting he was out of town for one of the key dates involved in Moody's narrative. Item by item, Shapiro fed pieces of Moody's story for Ford to deny. Ford's wife, Diane, followed him on the stand. She recalled an odd call from Roy she indicated came in late April or early May 1990, when Roy was still on the street.

"Well," she said, "the first thing he asked is where does Mike buy his gunpowder, which I thought was a very strange thing to ask anyway. And at that time everybody around him knew his phones had to be tapped."

Next came Judge Edward Baety of the Atlanta Traffic Court, a black man who had known Ford since about 1974 and said Ford never displayed a racist attitude or asked him to arrange dates with black women.

Benjamin Bayman was a nuclear physicist from the University of Minnesota, but he could have been from central casting, with his Dr. Zorba looks and his academically eccentric sneakers. The professor had lectured before about cold fusion.

Shapiro had asked him to review about twenty pages of the trial transcript. The prosecutor called the scientist's attention to portions regarding Moody's supposed experiments.

"Is what Mr. Moody describes himself as doing here at all related to cold fusion?" Shapiro asked.

"No."

". . . It is more akin to charging your battery?"

"Yes. Yes. Unless, unless there is something very special about the electromagnetic field that he refers to . . . which . . . makes his experiment unique and distinguishes his experiment, but about which he has told us nothing else."

Terry Byer, the ATF bomb expert, retook the stand. Howard Shapiro read the portion of Roy's testimony concerning the Chamblee device, where Moody said "a rod would not fit in that nut unless it was a specially made rod."

Byer recounted the purchase of a threaded rod during Moody's testimony.

"It wasn't specially made?" Shapiro queried.

"No, sir."

"It wasn't specially ordered?"

"No, sir."

". . . What I have handed you, is that a threaded rod, washer and nut?"

"Yes, sir."

"And does that fit with the Chamblee device . . . ?"

"Yes, sir, it does."

"Would you show the jury how you would assemble that using a threaded rod?"

"Yes, sir. I will." And Byer did.

Shapiro: "That took you less than a minute, is that fair to say?"

"Probably, yes, sir."

The next morning Louis Freeh handled the government's closing argument. He referred to Susan's testimony. Even Roy, he declared, corroborated 90 percent of what she'd said. Then he brought up Ted Banks.

"Mr. Tolley calls him a pirate. He is a pirate, an absolute pirate," Freeh conceded. "He would do anything for a buck. But he was Mr. Moody's pirate. He was the guy who worked for Mr. Moody year after year in fraud after fraud after fraud. Mr. Moody trusted him." And Moody, Freeh said, corroborated 90 percent of what Banks said too. The powder. The Chamblee device. The similarities to the 1972 bomb. Julie Linn-West. The prosecutor rattled it off. Motive was not so easy.

"Remember what the court said about Mr. Moody's error coram nobis? . . . They said it is too old, Mr. Moody, it is too old, rule of finality. You should have raised these claims before. It is too late.

"Can you imagine the rage—quiet rage, he is a very quiet man, very charming—the quiet rage when he read that, Judge Vance telling the black plaintiffs that remoteness . . . in time is not a bar? And his judge telling him, remoteness in time is a bar? The perfect target becomes Judge Vance."

Freeh admitted he couldn't say why Vance was targeted among other judges. But the bomber had victims in Georgia and the Jacksonville NAACP in Florida. Georgia, Florida and Alabama are the three states comprising the Eleventh Circuit. He *needed* a victim in Alabama.

"The only correct decision," the special prosecutor told the jury, "without any sympathy on your part for Mr. Moody, is that he did these crimes, he did them deliberately, he planned them, he carried them out, he did it in a way to protect himself. He did it in such a way that he could get up on a witness stand if he had to, like he did here, and tell you that somebody else did it. Blame somebody else. Ford and the KKK.

"And remember one thing more than anything else. Remember Mr. Robinson. Mr. Robinson is dead. Blown to bits. Dying three hours in a way nobody should ever have to die, because he wanted a diversion. He wanted to protect his butt someday when he had to. And that's why he killed that person."

On the stand, Ed Tolley's client had been like a snowman hammered by a warm front, melting away in plain view; now Tolley had to construct a closing argument from a handful of slush. Echoing his

opening, he told the jurors, "If the charges against Roy Moody today for this jury to consider were that he was a most unpleasant fellow, then, ladies and gentlemen, I would suspect you would find him
guilty of being a most unpleasant fellow.

"If the charges against Roy Moody were that he had on multiple
occasions been dishonest or had lied, then I suspect, ladies and gentlemen of the jury, that you would find him guilty of dishonesty and
lying. That is also not what he is charged with today.

". . . The true issue, ladies and gentlemen, and I am afraid that
Roy rambled and rambled and rambled for three days. But the true
issue . . . is not whether Roy Moody has proven to you who committed the crime, because that is not his burden. He could have said
nothing if he had chosen to; that is his constitutional right. The true
issue and the only issue is whether or not the government has
proven Roy Moody guilty beyond a reasonable doubt."

Tolley fell back on what might have once stood a chance, albeit
not an overwhelming one, of working: the argument about what the
government *didn't* have. Roy, however, had in his testimony bol-
stered both Susan's account of gathering what the government suggested became bomb componentry and Banks's account of the
metal fabrication and welding, though Roy maintained what his
buddy welded was not the same as the metal in the mail bombs.

"We can send a man to the moon, ladies and gentlemen," Tolley
said, "and we just about have in this case. But with all of their technical expertise, with all of their technical capabilities, there had
been found not one nail of the two million nails available, not just at
the Kroger stores, but throughout the United States of America—
not one nail in any car, any home, any storage facility, any footlocker
of Walter Leroy Moody.

"There has been found not one grain. And ladies and gentlemen,
we are talking grains. We are talking something you look at under a
microscope that can be inadvertently carried on your pants leg, your
shoe bottom, your hair or your fingernail. Not one grain of smokeless powder in anything connected to Roy Moody. Nobody is that
much of a master criminal, ladies and gentlemen, I submit to you."

The government got the last shot at the jury, and Shapiro handled it, answering Tolley's closing point by point, and pointing out
perhaps the most compelling witness of all.

"He sends the bombs to make the points he wants to make,"
Shapiro said. "He sends a bomb or prepares to, to a man who repos-

sesses his car for one hundred dollars. Is it going to bother him that he doesn't even know Robbie Robinson? Will he hesitate for a moment to take that life for no reason other than his own scheme?

"You have had a lot of time to look at him. You had a lot of time to hear him. You've had a lot of time to evaluate him. Do you doubt for a second that he would do that? There's no doubt, ladies and gentlemen. There's no doubt about that whatsoever."

It took the jury nearly two days, punctuated by several questions to the court, to come to the same conclusion. Just in time for live reports near the top of the five P.M. news shows in Atlanta, the court clerk read seventy-one guilty verdicts.

"What was the worst thing that Roy Moody did during the conduct of this case?" a reporter asked Tolley outside the courthouse.

"Well, obviously, taking the witness stand against our advice. Probably the second-worst thing he did or perhaps the first-worst thing he did was refusing to allow us to proceed with a mental-illness defense. Took our two big issues away from us."

Bob Vance Jr. and his mother had been there for the decision too. "I think this trial's been good therapy for us," the young Birmingham lawyer said. "And today's events just been the best medicine we could have asked for."

Helen Vance looked exultant. "I just feel like justice has been done," she said, beaming. "And that's a good feeling."

———

The handwritten letter was dated July 21, 1991, less than a month after the end of the trial. "Dear Susan," it began. "You have always been so beautiful to me. I wrote you a short note after I saw you the other day and ask [*sic*] Don, one of my attorneys, to get it to you through Sandra. He asked if he could read it first. I agreed so I doubt if you got it. So, I will repeat it here.

> *Susan, Susan, Susan.*
> *You look so wonderful. Your pearls look good too.*
> *Love Roy*

"Ed, my other attorney, has a hard time understanding my feeling for you.

". . . I'm sure no greater effort to destroy the relationship between a man and a woman has ever been made than that directed at us. They gave you the choice of absolute distruction [*sic*] or limited reward. In reality, that is not a choice, and no one could have taken a course of action different from the one you took."

The letter went on for close to thirteen pages, during which Roy reminisced, extolled Susan's virtues and professed an unconditional, endless love. "Regardless of where you are, what you are doing and when it is, I will love you," he wrote. "That truth has been made a part of every cell of my body for the last year."

He wanted to know, if things worked out, "would you be interested in spending a year or two in Europe with me? I may have a surprise for you." He said he needed to see something she had written or touch something she had touched, that the inability to communicate with Susan had "all but destroyed me."

Susan didn't respond to the letter, other than to turn it over to a federal agent.

Epilogue

In the cool of a courtroom in sultry, summery Brunswick, Georgia, Roy Moody faced Judge Alaimo and his reputation for brooking no nonsense from those caught in his imperious, begoggled gaze.

Moody was to be sentenced for his conviction on obstruction of justice, subornation of perjury, witness tampering and the other, related charges. Tolley stood beside his client.

"Do you know of any reason why I should not now pronounce sentence?" the judge asked.

"No, sir, your honor. We're ready," Tolley replied.

"I will be glad to hear anything either one of you or both of you has to say," said Alaimo.

Moody spoke in a low voice. "Your honor, I'd like to say that the culpability regarding this matter lies with me in its entirety. Susan's participation was an unwilling participation and primarily the result of . . . psychological coercion by me. And I'd ask the court to direct whatever punishment is so due to Susan to me instead."

Pause.

"All right," said Judge Alaimo. "That is the first admirable thing I have heard you say."

Not that everyone—or even anyone—in the courtroom unquestioningly accepted Moody's statements at face value, but they were still remarkable coming only two months after Susan's stunning performance in St. Paul. It was hard, of course, to know whether his

297

speech to the judge was born of undying love or his desire not to die in the electric chair in Alabama, where he would soon be indicted on state charges for Judge Vance's murder and where Susan's testimony again figured to be key to the prosecution.

Judge Alaimo sentenced Moody to a total of 125 months in prison, a $400,000 fine and three years supervised release, but the last component would never take hold in light of the sentence Judge Devitt would hand down in St. Paul on August 20.

Said Judge Devitt, "These murders and attempts and threats to kill other judges and court personnel and to bring harm and fright to black persons and the NAACP, and to instill widespread fear for public safety, and to encourage hatred for the courts and for minorities, were all part of this defendant's vicious criminal scheme, a scheme which caused such pain and personal loss to so many and occasioned disruption and challenge to constitutional government itself."

He sentenced Roy to seven life terms plus four hundred years. There is no parole in the federal system.

Tom Stokes still smokes and seems sorry to lose Hoback, who got a plaque from the president in the Rose Garden along with other key people in the mail-bomb case, then transferred home to Memphis where one of his brothers is also an ATF agent. Hoback is now a member of ATF's National Response Team, which does crime-scene investigations for major arson and explosives cases, and lectures about the mail-bomb case to classes at the Federal Law Enforcement Training Center. Somewhere, amid the hundreds of government recordings made when Moody's prison space was bugged, there is a tinny recording of Roy Moody's whispered voice. "Hoback . . ." he says in bitter, breathy tones. "You slimy son of a bitch."

Joe Gordon was transferred to Atlanta where he served as public information officer, then to Colorado Springs, Colorado, where he is the resident agent-in-charge. Frank Lee retired from ATF about six months after the bomb trial and started Lee Investigative Services, which primarily handles fire investigations for insurance companies. Bill Hinshaw retired from the FBI in 1992 and was hired as the Inspector General for the Tennessee Valley Authority. Two years later he went into the home-building business in metro Atlanta. John Sheddan retired from the sheriff's department but still teaches explosives classes. Bob Holland and J. W. Powell also retired from their government jobs. In early 1991, Ray Rukstele took a job as a federal prosecutor in Las Vegas, Nevada, where he had worked before going to Georgia. He remains particularly proud of the role the U.S. Attorney's Office in Atlanta played in the Julie Linn-West case, which he considers a turning point in the investigation of Roy Moody.

Judge Devitt was hospitalized with terminal cancer. Tolley, Freeh and an FBI agent who assisted with the trial met in St. Paul, smuggled a bottle of Scotch into the hospital room and drank a toast. A few days later, Judge Devitt died.

Freeh was appointed a federal judge the month following the mail-bomb trial but did not hold the job for long. Barely more than two years later he was sworn in as director of the FBI. Even before Freeh's arrival, Larry Potts, the inspector who had been brought down to Atlanta to head the mail-bomb task force, was appointed the FBI's assistant director in charge of the criminal investigative division. Howard Shapiro went from precocious prosecutor to precocious professor, teaching law at Cornell. But he was once again lured by Freeh and has become the FBI's general counsel, one of the bureau's highest-level jobs.

Robert Wayne O'Ferrell and Mary Ann O'Ferrell have brought suit in federal court against the U.S. Department of Justice. Brian Fleming blames the publicity about the mail-bomb investigation in part for his conviction on the weapons-related charges he was facing. He says he helped start a prison ministry during more than two and a half years in a federal penitentiary. He's out now, and Georgia Fleming says things have returned to normal at their print shop. Wayne O'Ferrell, she told me, has come in a time or two for copying services.

Julie Linn-West told me recently that, long before the mail bombs turned up, she knew what she had done for Roy Moody would come back to haunt her some day. And even after her splendid undercover work, even after her steadfast testimony, even after the mail-bomb trial was over, it haunted her still. She was ashamed. Julie says she sunk into a deep depression and functioned too poorly to hold a job. Only in the past year, she told me, has she made peace with herself, accepted how vulnerable she was when she met Roy Moody and accepted that she couldn't change the past. She finally accepts, too, that when the government gave her the chance to help change the future, she took it. She recently started a new job and considers herself productive once more.

In November 1992, running for the first time for public office at age sixty-six, Willye Dennis was elected to the state legislature in Florida. Reportedly, Earl Shinhoster was under consideration for the NAACP's top job, became the organization's national secretary instead, then was named interim chief after the controversial firing of Benjamin Chavis. Helen Vance spends lots of time with her grandchildren, neither of whom her husband lived to see. She sold the big house on the hill but still lives in the Birmingham area where she says she has a good life today, though not the one she once would have pictured. "I miss my friend," she told me recently.

With Howard Shapiro and government agents vouching for her, Susan was sentenced to probation for her role in the obstruction case. She has become a model of independence and resilience, opening, with her friend Eva, a new restaurant in metro Atlanta, which appears to be a raging success. I stop by there frequently and it is common for every table to be taken at lunchtime. I sense few of her customers know who she is—more accurately, who she was. Not long ago, I attended a wedding reception there. Hers.

At this writing, Roy Moody is still writing writs, with his life on the line as the State of Alabama, represented by Attorney General Jimmy Evans, presses on with its death-penalty prosecution. Wrote Roy in one recent filing, ". . . Jimmy Evans is attempting to advance his career by using the same tainted evidence that was fabricated under the direction of Louis Freeh and wrongly used by him to advance his career from Assistant U.S. Attorney to Director of the FBI in record time." Among the targets in a recent lawsuit Roy filed were two lawyers who had been representing him in the state prosecution, and the possibility appears significant that Moody might represent himself if the long-delayed state murder trial finally commences. He seems to have at least one important ally, someone who lined up against him in the federal case: Ted Banks.

Banks now tells me he firmly believes Roy Moody is innocent. Released from jail less than a month after the St. Paul verdict, Banks says he intends to testify in Moody's behalf if the Alabama murder case comes to trial and that he has already assisted Roy's legal team in a number of ways. According to the aging Floridian, the one recovered pipe bomb he recalls being shown was not one of the pipes he welded.

After a long hiatus, I resumed contact with Roy in several phone conversations in 1994, making clear my willingness to discuss with him each portion of the book in which he was involved so that, in the interest of fairness, he could offer input. He said he did not have an attorney he trusted with whom he could discuss the matter. "If I had a client and you came to one of my clients with that proposal I would say, in view of the fact this is a capital case, don't talk to anybody about anything," Roy said. "I wouldn't even analyze it to try to determine the pros and cons of it. I would just say keep your mouth shut." I sensed he, too, saw the irony of this in light of his St. Paul testimony. "You know, I have the bad trait of thinking for myself occasionally," he added with a laugh. Roy conceded he testified in Minnesota "more or less just out of a state of shock and confusion," suggesting it was in response to the realization Tolley would not pursue the defense Moody wanted. Roy left the clear impression he wants the Alabama case to go to trial, as a sort of second shot at his day in court. Of course he is still appealing the federal conviction.

Acknowledgments

One Saturday, just before lunch, Helen Vance took me to a vacant house where she and her husband had lived, the house where Judge Vance died. We stood in the kitchen while she unfalteringly walked me through her recollections of what happened when the bomb had detonated in that very room. I was humbled that this strong, gracious woman would do this for me, as I was by the extensive cooperation given me by many involved in the mail-bomb case, and even a few who were not. Many of these folks not only submitted to interviews but allowed me to call on them again and again as I double-checked and rechecked, helping me synthesize and reconcile multiple accounts of the same incidents. Some of the most important sources of information I will not single out here; I suspect for them the accurate telling of their roles in the mail-bomb case is sufficient acknowledgment.

Ed Tolley, while respecting the bounds of the attorney-client relationship, has been helpful from the beginning of this project. His secretary, Nancy Bachman, and the entire staff of his firm, Cook, Noell, Tolley and Wiggins, has been supportive and patient with my frequent intrusions. Janet Westbrook, Tolley's paralegal, has been especially so and has become a close friend. Lawyers Peter Canfield, who successfully represented news organizations seeking to open up the February 1990 court proceedings, Sandra Popson, John Malcolm, Scott Winne, Martin Weinstein, Gilbert Johnston Jr., Holly

303

Barnard and Jeremy Nussbaum were also very helpful while respecting their professional responsibilities. The same can be said of Atlanta FBI SAC D. Caroll Toohey and Atlanta ATF public information officer Bobby Browning. Clifford Fulford and Max Pope offered an important perspective on Judge Vance's early political career. I thank John Johnson and William Gibson with the NAACP. Leon Blakeney supplied valuable FBI insight. Delores Cumming and Bobby Moody were always kind. Jim Jennings provided able accounting assistance. Echo Garrett, Melissa Fay Greene, Jack Simms, Chris Winne and Dr. and Mrs. Jim Sievert were among those who encouraged me to pursue this project. I should thank WSB-TV general manager Greg Stone for making the contractual allowances for me to do the book, and news directors Dick Moore and John Woodin for their support. I also commend the court reporters whose transcripts proved so useful in this project, particularly Jeanne Anderson and Martie Saphir in St. Paul. Editor Lisa Drew, her assistant Katherine Boyle, literary agent Denise Marcil and her staff have been dreamlike. My parents, Brig. Gen. (ret.) and Mrs. Clinton H. Winne Jr., provided not only moral support but historical research in Brunswick.

I also want to acknowledge the storytelling abilities of many of the characters in this book. The natural narrative talents of, for instance, Willye Dennis, John Sheddan and Joe Gordon made richer the chapters in which they were involved. Warren Glover's gripping version of the incident in the Florida Keys was adapted with very few changes, other than omitting lawyer questions and changing voice and tense. The detail and quality of investigators' reports and affidavits also required only slight adaptation and at times only slight adaptation was possible in order to ensure accuracy.

Brian Hoback sometimes expressed concern that the emphasis on his role in the case might give the appearance he was taking disproportionate credit for the outcome. I believe the finished product should allay those fears. However, it is important to note that in an investigation of this size there were some major contributions that may get scant mention, or none, here. During the outline stage I realized my mission was not to produce an encyclopedic record of the case but a readable, compelling and accurate story.

My two young sons have been wonderful, patient and inspirational. Finally, it is difficult to imagine finishing this project without my first-line editor, bookkeeper and partner, my wife Kate.

Index